Giotto

On cover
The Last Judgement, *detail of* Christ seated in a mandorla.
Padua, Scrovegni Chapel.

Texts by Stefano Zuffi
Translation by Richard Sadleir

Photograph Credits
Sergio Anelli, Milan

Elemond Archives, Milan

Foto Saporetti, Milan

Scala, Florence

Printed for Electa
by Fantonigrafica - Elemond Editori Associati

Giotto

Electa / Art Books International

4

The Cycle of Paintings in the Scrovegni Chapel

Scenes from the Life of Joachim and Anne
1. Joachim expelled from the Temple
2. Joachim withdraws among the Shepherds
3. The Annunciation to St Anne
4. Joachim's Sacrifice
5. Joachim's Dream
6. The Meeting of Joachim and Anne at the Golden Gate

Scenes from the Life of Mary
7. The Birth of Mary
8. The Presentation of Mary in the Temple
9. The Handing over of the Rods
10. The Prayer for the Flowering of the Rods
11. The Wedding of Mary and Joseph
12. Mary's Bridal Procession

13. God the Father instructs the Archangel Gabriel to make the Annunciation to Mary – The Annunciation

Scenes from the Life and Death of Christ
14. The Visitation
15. The Nativity of Jesus
16. The Adoration of the Magi
17. The Presentation of Jesus in the Temple
18. The Flight into Egypt
19. The Slaughter of the Innocents
20. Christ among the Doctors
21. The Baptism of Christ
22. The Wedding at Cana
23. The Raising of Lazarus
24. The Entry of Christ into Jerusalem
25. The Expulsion of the Merchants from the Temple
26. The Betrayal by Judas
27. The Last Supper
28. The Washing

of the Feet
29. The Seizure of Christ
30. Christ before Caiaphas
31. Christ Mocked
32. The Ascent of Calvary
33. The Crucifixion
34. The Lament over the Dead Christ
35. "Noli me tangere"
36. The Ascension
37. Pentecost
38. The two "Small Choirs"
39. The Last Judgment

The Virtues and Vices
a. Prudence
c. Fortitude
e. Temperance
g. Justice
i. Faith
m. Charity
o. Hope
p. Despair
n. Envy
l. Faithlessness
h. Injustice
f. Wrath
d. Inconstancy
b. Foolishness

Giotto

The greatest achievement of Italian culture at the start of the fourteenth century was the awareness of the active presence of the individual in history and the world. The new language was taking shape: the vernacular Italian used by Dante and Boccaccio, and at the same time sculpture, in the works of Arnolfo di Cambio and Giovanni Pisano, also achieved its full expressive range, from vibrant animation to solemn calm.

As his contemporaries said, Giotto changed the language of art "from Greek to Latin." And yet his apprenticeship was spent in a figurative training still influenced by Byzantine art. This tradition stemmed from the Imperial court in Byzantium and created a tradition which regulated all the images used in a very specific code of representation. From his earliest known works, Giotto adopted a totally different approach, and in doing so achieved one of the great breakthroughs in Western art. It is highly likely that Giotto made a journey to Rome when still a young man, and that this stimulated him to develop his clear and personal interpretation of ancient art, seen as a model of restraint and harmony, together with a subtle and acute understanding of nature and human sentiments. The late thirteenth-century artists in Rome had already begun moving in the same direction, but it was only with Giotto that this movement triumphed soon to spread through the influence of his works in Assisi, Rome, Rimini, Padua, Naples and Milan. Within a few decades there were schools of his followers in all parts of Italy: but it was Florence in particular that embraced the teaching of her illustrious son. When Renaissance painting began to flower early in the

fifteenth century, Giotto was always acknowledged as its strong, enduring
root. Though it sounds like a paradox,
the truth is that Giotto (like Dante) has
been thought of as a "modern" for over
seven hundred years because he lived
and acted as a man of his own age.

Legends and Reality of Giotto's Youth, Down to the Revelation of the Assisi Frescoes (1267–1300)

We know very little about Giotto's
childhood and early training, not even
wheter "Giotto" was his original name
or merely a diminutive of Biagio or Agnolo. The year of his birth is not recorded in any document but deduced
from the fact that the painter died in
January 1337 at the age of seventy.
However 1267 is a very likely date and
follows closely after that of Dante in
1265.

Born into a peasant family at Colle di
Vespignano, not far from Florence,
Giotto was described by early commen-
tators as an infant prodigy. The encounter between the great master Cimabue and the shepherd boy scratch-
ing a drawing of sheep on a stone at
Mugello, on the road to Bologna, is one
of the most widely quoted examples of
"natural talent" in the whole history of
art. However implausible the ancient
legend, there was definitely a close relationship between Cimabue and Giotto, so that it is quite possible that master
and pupil may have worked together
on some paintings, such as the Madonna of the prepositorship at Castelfio-
rentino.

Cimabue's style marked the final development of Byzantine art in Italy:
the poses of the figures, their gestures
and lineaments, and his lack of interest
in the representation of space all corre-
spond to the rules dictated by Eastern
tradition. But Cimabue also possessed
a lofty and dramatic vision of sacred
history, a sense of the conflict between
good and evil which he translated into
a new plastic energy in his paintings,
with a powerful and expressive emotional impact.

The apprenticeship to Cimabue was
followed by another equally important
experience of Giotto's youth, a journey
to Rome. Amidst the rubble of ancient
Rome emerged the splendid early
Christian basilicas, many of them decorated with mosaics and frescoes in the
course of the thirteenth century.

There was also an important school of
Roman painting, led by artists such as
Piero Cavallini, Jacopo Torriti and Filippo Rusuti. These Roman painters
and mosaic-workers were recreating
the monumentality of classical art: the
papal city was giving birth once more
to an imperial city, and one of the artists involved was the Tuscan sculptor
and architect Arnolfo di Cambio.

Critics agree on the decisive importance of the sojourn in Rome, so that it
is debated wheter Giotto came to Assisi
in the train of Cimabue or as one of a
group of artists coming from Rome. Be
as it may, the 1290s mark the beginning
of his close relationship with the Franciscan order, which commissioned
many of his later works.

The great architectural complex of the
Convent and Basilica of San Francesco
in Assisi began to be built only two
years after the death of the saint in
1226: work went ahead rapidly, and it
grew into the most important monument of Italian architecture and painting in the thirteenth and fourteenth
centuries. An under-
ground crypt formed the lowest level
and contains the tomb of Saint Francis.
Above the crypt stands the large, shal-

low Lower Church, its architecture still Romanesque, completed shortly after 1230. Above it rises the Upper Church (Plate 1), consecrated in 1253. Like the church below, it has a broad nave without side aisles but is much taller, wholly Gothic in style. Great mullioned windows with stained glass make the interior bright, in contrast with the gloom and silence of the Lower Church, and the space is rhythmically divided into four simple cross-vaulted bays. The great walls were left bare, ready to be decorated with frescoes. Work went ahead simultaneously inside the two churches, but while the Lower Church, with its more highly articulated plan, provided a variety of chapels and other surfaces that could be entrusted to different artists, the great walls of the Upper Church suggested the need for a single coherent scheme of decoration. The *Scenes from the Old and New Testaments* are linked to passages from the *Legenda Maior*, the story of the life and miracles of Saint Francis by Saint Bonaventura, written in 1260–1263. In the years around 1277–1280 Cimabue made an outstanding contribution to the decoration of the left transept, including the vaulting, with frescoes that included the dramatic scene of the *Crucifixion*. Later, in around 1285, though Cimabue retained the supervision of the work, the execution of the frescoes passed to his collaborators. Work thus began on the decoration of the upper parts of the nave, especially the spaces between the windows, with the *Scenes from the Old and New Testaments* set one above the other on two levels. It is in this phase that Giotto's hand first appears in the work, in the fourth bay. Divided into regular squares measuring three metres per side, these scenes are one of the most important sources for

The Presentation of Mary in the Temple. Padua, Scrovegni Chapel.

The Wedding at Cana. Padua, Scrovegni Chapel.

the study of Italian painting at the end of the thirteenth century. The personality of the youthful Giotto is at once evident, especially in the two *Scenes from the Life of Isaac* (Plates 2, 3) and the fragmentary *Entombment*, in the subtle attention paid to the interplay of expressions and feelings, while the narrative is based on deliberate, regular, classical rhythms, and not the urgently dramatic rhythms of Cimabue. While Giotto collaborated with other important artists in *Scenes from the Old and New Testaments*, measuring himself against them, in the lower series he was working on his own. The *Scenes from the Life of Saint Francis* (Plates 4–9) mark the appearance of a new idea in art. Composed during the later 1290s, they tell the study of the life of Saint Francis from adolescence down to the miracles performed after his death. Without any iconographic precedents (save for the features of the saint), Giotto was free to handle the scenes as he chose. Only in some of the last scenes does a certain falling-off of the quality appear, a sign of the intervention of pupils. The novelty of these frescoes lies in the depiction of a flesh-and-blood Saint Francis (see the partial nude in the scene of *Saint Francis Renounces his Worldly Goods*, Plate 5), in the midst of his people (often represented as acting in unison, as in the *Death of the Knight of Celano*, Plate 9), in concrete, recognizable places (the square of Assisi forms the background to the *Saint Francis Honoured by a Simple Man of Assisi*, Plate 4); and above all in architectural or natural settings conceived in three-dimensional depth and closely related to the scene depicted. For example, the line of the hills in the *Saint Francis Giving His Cloak to a Poor Man* converges towards the saint's head, which thus becomes the vertex not just of the episode but of the whole landscape. Or in the *Miracles of the Crucifix* and the *Confirmation of the Rules*, the architectural settings are spatial "sets," depicted with an unprecedentedly three-dimensional vision, anticipating later studies of perspective. The iconostasis seen from behind in the *Christmas Crib at Greccio* (Plates 6, 7) is a notable example of this.

Without giving in to a purely biographical account, yet following the iconographical programme closely, Giotto produced a sequence of realistic images, figures and settings. The harmony of his scenes creates a moving and exciting narrative for the uninstructed faithful, while at the same time the frescoes are rich in interest and innovations for artists and men of culture. In 1300, when he had probably completed the *Scenes from the Life of Saint Francis*, Giotto returned to Rome and was present at the Jubilee celebrations held by Pope Boniface VIII. In this period he painted a number of frescoes recorded in documents now mostly lost: there still exists a fragment of *Boniface VIII Proclaiming the Jubilee* in the church of San Giovanni in Laterano. After Assisi and Rome, Giotto finally returned to Florence. Significant traces of his first period in Florence remain in the *Madonna* in San Giorgio della Costa, in some remnants of frescoes in the church of the Badia (which also possessed a polyptych, now in the Uffizi), and above all in the great *Crucifix* on a panel in the sacristy of Santa Maria Novella (Plate 11). This is the first version of a subject that Giotto repeated a number of times, and it shows his rejection of the elegant, rigid Byzantine style for a more direct anatomical representation.

The Scrovegni Chapel and the Central Years of Giotto's Maturity (1300–1320)

Between 1304 and 1306 Giotto was working in Padua on the frescoes of the chapel erected by Enrico Scrovegni to expiate the sin of usury committed by his father. The structure is simple, essential, and the interior is perfectly functional as a container for a complex fresco cycle: a single space, a nave without side-aisles, with narrow windows on one side only, the barrel-vaulting of the ceiling being painted as a starry sky with a number of divine figures (the *Madonna and Child*, the *Christ Blessing*, the *Evangelists*, the *Four Church Fathers*) within medallions. The iconographic scheme exalts the figure of the Madonna as the mother of Christ, who worked our Redemption, the means of salvation for mankind, who travel on their path between good and evil (represented in the fanciful *grisaille* allegorical figures decorating the base), towards the Last Judgement. This is the scene painted on the great end wall (Plate 13), organized around the energetic figure of Christ, surrounded by compact ranks of angels dividing the blessed from the damned, who hurtle downwards amid the fearful torments of hell. The same wall contains the portrait of Enrico Scrovegni dedicating the model of the chapel to the Madonna. Along the sides and on the triumphal arch, ranged on three levels, run the *Stories from the Lives of Joachim and Anna* (Plates 16–19) and the *Scenes from the Life and Passion of Christ* (Plates 20–23; 25–27), for a total of thirty-six scenes. They are meant to be read in the same order as the *Scenes from the Life of Saint Francis* (Plates 4–9). Painted in a fairly brief period of time, the Paduan frescoes are the work in which Giotto first shows his mature powers, apparent in their great stylistic coherence, continuous formal mastery and their solemn affirmation of the dignity of the human figure and its central place in the episodes recounted. The chronological order of the scenes begins with the vicissitudes of the parents of the Madonna. The scenes depicting the father of Maria an exile in the desert (for example *Joachim with the Shepherds*, Plate 15) are typical of the "psychological" arrangement of the elements of nature and the landscape, with solitary figures, as harsh and rugged as the hills in the background. The deep sentiments that form a bond between Joachim and Anna appear in the *Meeting at the Golden Gate* (Plates 18, 19), one of the fullest examples of Giotto's expressive powers, here embodied in the tender kiss exchanged by the two central figures. With the *Nativity of the Virgin* (placed in the same architectural setting as *Annunciation to Saint Anne*), also in the upper row of frescoes, we pass on to the left-hand wall. Of the various scenes into which the episode of the *Virgin's Wedding Feast* is divided, that of the *Watching of the Rods at the Altar* is highly moving and shows great energy in its composition: the group of priests and the suiters for the Virgin's hand form imposing masses. The figures of the *Archangel Gabriel* and the *Annunciation* on the triumphal arch link the left-hand wall with the right-hand one: they are set within identical architectural scenes, foreshortened, forming two full, sturdy masses, very different from the more sinewy outline of Giovanni Pisano's *Madonna and Child* placed on the altar. The childhood of Christ, which begins with the *Visitation* in the triumphal arch, in the middle row of frescoes, opens with a

The Raising of Lazarus. Padua, Scrovegni Chapel.

The Entry of Christ into Jerusalem. Padua, Scrovegni Chapel.

number of episodes that are movingly intimate: the Madonna has her hair braided (a common hairstyle in the Veneto in the early fourteenth century). In the *Nativity* she is shown reclining, a pose unusual in painting but here very natural (Plate 20). In the *Flight into Egypt* (Plate 21), Giotto once again uses natural features of the landscape to intensify the psychological expressiveness of the figures. The Madonna and Child appear compact, clinging together, and set within the outline of a rock in the background. An inversion of this effect is seen in the *Baptism of Christ*, where the hillsides seem to open out symmetrically. This scene opens the sequence devoted to the miracles and Passion of Jesus, the *Betrayal of Judas* placed on the triumphal arch, links the two walls and indicates a shift to the lower series of frescoes. The features of the traitor are caricatured in those of the dark devil behind him.

The *Last Supper* (one of the episodes, together with the scene of the *Way to Calvary* and the *Ascension*, in which the hand of a collaborator is most evident), and the *Washing of the Feet* are placed within an identical pavilion, shown in perspective, which gives the scene an air of solemnity and deliberation, very different from the *Kiss of Judas* (Plates 22, 23), with the chaotic atmosphere surrounding the figure of Judas, petrified by the serene, severe gaze of Christ. The movement of the agitated crowd of figures derives from the dynamic composition, underscored by the waving of lanterns and pikes. The central scenes on the wall (*Crucifixion*, *Lamentation over the Dead Christ*, Plates 25, 26; *Noli me tangere*, Plate 27), form almost a triptych. The grief of the angels around the Crucifixion in yet another demonstration of Giotto's sensitivity to human expression. The resurrected Christ, appearing to Mary Magdalene, moves lightly, elegantly, which has led to comparisons with the carvings of Pallas Athene by Phidias. In the scene of mourning in the *Lamentation*, the figures are set in a sequence of different visual planes that recede into the background, starting with the innovatory presence of the two figures seen from behind. Saint John, stooping over the body of Jesus, opens out his arms at right angles to the plane of the painting, making another breach in the two-dimensional space.

A *Crucifix*, painted on panel, was also painted for the Scrovegni Chapel and is now in the Civic Museum in Padua (Plate 29): some scholars hold that it was painted by Giotto during a second sojourn in Padua in 1317, when he decorated the Palazzo della Ragione with frescoes that are now lost.

The period between the Scrovegni Chapel and the frescoes in the Bardi and Peruzzi chapels in Santa Croce (in Florence), that is from about 1305 to 1320, is the "classical" phase of Giotto's work. During these years he still travelled widely, working in Rimini (where he produced the splendid *Crucifix* in the Tempio Malatestiano, Plate 31, and Rome, where he returned in 1310 to execute the great mosaic with the *"Navicella" of Saint Peter* for the exterior of the Basilica Vaticana: nothing remains of this work save some heavily restored fragments. His reputation and status grew steadily: financially and socially he was secure. The paintings of this period are solemn, harmonious compositions, in which the figures are arranged regularly, without expressive excesses or unpleasing deformities. To this period belong works on a large scale, such as the *Ognissanti Altarpiece* in the Uffizi (Plate 30) and the later *Dormition of the Virgin* in the museum of Berlin.

The Florentine Frescoes and the Last Phase: From Giotto to his Followers (1320–1337)

From 1320 on Giotto appears to have been particularly busy in Florence. Many of the works mentioned in the historical sources have been lost; others are scattered in different museums all over the world. This is the case with a great polyptych, consisting of five cusped panels and a predella with *Scenes from the Life and Passion of Christ*, laboriously reconstructed, starting from a *Saint Stephen* in the Horne Museum in Florence and the *Madonna with Child* in the National Gallery of Art in Washington. Between 1320 and 1325 Giotto worked assiduously in the chapels of the Florentine families that are to be found in the apse of the great church of Santa Croce. The records tell us that he frescoed no fewer than four of the chapels; of these two remain, both belonging to banking families, on the right of the central apse.

The Peruzzi Chapel contains *Scenes from the Lives of Saint John the Baptist and Saint John the Evangelist*, on the two side walls facing each other. Giotto's interest in perspective is even clearer here. He makes allowance for the point of view of the observer in this narrow, tall chapel. The architecture of the buildings in the paintings is very complex (as in *The Feast of Herod*, with interiors of different sizes and depths; even in the outdoor scenes (*Resuscitation of Drusiana*) the articulation of the urban and architectural spaces is unusually varied. The fresco of the *Vision of Saint John in Patmos* (Plate 36) is extremely powerful: it shows the saint sleeping and surrounded by the symbols of the Apocalypse appearing to him in a dream.

The adjacent Bardi Chapel repeats the theme, dear to Giotto, of the *Scenes from the Life of Saint Francis* (Plates 33–35), starting from the large fresco of *Saint Francis Receiving the Stigmata* on the entrance arch (Plate 35). Compared with the Assisi cycle, painted thirty years earlier, Giotto displays a firmer, more serene handling that extends more fully in space. Even the strongest feelings appear to be restrained by a sense of peace, which is also embodied in the broad, harmoniously distributed structures of the compositions. A good example is the *Examination of the Stigmata*, with the moving grief of the friars, mourning for the death of Saint Francis.

In the Baroncelli Chapel, also in Santa Croce, there is the *Polyptych of the Coronation of the Virgin*, probably painted soon after the frescoes in the Bardi Chapel. Here there is extensive evidence of the work of pupils in the massed array of angels praising the Virgin and also in the massive figures in the central section. The individual collaborators who worked with Giotto in Assisi and Padua had by this time been replaced by a well-organized workshop, among whom certain relatives of Giotto and artists with a definite personality of their own were beginning to emerge. In 1327, together with Taddeo Gaddi and Bernardo Daddi, Giotto enrolled in the Guild of Physicians and Druggists, then opened to artists. A confirmation of the contribution of his assistants to the *Baroncelli Altarpiece* is given, paradoxically, by the fact that this work bears Giotto's signature, as if he were concerned to certify his supervision of the work.

Between 1328 and 1333, after a decade spent working in Florence, Giotto set out on his travels again. He returned to Naples several times; there Robert of Anjou employed him on a number of works, all now lost. In about 1330 he went to Bologna, where he coordinated the execution of the *Altarpiece in Bologna* (now in the Pinacoteca Nazionale, Plate 37), which he also signed conspicuously but was largely the work of pupils. Even more important was the *Stefaneschi Altarpiece* (Pinacoteca Vaticana, Rome, Plates 38, 39), dedicated to Saint Peter and commissioned by the cardinal Jacopo Caetani Stefaneschi for the high altar of the Basilica of Saint Peter. The polyptych, with its predella, was painted on both sides of the panel; on one side Christ in glory is flanked by depictions of the martyrdoms of Saint Peter and Saint Paul; on the other, Saint Peter is seated on his throne as the first pope amidst other saints. The donor is shown in the act of donating the polyptych. Though it shows numerous signs of the work of an assistant, much of the work is of high quality, directly from Giotto's own hand, while the figure of the kneeling donor shows his insight as a portraitist. The Bologna and Rome polyptyches are among the last works by Giotto to come down to us. On 12 April 1334, the artist was appointed the *magister et gubernator* of the Opera di Santa Reparata, i.e. overseer of the construction of Florence cathedral. Between 1335 and 1336 Giotto, accompanied by his pupils, moved to the court of Azzone Visconti in Milan. As at Naples, there is now no trace of his work in Milan, save in panels and frescoes by his followers. Giotto then returned to Florence to supervise work on the bell tower. He died in his seventies on 8 January 1337, and was buried in the cathedral with great public honours.

The Legacy

Giotto's frequent travels fostered the birth of schools of followers all over Italy. The use of perspective and geometrical organization was to take root most strongly, however, in Florence, which took the place of Assisi as the avantgarde of artistic development during the fourteenth century. In the same places as Giotto had once worked, starting from the church of Santa Croce, masters such as Maso di Banco, Agnolo Gaddi, Bernardo Daddi and the relatives of Giotto Stefano and Giottino formed a compact group, inspired by a solid sense of realism.

As Millard Meiss has amply demonstrated, the "Black Death" of 1348 led to a far-reaching revision of attitudes in Tuscan culture and art. Painting returned to a vision of man's destiny as depending on the will of God, which Giotto's paintings had to some extent limited. The *novelle* of Boccaccio and Sacchetti recall the historical figure of the master, as ugly as he was shrewd; there emerges from their writings a nostalgia for a kind of art that no one was now capable of practising. The *Libro dell'Arte* written at the end of the fourteenth century by Cennino Cennini is a compendium of Giotto's technique, minutely descriptive of every phase of preparation and execution of the work of art.

At the start of the fifteenth century Giotto's example became the essential basis for humanism. Masaccio was hailed as "Giotto reborn" for his application of the rules of perspective to the painting of both figures and architecture. At a time when the rich and or-

The Expulsion of the Merchants from the Temple. Padua, Scrovegni Chapel.

The Last Supper. Padua, Scrovegni Chapel.

nate late-Gothic school was dominant, Giotto's strong, plain style returned to favour with the linearity of Brunelleschi's architecture and the plastic energy of Donatello's sculptures. The revival of Giotto, seen as the forerunner of the Florentine Renaissance, was ratified by a public decree to raise a monument to him, with a sculpture by Benedetto da Maiano and an inscription by Politian. In the same period the young Michelangelo was practising by copying Giotto's frescoes, deriving from them his taste for figures that occupied a robust volume.

From the Cinquecento on, despite the high praise bestowed by Vasari and all subsequent art historians, Giotto's reputation and that of all the "primitives" tended to suffer an eclipse. The painters from before the mid-fifteenth century were regarded as mere "curiosities" by the learned, and many of their works were irremediably destroyed or damaged. In the course of the nineteenth century, Giotto was given increasing attention, and his works were rediscovered and sometimes restored injudiciously. Towards the end of the century the frescoes in Assisi were being studied in depth: the work of Rintelen (*Giotto und die Giotto-Apokriphen*, published in 1912) began the long polemic over attributions. While the critics were divided, Giotto was also an important model for painters: Cézanne and the Cubists regarded him as an important point of reference, and Carlo Carrà made him the basis of the Italian school known as the Novecento. The critical research of the postwar period, with restoration work and further discoveries, has covered a wide range of topics, with particular attention to Giotto's representation of space, the chronology of his works, and his early training.

1

1. Upper Church, Assisi, interior. The bright interior, one of the prototypes of Italian Gothic, was planned with a view to its decoration with a complex series of frescoes. Work began on them in 1280, and they were distributed in all the available spaces. The iconographic scheme required a close symbolical relationship between the Scenes from the New and Old Testaments *(Plates 2,3), painted in the upper sections of the nave and along the transept, while the* Scenes from the life of Saint Francis *(Plates 4–9) are ranged along the plinth and meant to be read as the exemplary fulfilment of the teaching of the Bible. The decoration began in the transept and continued along the sides in the upper section. After the first scenes had been painted by unknown artists, Cimabue was made responsible for the work, aided by collaborators and a group of painters from Rome. Giotto gradually made his first contributions in the last decade of the thirteenth century, painting one of the vaults and some of the Biblical scenes (which have deteriorated badly) level with the windows. Later he became the leading figure in the work, and began the decoration of the lower part of the wall with the* Scenes from the Life of Saint Francis. *By the time he was thirty Giotto was able to display his own highly personal style, not just in the articulation of the separate scenes, but also in the narrative coherence of the whole cycle. Many years later Giotto returned to Assisi to supervise work on fresco cycles in the Lower Church.*

2

2, 3. Isaac Rejects Esau,
c. 1290, fresco.
Upper Church, Assisi.
The attribution of this fresco
to Giotto is supported by many
critics. It belongs to the
Scenes from the Old and
New Testaments, frescoed in
the strip between the windows,
initially under the supervision
of the Roman artists Filippo
Rusuti and Jacopo Torriti.
Despite the precarious state
of conservation of this work,
the young Giotto here gives us
a precocious sample of spatial
coherence and a sensitive
rendering of the expressions
of the figures, throwing off
the rigid conventions
of Byzantine tradition.

4

4. Saint Francis Honoured
by a Simple Man of Assisi,
1295–1300, fresco.
Upper Church, Assisi.
One of the moments in Saint
Francis' youth, with an urban
setting based on reality. A man
is laying his mantle before

Saint Francis in the central
square of Assisi, with the
classical elevation of the Roman
temple dedicated to Minerva
and the Palazzo Comunale.
Identification of the buildings
is facilitated by the fair state
of preservation of the fresco.

5

5. Saint Francis Renounces his Worldly Goods, 1295–1300. Upper Church, Assisi. Saint Francis' decisive rejection of his father and his wealth is underscored by means of a sharp break in the composition. The saint, half-naked and clad in the cloak of the bishop of Foligno, looks up at a hand emerging from the sky, while the people of Assisi cluster around his father and restrain him. Two complicated buildings, naively foreshortened but drawn with a highly developed feeling for volume, stress the division of the action into two blocks.

6

6, 7. The Christmas Crib at Greccio, *1295–1300, fresco. Upper Church, Assisi. The scene is clearly related to that of the* Nativity *in the* Scenes from the Old and New Testaments *(Plates 2, 3), frescoed in the upper section of the nave and forming a "precedent" for episodes from the life of Saint Francis. Giotto's ability to measure space in depth here creates a scene of great intensity, with the iconostasis seen from behind, hence with the Crucifix shown in outline, as are the other objects that project toward the background of the fresco, crowded with the faithful.*

7

8

8. Saint Francis Preaching
before Pope Honorius III,
1295–1300, fresco.
Upper Church, Assisi.
Giotto's study of space
gradually develops
in awareness.
The three-dimensional "box"
of the chamber in which the
debate takes place is stressed
by the skilful arrangement
of the architecture and the
human figures, who serve
as a yardstick for the
volumes. Like all the scenes
from this cycle, this has
suffered from heavy
restoration.

9

9. The Death of the Knight of Celano, *1295–1300, fresco. Upper Church, Assisi.* The subject records the instantaneous realization of a prophecy of Saint Francis, that the Knight of Celano would receive eternal salvation but also that his death would be immediate. The opposition of the voids and solids in the composition links the figures with the setting. The figure of the saint acts as a link between the two spaces. In the mourners around the body of the Cavaliere, Giotto expresses a choral drama, with a wide range of feelings and expressions.

10. Saint Francis
Receiving the
Stigmata, *c. 1300,
panel, 314 × 162 cm.
Louvre, Paris. This
well-preserved work
comes from the church
of San Francesco in
Pisa, so confirming the
close link between
Giotto and the
Franciscan Order
throughout his career.
The use of the
traditional gilt
background limits the
effect of depth obtained
in the Assisi frescoes
but it endows the
scenes—especially the
three small images at
the bottom—with a
delicate poetry.*

11. The Crucifix, *c.
1300, panel,
578 × 406 cm.
Sacristy of Santa
Maria Novella,
Florence.
This is the earliest of
Giotto's shaped panel
paintings of the
Crucifix. The
divergence of Giotto's
approach from the
Byzantine scheme is
already notable. This
appears in the
naturalness of the pose,
the delicate lineaments,
the simplicity of the
loin cloth and the
superimposition of the
feet, pierced by a single
nail.*

10

11

12

12. Scrovegni Chapel, Padua, *view of the interior toward the rear wall. Commissioned by Enrico Scrovegni in atonement of the sin of usury committed by his father, the chapel is simply planned, with tall single light windows running down one side only. In the lower section runs a series of* grisaille *allegorical figures of the vices and virtues. Along the walls and the triumphal arch that closes the little choir of the chapel, there are three superimposed orders of* Scenes from the Life of Joachim and Anna, *and* Scenes from the Lives of the Virgin and Christ. *On the ceiling there are medallions with the* Evangelists *and the* Four Church Fathers. *The iconographic scheme is based on the redemption of man through the life of Jesus, and is completed by the* Last Judgement *on the end wall.*

13. Enrico Scrovegni Dedicating the Chapel to the Madonna, *detail of the* Last Judgement, *1304–1306, fresco. Scrovegni Chapel, Padua.*

15

14. Inconstancy,
1304–1306, fresco.
Scrovegni Chapel, Padua.
This is one of the emblems
of the vices and virtues that
run along the opposite sides
of the plinth. Giotto uses
a grisaille *technique*
to suggest bas-reliefs.
They comprise a very vivid
series of symbolic figures,
freed from the traditional
canons of art and based
on visual impact.

15. Joachim with the
Shepherds, *1304–1306,*
fresco. Scrovegni Chapel,
Padua.
The sequence of the scenes
begins from the end of the
chapel at the top of the left-hand
wall. Giotto uses the landscape
to intensify the psychological
effect of the situations of the
characters. In this case the
rugged background stresses the
solitude of the sturdy masses
of the three figures.

16

16, 17. Joachim's Dream,
1304–1306, fresco.
Scrovegni Chapel, Padua.
The identification of the
human figure with a regular
geometrical form is
significantly confirmed here by
the "cubic" shape of the
sleeping Joachim. The silence
of the scene is broken by the
flock of sheep. Giotto here
returns to a naturalistic
subject reminiscent of his
legendary meeting with
Cimabue as a boy.

18

18, 19. Meeting at the
Golden Gate, *1304–1306,
fresco. Scrovegni Chapel,
Padua.
Joachim is greeted on his
return by Anna's affectionate
embrace. This is one of the
most celebrated scenes in the
whole cycle. Here Giotto takes
advantage of the dramatic
situation to represent human
expressions that had been
absent from art for almost a
thousand years: a smile, a kiss,
personal emotion.*

20

20. The Nativity,
1304–1306, fresco.
Scrovegni Chapel, Padua.
This belongs to the stories
of the childhood of Christ,
which begin on the right-hand
side. Starting with the middle
series, the tone of the frescoes
grows more familiar.

The departures from the
conventions of the past are
increasingly frequent, adding
to the sense of spontaneity
in the narrative. Note the
reclining position of Mary,
who places Jesus in the
manger with an expression
of deep tenderness.

21

21. Flight into Egypt,
1304–1306, fresco.
Scrovegni Chapel, Padua.
The landscape is again used to
intensify the effect of the whole
and give a structure to the
composition: the hillsides
follow the rhythm of the action,
isolating the figures.

22

22, 23. The Kiss of Judas,
1304–1306, fresco.
Scrovegni Chapel, Padua.
This scene is one of the most
animated and crowded, though
it centres on the motionless
heads of Judas and Christ.
The gesture of betrayal can be
compared with the embrace of

Joachim and Anna, on the
same wall. Giotto, who is
normally more restrained and
deliberate, here confers a
dramatic dynamism on the
nocturnal scene of the
betrayal, heightened by the
pikes, torches and lanterns
waving in the air.

25

24. Jonah Swallowed by the Whale, *1304–1306, fresco. Scrovegni Chapel, Padua. Along the left-hand walls of the chapel there are no windows and Giotto used the space available to insert broad decorative bands, with small biblical scenes meant to prefigure events in the Gospels. The prophet swallowed by the whale and emerging after three days in its belly is painted between the scenes of the* Crucifixion *and the* Lamentation *(Plates 25, 26)*

to foreshadow symbolically and iconographically the death of Christ and His resurrection after three days.

25, 26. The Lamentation over the Dead Christ, *1304–1306, fresco. Scrovegni Chapel, Padua. This scene epitomizes many of Giotto's innovations at Padua: the use of the landscape as an important element in the composition and not as a mere neutral backdrop; his concern for human feelings; the sophistication of the narrative*

scheme, with figures seen from behind and the variety of despairing gestures among the angels. The way the different elements are arranged in depth has reached a high degree of development here: the two Marys are seen from behind, then there is the body of Christ, then the Madonna, with three different planes ranged toward the back of the scene. Saint John, with his arms outstretched at right angles to the plane of the picture further dilates the pictorial space.

27

27. Noli Me Tangere,
1304–1306, fresco.
Scrovegni Chapel, Padua.
Thje elegant "cross-step" taken
by Christ as he moves away
from Mary Magdalene is
combined with the inert sleep
of the soldiers by the empty
sepulchre. The theme of "Noli
Me Tangere" is thus united
with that of the Resurrection.

28

28. "Coretto" or Votive
Chapel, *1304–1306, fresco.*
Scrovegni Chapel, Padua.
On the triumphal arch of the
chapel, on the bottom level,
Giotto has imitated two little
cross-vaulted chapels with
Gothic windows. This was the
first example of "pure"
perspective, without figures,
simply to create the illusion of
space opening out beyond the
surface of the painting.

29. Crucifix, *1304–1306/*
1317?, panel, 223 × 164 cm.
Musei Civici, Padua.
The shaped panel of medium

dimensions and in a fair state
of preservation comes from the
Scrovegni Chapel. It is not
clear if it is of the same period
as the frescoes or was painted
in a second sojourn in Padua
in 1317.

30. Enthroned Madonna
(Ognissanti Altarpiece),
1306–1310, panel ,
325 × 204 cm. Florence,
Uffizi.
This composition, in a good
state of conservation and
recently restored, belongs to the
Tuscan tradition of the
Madonna with a gilt

background on a pentagonal
panel. The solid volumes of
Giotto's figures, deliberately
related to geometrical solids,
stand out within a throne of
Gothic architecture, slender
and elegant. The gesture
of the two kneeling angels,
supporting vases of flowers,
is unusual.

29

31

32

31. Crucifix, *c. 1310, panel,*
430 × 303 cm.
Tempio Malatestiano, Rimini.
Evidence of a period spent in
Rimini (in c. 1310) and a
landmark in the development
of painting in the area, this is
the finest example of this
particular genre. The careful,
delicate study of anatomy is
favoured by a sensitive use of
light, which glances off the
elongated limbs. Christ is

shown as already dead, and
his features do not show
the grimace typical of earlier
tradition. The plate is in good
condition, though the small
figures at the ends have been
removed.

32. Saint Stephen,
1320–1325, panel,
84 × 54 cm.
Museo Horne, Florence.
This panel is in excellent

condition. It was originally
part of a polyptych, now
divided up between various
museums.
The central panel is of the
Madonna, *and is now in the*
National Gallery of Art in
Washington. This Saint
Stephen *is one of Giotto's*
works which shows most care
for the transparency of the
colours, laid on with rare
delicacy.

33

33, 34. Saint Francis
Renounces his Worldly
Goods, *fresco, c. 1325.*
Santa Croce, Bardi Chapel,
Florence.
Giotto's most intense activity in
Florence was concentrated on
the church of Santa Croce.
The records tell us that no
fewer than four chapels were
decorated with frescoes by him.
After the destruction of some
and the repainting of others

(partly because they were
regarded as "primitive"
works in the eighteenth and
nineteenth centuries) the cycles
in the two chapels of the
bankers Peruzzi and Bardi, to
the right of the great chapel,
alone survive. They were
painted after 1320. Covered
with whitewash in the past,
they are in poor condition but
they reveal the direction of
Giotto's development after he

left Padua. He enriched the
expressive and dynamic
resources of his work, without
losing any of the dignity
of the volumes of the human
figures and architectural
elements.
The Bardi Chapel, which was
dedicated to Saint Francis,
enables us to compare the
treatment of certain scenes
with the cycle in Assisi of thirty
years earlier.

35

35. Saint Francis Receiving
the Stigmata, *c. 1325, fresco.*
Santa Croce, Bardi Chapel,
Florence.
Painted on the arch of the
entrance to the Bardi Chapel,
the fresco testifies to Giotto's
achievements in the
representation of the human
body. Compared with his work

in Padua, where the figures
were composed as regular
geometrical shapes, this Saint
Francis has a complex volume,
achieved through the
combination of various solid
figures. As in the Peruzzi
Chapel, Giotto allows for
the position of the viewer below
the picture.

36

36. Vision of Saint John
in Patmos, *c. 1325, fresco.*
Santa Croce, Peruzzi Chapel,
Florence.
The Peruzzi Chapel is
dedicated to Saint John the
Evangelist and Saint John the
Baptist. The frescoes have
faded somewhat. They possess
great dramatic intensity. This
lunette shows Saint John with
the jagged outline of the island
of Patmos, during his vision of
the Apocalypse, whose symbols
appear in the semicircle
in the sky.

37

37. Altarpiece in Bologna,
c. 1330, panels,
91 × 340 cm. Pinacoteca
Nazionale, Bologna.
An important example
of Giotto's late work and his
relationship with his well-
organized workshop. The
polyptych is important in the
development of the Bologna
school of painting in the
fourteenth century.
The structure of the
whole is overshadowed
by the prominence of the
individual, solid figures
of the saints and the Madonna.

38

38, 39. Stefaneschi
Altarpiece, *c. 1330, panel,*
220 × 245 cm. Pinacoteca
Vaticana, Rome.
Intended for the high altar of
the Basilica of San Pietro, this
is the best preserved of all
Giotto's paintings executed for
Rome. The client who
commissioned it was the
cardinal Jacopo Caetani
Stefaneschi, who is portrayed
on the altarpiece, which is
painted on both sides. The
cardinal's gesture is curious:
he is holding a representation
of the polyptych in which a
diminutive image of the
cardinal appears holding the
painting.

Where to See Giotto

Of all the painters who lived before the fifteenth century, Giotto is the one whose life and artistic evolution can be traced with the greatest precision. The master's seventy years of life are densely studded with anecdotes, documents, recollections, and citations. Around thirty panels, four impressive cycles of frescoes, and other works carried out in collaboration with his *bottega* constitute a corpus of unusual size for a mediaeval artist. Nor should we forget Giotto's activity as an architect, to which the campanile of Florence Cathedral stands witness.

Naturally, a number of important questions of attribution remain unresolved, especially with regard to significant sections of the decoration of San Francesco in Assisi. There is also a long list of paintings to which the old sources gave much emphasis but that have subsequently been lost. The most painful gaps regard whole cycles of frescoes that have completely vanished. The chroniclers (though their testimony is not always reliable) record works in Arezzo, Avignon, Ferrara, Gaeta, Lucca, Pisa, Ravenna, Venice, and Verona of which no trace remains.

There is more direct evidence (payments, contracts, and other documents) for the frescoes and polyptyches he left in four chapels belonging to noble families in Florence's Santa Croce (the frescoes of the Bardi and Peruzzi Chapels and the *Baroncelli Polyptych* have survived). Our knowledge of his activity in Rome is full of blanks: the frescoes in the apse of the old basilica of Saint Peter's in the Vatican were destroyed and even the mosaic of the *Navicella* has been almost completely reworked.

During the years he spent in Naples, Giotto had frescoed the chapel and the baronial hall of the Angevin Keep, as well as a chapel in Santa Chiara. Finally, nothing is left of the *Glory of Illustrious Men* he frescoed for Azzone Visconti in Milan.

Works in Italy

The distribution of Giotto's paintings more or less follows the route taken by the artist in his wanderings, even though little or nothing remains from some of the places where he worked. Naturally the greatest concentration of Giotto's pictures is in Florence; Assisi offers the largest sample of his frescoes; the best-preserved cycle is to be found in Padua.

Florence

A tour of Giotto's works in Florence, always in the shadow of the campanile built to plans drawn up by the master, might start with the Franciscan basilica of Santa Croce. In the row of side chapels are to be found two cycles from the mature period of Giotto's career: the Peruzzi Chapel (*Scenes from the Life of Saint John the Evangelist*) and the Bardi Chapel (*Scenes from the Life of Saint Francis*). In addition, there is the *Baroncelli Polyptych*, thronged with figures and set in a Renaissance frame, whose central panel depicts the *Coronation of the Virgin*.

The Dominican basilica of Santa Maria Novella, at the

opposite end of the city's historic centre, can boast no frescoes by Giotto but does contain, in the sacristy, a large *Crucifix* on a shaped panel.

Two more *Crucifixes* attributed to Giotto are in the churches of Ognissanti and San Felice di Piazza.

A few traces of a cycle of frescoes survive in the church of the Badia: the *Badia Polyptych* is now in the Galleria degli Uffizi, where other works from Giotto's circle can be found. Outstanding among these are the juvenile *Enthroned Madonna* and above all the large pentagonal panel of the *Ognissanti Maestà*: one of the artist's best-known masterpieces, it is set in the middle of the museum's first room, in accordance with a celebrated decision to present Vasari's view of the artist from a critical viewpoint, underlining the central role that Giotto played in the history of Italian art.

The Museo Horne possesses an extremely delicate figure of *Saint Stephen*, a panel from a dismembered polyptych that was probably originally in Santa Croce.

The attribution of the *Polyptych* painted on both sides and now in the Museo dell'Opera of the Cathedral is controversial, while the frescoes in the chapel of the Palazzo del Bargello, although probably begun by Giotto, have been repainted several times.

Not far from Florence, in the Berenson Collection at Villa I Tatti in Settignano, there are two fine panels: a *Deposition*, part of a dismembered altarpiece, and a vigorous, juvenile *Saint Anthony*.

Assisi

The cycle of *Scenes from the Life of Saint Francis*, frescoed on the lower part of the walls of the upper basilica of San Francesco over the course of the last decade of the thirteenth century, is universally known.

The question of other interventions by Giotto preceding and following the *Life of Saint Francis* is more delicate. The hand of Giotto, at a time when he had only just left Cimabue's workshop, has been recognized in some of the *Scenes from the Old and New Testaments* in the middle row of the walls of the upper basilica. In the lower basilica, on the other hand, the authorship of the four vaulting cells above the high altar, frescoed with *Franciscan Allegories*, is much more controversial.

Giotto, assisted by his workshop, intervened in the frescoes of the Chapel of the Magdalen. The *Maestà* in the Pinacoteca Civica of Assisi may be the work of Giotto's assistants.

Padua

The Scrovegni Chapel, with the cycle painted for Enrico Scrovegni and dedicated to the redemption of Man through Christ, contains the most complete example of the technique used by Giotto in his early maturity.

The frescoes cover the whole of the side walls, the vault, the inside of the facade, and the triumphal arch. The ones in the chapel's small chancel and apse are by another artist.

The Scrovegni Chapel originally housed a delicate *Crucifix* on a shaped panel, which can now be seen in the adjacent Museo Civico.

Rome

Despite the frequency of Giotto's stays in Rome, very little signs of his activity there remain. The most interesting work in the city is the *Stefaneschi Polyptych*: painted on both sides and originally located on the high altar of the basilica of Saint Peter's, it is now in the Vatican Art Gallery. On one door of the basilica is set what remains of the mosaic depicting the *Navicella*, or Saint Peter's Boat, originally made to cartoons by Giotto but completely reworked. Two fragments of the original mosaic (*Angels*) survive, and are kept in the Vatican Grottoes and the church of San Pietro at Boville Ernica (Frosinone) respectively. The basilica of San Giovanni in Laterano still contains part of the fresco depicting *Boniface VIII announcing the Jubilee Year in 1300*, but it too, unfortunately, has been heavily repainted.

Emilia Romagna

Traces of Giotto's stay in *Rimini* survive in the form of a lively fourteenth-century local school of painting and an elegant *Crucifix* in the Tempio Malatestiano.

The Pinacoteca Nazionale in *Bologna* has an expressive *Polyptych*, a testimony to Giotto's visit to the city at an advanced age.

Works Located Abroad

There are no more than fifteen or so of Giotto's works outside Italy, with the actual number varying as a result of changes in attribution. It is difficult, in view of their scarcity, to present a true guide to their location. It is possible, however, to point to a certain concentration of panels in Germany and the United States.

Germany

The Staatliche Museen in *Berlin* houses two works of considerable importance. The grand and solemn *Dormitio Virginis*, on a cuspidate panel, comes from the Florentine church of Ognissanti, where it was studied and appreciated by Michelangelo. The small *Crucifixion*, on the other hand, should be seen in connection with a panel depicting a similar subject in the Strasbourg Museum. Another *Crucifixion*, together with a *Last Supper* and the *Descent of Christ into Limbo*, forms a small but consistent group of Giotto's works in the Alte Pinakothek in *Munich*. The three small panels were originally part of a single altarpiece.

United States

The activity of collectors has brought a number of Giotto's pictures to American museums. Most of them are parts of polyptyches that have been broken up. The work of piecing together these groups of paintings is a constant preoccupation among scholars.

The Metropolitan Museum in *New York* and the Isabella Stewart Gardner Museum in *Boston* possess two more panels from the Franciscan altarpiece depicting scenes from the life of Christ that has already been mentioned in connection with works in Settignano and Munich: they are, respectively, the *Adoration of the Magi* and the *Presentation of Jesus in the Temple*. The seventh panel in the series, representing *Pentecost*, is in the National Gallery in London.

The North Carolina Museum in Raleigh houses the five panels of the *Peruzzi Polyptych*, in all likelihood from the family's chapel in Santa Croce, although they may not be entirely the work of Giotto. The beautiful *Madonna and Child* in the National Gallery in Washington comes from another dismembered polyptych, again from the Franciscan church in Florence. Other panels from the same altarpiece are the aforementioned *Saint Stephen* in Florence's Museo Horne and the two panels depicting *Saint John the Evangelist* and *Saint Lawrence* in the Musée Jacquemart-André in Paris.

Returning to the United States, it is also worth mentioning the small cuspidate panel representing the *Eternal Father* in the San Diego Museum, a fragment of the *Baroncelli Polyptych*.

Paris

The Musée du Louvre contains the largest picture by Giotto outside Italy, the juvenile altarpiece depicting *Saint Francis Receiving the Stigmata*, complete with a predella and over three metres tall. It originally came from the church of San Martino in Pisa.

The same museum in Paris also has a *Crucifix* on board, a recent and still controversial addition to Giotto's catalogue.

Anthology of Comments

Cimabue believed he held sway/ In the field of painting,/But now Giotto is all the cry/ So that the other's fame is eclipsed.
(Dante, *Purgatorio*, Canto XI, c. 1310)

Giotto possessed an intellect of such excellence that nothing of nature, the mother of all things and responsible for the continual turning of the heavens, did he fail to paint with stylus and pencil and brush similar to the original... so that often the things he painted led men's eyes to fall into error, believing them real. For this reason, having restored art to the light, which for many centuries has been buried under the errors of those that sought to delight the ignorant rather than please the intellect of the wise, he can truly be called one of the leading lights of the glory of Florence; and all the more so, since with great humility he, a master of others in his art, always refused to let others call him *maestro*; which title, rejected by him, shone all the more brightly in him, in proportion as it was avidly usurped by those that knew less than he or by his pupils.
(G. Boccaccio, *Decamerone*, VI Day, V Novella, c. 1350)

He translated the art of painting from Greek into Latin and made it modern; and he possessed the most accomplished art that anyone has ever had.
(C. Cennini, *Il Libro dell'Arte*, c. 1390)

Among the other questions raised, one, whose name was Orcagna, the master builder of the noble oratory of Nostra Donna d'Orto San Michele (the church of Orsanmichele in Florence), asked: "Who was the greatest master of painting, apart from Giotto, down to the present day?" Some said Cimabue, others Stefano, others Bernardo (Daddi] and still others Buffalmacco, and some said one, some said another. Taddeo Gaddi, who was of the company, said: "Certainly there have been very fine painters, who painted in such a way that human nature is unable to do better. But that art is gradually disappearing day by day."
(F. Sacchetti, *Novelle*, CXXXVI, c. 1395)

The art of painting began to rise in Etruria, in a place near Florence, Vespignano. A boy was born of wonderful intellect, who happened to be drawing a sheep when Cimabue the painter passed by that way along the road to Bologna, and saw the boy sitting on the ground and drawing a sheep on a stone. He was filled with admiration for the lad, who though young was drawing so well. Seeing that he was naturally gifted as an artist, he asked the lad what his name was. "My name is Giotto and my father's is Bondone and he lives in this house near at hand," the boy said. Cimabue went with Giotto to his father (he made a very fine appearance), and asked the father to entrust him with the boy. The father was very poor. He allowed the boy to go with Cimabue, and so Giotto became his pupil.
(L. Ghiberti, *Commentarii*, II, c. 1450)

He went to Assisi, a city of Umbria, being summoned there by Fra Giovanni di Muro della Marca, then the general of the friars of Saint Francis. There, in the upper church, he painted frescoes under the strip traversing the windows on the two sides of the church, with thirty-two stories of the life and works of Saint Francis, sixteen on either side, so perfectly painted that he won great fame. And truly there can be seen in this work a great variety not just in the gestures and attitudes of the different figures, but also in the composition of all the stories. It is also wonderful to see the diversity of the garments of those times and certain imitations and observations of the natural world.
(G. Vasari, *Le Vite dei più eccellenti pittori, scultori et architettori*, 1568)

He was also a sculptor and his models were preserved down to the age of Lorenzo Ghiberti. Nor did he lack good esamples. There were ancient marbles in Florence, which can now be seen at the cathedral (without mentioning what he later saw in Rome), and their merit, already acknowledged by Niccola and Giovanni Pisani, could hardly have been ignored by Giotto, whom nature had endowed with a sensibility for the true and the beautiful.
When one looks at certain of his male heads, certain squared forms, so remote from the slender forms of his contemporaries, or his feeling for rare, natural, majestic draperies, and certain poses of his figures, which have an air of decorum and restraint, then it is very hard to believe that he did not learn a great deal from ancient marbles.
(L. Lanzi, *Storia pittorica dell'Italia*, 1795–1796)

Giotto changed the method of preparing colours hitherto in use and changed the concept and direction of pictorial representation.
He kept to the present and to reality; and his figures and effects were used to represent the life around him.
Together with these tendencies, there was also the fortunate circumstance that not only did costume become freer and life gayer in Giotto's time, but the cult of new saints also came about then, saints that had flourished in times not long before the painter's own lifetime. In the content of his paintings, the naturalness of the bodily figures themselves was thus implicit, as well as the presentation of definite characters, actions, situations, attitudes and movements. Because of this tendency, there was a gradual (though relative) loss of that grandiose, sacred austerity that was the foundation of the previous school of art. Worldly attitudes took root and spread, and in keeping with the spirit of the time, Giotto, too, accepted burlesque alongside pathos. (G.F. Hegel, *Vorlesung über Aesthetik*, 1829)

With the achievements of Giotto and Duccio began the eclipse of the mediaeval figurative vision. For the depiction of a closed, interior space conceived as a concave body signifies more than a simple consolidation of objects; it entails an authentic revolution in the formal valuation of the painted surface: it is no longer the wall or panel on which the forms of individual things or figures are laid, but it has once more become the transparent plane through which we may believe we are looking at an open space, though circumscribed in all directions: a "figurative plane" in the fullest sense of the word.
(E. Panofsky, *La prospettiva come "forma simbolica,"* 1927)

Under the burden of my years I traverse the field from which emerge the walls of the ancient arena, like the bones of a skeleton picked clean; but when I cross the threshold of the Scrovegni Chapel, time suddenly winds backward and I am a child again, in my playroom. Toys to right and left of me. A double row of toys, in the midst of which the man, now a child again, passes solemn and lightly, in the always-young light of earthly immortality. Giotto's painting is the mother of toys. This is his supreme quality, his secret quality. The composition follows the instructions for "Little Architects." These pure, vivid colours are like those that shone on the balls and ninepins and dice of my childhood. And there I can see my rocking horse. Art always rekindels the lights of the lost paradise, which the gloomy hands of non-artists return always to extinguish. But Giotto revives not just the image of that lost paradise, but also the games that took place in that light that was soft to the touch, in that life that seemed to be enclosed in pearl, the games we played to pass the timeless time. Here, as in the art of ancient Greece, nothing is stronger than the strength of men, everything is made to be dismantled and then assembled differently, everything is portable. Nothing has yet been darkened by the shadow of sin. No cloud has yet formed in that clear sky. Silver nails secure this unchanging serenity, this intense boundless turquoise. (A. Savinio, *Ascolto il tuo cuore, città*, 1944)

No scientific treatise can describe human events of the earth and the heart with such great immediacy and effectiveness as does painting, through the use of form, which is incarnation and purification, through style, which is the enduring shape of passions suffered and dominated. This was how Giotto *saw* and felt the value of the human figure first: he possessed a feeling for large, imposing composition, a sense of the weight and volume of things, and to his language submits the exquisite colour that enlivens unpredictably changing surface, which a wholly Tuscan sense of form has drawn and caught with precision. A quality that until the coming of Michelangelo remained intact even when confronted by the allurements of Leonardo's softer colours. He understood space, atmosphere, different planes, he was the first person to have a feeling for the external world, meaning landscapes, mountains, trees and rocks, whose aus-

terity and heroism, like his human figures, bear the singular and unifying touch of a cosmic vision. (G. Delogu, *Antologia della pittura italiana*, 1947)

If one stands at the centre of the paving of the Scrovegni Chapel, in the spot best suited to take in at a single glance the wall in which the apse is set, it at once becomes plain... that the two *trompe-l'oeil* apertures have the effect of "opening up" the wall, with the aim of affecting the architecture of the votive chapel. The convincing illusion thus created is underscored by the two Gothic vaults running towards a single centre which lies on the axis of the church, that is in the real, existential depth of the apse. The internal light starts from the centre and spreads through the two bays, even onto the columns and jambs of the apertures of the windows not with "abstract" ultramarine but a pale azure colour, which combines with the real blue outside the windows in the apse: so real is the illusion that one feels an impulse to wait and see the swallows swooping down from the nearby eaves of the church of the Eremitani. (R. Longhi, "Giotto spazioso," in *Paragone*, 31, 1952)

Between 1260 and 1290 Cimabue, who worked in Rome and Florence, was undoubtedly an Italian—and even European—painter of outstanding greatness and poetical energy; and he was also the painter possessed of the highest and most complex culture in the great medieval tradition. In him we

find a moral force, an evocative and expressive power, that can still be felt pressing against the mediaeval forms and transforming them until they became something new, but always within limits that he seems to have suffered from dramatically, seeking to overcome them, yet that still hemmed him in. And in this clash that strength swelled and was exalted, displaying itself in dilated, superhuman forms. Giotto inherited the poetic message of Cimabue, but at once added the awareness that mankind now had other means to express their truth, in all its fullness and variety and not merely in that vertical ascent or unmeasurably profound sense of drama. With Giotto a new cycle opened in serenity. Cimabue was heroic passion dilating and overwhelming humanity. Giotto was harmony and measure dominating and containing the passions, the greatness of man. (G. Gnudi, under the entry "Giotto," in the *Enciclopedia Universale dell'Arte*, VI, 1958)

In the commentary on the *Commedia* by an anonymous Florentine we find it said that the painter, having become a master builder in his old age, "composed and designed the marble bell tower of Santa Reparata in Florence: a noteworthy bell tower and very costly. He committed two errors: the first that it had no foundations, the second that it was too narrow. These things struck his heart with such sorrow that he fell ill and died." The "errors" were merely the gossip of back-

biters, for the bell tower showed clearly that the foundations were strong and the marble shaft was, in fact, of the right proportions. But the pupil of Arnolfo, the artist who had painted so many bold, elaborate works of architecture, may actually have died, on January 8 1337, when the bell tower was only a few yards high, nursing the doubt that he had erred in his only real work of Architecture.
(P. Bargellini, *Belvedere. L'Arte Gotica*, 1961)

The Scrovegni Chapel was built in the place of a more modest and ancient structure, before which a sacred play was represented every year on the theme of the Annunciation and the other Stories of Maria. There was nothing more natural than that Giotto, so observant of whatever went on about him, should have watched the sacred play of Padua while preparing to paint those same scenes on the walls of the chapel then being built..., and recalled the emotions and the narrative clarity in the arrangement of the various phases of the performance, together with the evocative value of certain architectural backdrops. So that he left on the chapel walls a more enduring spectacle, which was the official recognition, the seal and lasting record of the sacred play... It is impossible to ignore the possibility that alongside Giotto the architect there also exists what, in modern terms, might be described as a Giotto the "set-designer" –Giotto as the supreme director of gestures and feel-

ings adapted to the actors in an episode, stage-managing his creations, those simple yet very modern actors that he set out in his magical "living picture," asking of each one of them, and hence of himself, the greatest intensity of expression with the greatest economy of means. (M. Bucci, *Giotto*, 1966)

On the threshold of the year 2000, which may well loom up with greater terrors than the first millennium, this exploration of the ethical and poetical unity of the whole Middle Ages–and with the highly tangible example of Giotto, from the lyrical Giotto of Assisi to the tragic artist of Padua–is a profound lesson, and may even be a summons to salvation. Our age, and even more the millennium about to be born out of the current throes of the planet, seems to promise to be more mediaeval than classical or Renaissance... Even the modern age... has already created more than one "summa," perhaps desecrated but restorative. But until the recent past we were barely capable of a merely unambiguous and unilateral "summa," which aimed at isolated values but perhaps tomorrow like Giotto we will be willing to create a "summa" that is once more unified yet many-sided.
(G. Vigorelli, "Giotto e l'invito all'unità," in *L'opera completa di Giotto*, edited by E. Bacceschi, 1967)

In presenting the faithful with the life of Saint Francis (in the Assisi frescoes), Giotto is now tender, now solemn, now dramatic, now serene, now familiar,

now lyrical, now mystical, now popular, now apostolical, now a chronicler. He alternates observation of the contemporary world with the admonishment of the eternal, the miraculous with the everyday. Intended as hagiography, this fresco cycle seems to have been inspired by a natural heroism, a familiar sense of the supernatural, unattainable yet accessible (isn't all great poetry like this?). The saint is the hero of the human: not a model, but an example, and in the infinite distance that separates us from sanctity we yet share in his life. In this sense the stories of Saint Francis in Assisi are one of the least clerical monuments of all religious art.
(G. Pampaloni, *Giotto ad Assisi*, 1981)

What is more modern in all Western art in around 1290–1295 than these stories of Saint Francis? And not just in the reappropriation of the visible world in terms of spaces and volumes: this feature of his work, which after almost a thousand years meant once more seeing a value in the world of phenomena that man can verify through his own experience (as opposed to the so-called realism of the Middle Ages, which conceived the physical world as a symbol of the "true" reality, that of the next world), was part of a much wider reconsideration of the world and man in more natural and earthly terms. All those conventional graphic deformations of Byzantine origin disappeared from the human figure, whereas Cimabue and the young Duccio had only softened them...

The human anatomy grew normal again, acquiring a degree of truth never achieved before. A quite good example is the partial nude in *Saint Francis Renounces his Worldly Goods*, which—despite its chrysalid-like awkwardness that was typical of nudes all through the fourteenth century—reveals a remarkable degree of truthfulness in the depiction of the shoulder blades and ribs which must have amazed his contemporaries. The profiles of his faces re-acquire that positive value that had been denied for almost a thousand years, or at least the neutrality and normality typical of everyday experience. For the first time figures were again shown smiling in a painting.
(L. Bellosi, *La pecora di Giotto*, 1985)

T he first to be amazed by Giotto's great talents not just as an artist, but also as an entrepreneur and a man who made his own fortune, were his contemporaries. Giotto's legend spread rapidly because his artistic career developed at a wholly unprecedented speed, with exceptional powers of innovation and also thanks to the fact that the new and modern features of his work were so outstanding. And it is also clear that Giotto's works made the old methods followed by his predecessors look old-fashioned, both because of the way he organized his workshop and also because of the great refinement of his aesthetic achievement.
(S. Bandera Bistoletti, *Giotto. Catalogo completo*, 1989)

Essential Bibliography

M. Bacci, *Giotto*, Florence 1966.

L'opera completa di Giotto, edited by E. Baccheschi, Milan 1967.

F. Bologna, *Novità su Giotto. Giotto al tempo della cappella Peruzzi*, Turin 1969.

Giotto e il suo tempo, papers from the conference for the eighth centenary of Giotto's birth (Rome 1967), Rome 1971.

G. Previtali, *Giotto e la sua bottega*, 2nd ed., Milan 1974.

Da Giotto al Mantegna, exhibition catalogue edited by L. Grossato, Palazzo della Ragione, Padua 1974.

L. Bellosi, *Giotto*, Florence 1981.

C. Brandi, *Giotto*, Milan 1983.

L. Bellosi, *La pecora di Giotto*, Turin 1985.

G. Bonsanti, *Giotto*, Padua 1985.

S. Bandera Bistoletti, *Giotto. Catalogo completo*, Florence 1989.

CREATIVE
TOURISM
A Global Conversation

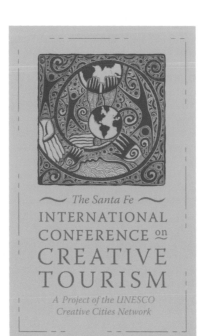

The Santa Fe

INTERNATIONAL
CONFERENCE on
CREATIVE
TOURISM

A Project of the UNESCO
Creative Cities Network

CREATIVE TOURISM
A Global Conversation

How to Provide
Unique Creative Experiences for Travelers Worldwide

Originally Presented at the 2008 Santa Fe & UNESCO International Conference
on Creative Tourism in Santa Fe, New Mexico, USA

Edited by
Rebecca Wurzburger
Tom Aageson, Alex Pattakos and Sabrina Pratt

SANTA FE

The 2008 Creative Tourism Conference logo was designed by artist Joel Nakamura
and Renee Innis of Cisneros Design in Santa Fe, New Mexico, USA

Sunstone books may be purchased for educational, business, or sales promotional use.
For information please write: Special Markets Department, Sunstone Press,
P.O. Box 2321, Santa Fe, New Mexico 87504-2321.

Book and Cover design ~Vicki Ahl
Body typeface ~ Adobe Garamond Pro
Printed on acid free paper

Library of Congress Cataloging-in-Publication Data

Santa Fe & Unesco International Conference on Creative Tourism (1st : 2008 : Santa Fe, N.M.)
Creative tourism : a global conversation : how to provide unique creative experiences for travelers
worldwide : as presented at the 2008 Santa Fe & UNESCO International Conference on Creative
Tourism in Santa Fe, New Mexico, USA / edited by Rebecca Wurzburger ... [et al.].
        p. cm.
Includes bibliographical references.
ISBN 978-0-86534-724-3 (softcover : alk. paper)
1. Tourism--Social aspects--Congresses. I. Wurzburger, Rebecca. II. Title.
G154.9.S26 2008
338.4'791--dc22
                    2009020393

WWW.SUNSTONEPRESS.COM
SUNSTONE PRESS / POST OFFICE BOX 2321 / SANTA FE, NM 87504-2321 /USA
(505) 988-4418 / ORDERS ONLY (800) 243-5644 / FAX (505) 988-1025

Contents

ACKNOWLEDGMENTS

In thinking about what was created at the Santa Fe International Conference on Creative Tourism, which this book documents, I am reminded of the famous saying, "It takes a village to raise a child." It did, indeed, take an international village of creative thinkers, planners, funders, and implementers to bring this unique conference to fruition.

To begin, we acknowledge the UNESCO visionaries who initially developed the Creative Cities Network: Milagros del Corral and Indrasen Vencatachellum, as well as the current Creative Cities Network Program Director, Georges Poussin. We also thank the first members of the Creative Cities Network who helped form the definition of Creative Tourism (underlying the conference), as well as our overall program concept. This includes: Ali Bowden, Edinburgh, Scotland (City of Literature); Ossama Meguid, Omar M. Osman and Mohamed S. A. Hamid, Aswan, Egypt (City of Folk Art); Guillermo Alberto González, Alvaro Garzón López and Aurelio Velasco Mosquera, Popayan, Colombia (City of Gastronomy); Benedetto Zacchiroli and Enrico Levi, Bologna, Italy (City of Music); Marc Tremblay, Montreal, Canada (City of Design) and Vicky Salías and Silvia Ramajo, Buenos Aires, Argentina (City of Design).

For more than a year, Santa Fe's Creative Tourism Planning Committee worked together on every decision: from speaker selection, detailed program design and graphic design to conference advertisement, public relations and fundraising. Special thanks goes to the following individuals who, indeed, were the local visionaries and implementers: Tom Aageson (Museum of New Mexico Foundation); Jackie M (The Georgia O'Keeffe Museum); Dena Aquilina (Creative Santa Fe); Keith Toler (Santa Fe Convention & Visitors Bureau); Tom Maguire (City of Santa Fe Arts Commission) and Sabrina Pratt (City of Santa Fe Arts Commission). We also acknowledge the hard work of our conference management team: Tom Maguire, who served as the city's project manager and Recursos de Santa Fe, including Ellen Bradbury Reid, Sandy Vaillancourt, Nancy Johnson and Dawn Hoffman and the team of volunteers Recursos gathered. Invaluable professional support in marketing was provided to us by Steve Lewis of the Convention & Visitors Bureau and Sarah Robarts and staff at Ballantine PR. We also want to salute Cisneros Design, Joel Nakamura and designer Renee Innis for the beautiful graphic design throughout the project.

Certainly the conference would never have occurred without the generous funding support of the Santa Fe City Council, New Mexico Department of Tourism, Thaw Charitable Trust, McCune Foundation, and the New Mexico State Legislature. We particularly thank Senator Peter Wirth and Representatives Luciano "Lucky" Varela and Jim Trujillo, as well as Speaker of the House, Ben Lujan. In addition, scores of local restaurants and business sponsors provided thousands of dollars of in-kind and cash support for which we are most grateful.

It is one thing to have a plan for a global conversation; it is quite another to experience the implementation of that plan, beyond one's imagination and expectations. This is truly what actually happened at our conference, not only because of the brilliance, creativity, and practical experience of our keynote speakers and UNESCO Creative City colleagues, but also because of the participants who came from 16 countries around the world. Our gratitude to all who came and actually made the conversation a reality can never be overstated.

This book documents the provocative and informative conversations that occurred in Santa Fe in September/October 2008. Its genesis came from a dynamic brainstorming session among several conference speakers including Greg Richards, Eric Maisel, Crispin Raymond, Alex Pattakos, Tom Maguire and myself. Twenty presenters positively responded to our request for papers and it is their thoughtful contributions that made this book possible.

However, credit and sincere gratitude for the real work of formatting, reading drafts, preliminary coordination with our publisher, and initial proof-reading must go to Tom Maguire.

Finally, special thanks is given to Celeste Valentine, Laura Banish, and Melissia Helberg for their roles in transcribing and editing drafts from our authors, to Maria Clokey for her assistance with the photographs, and to James Clois Smith, Jr. at Sunstone Press for being our publisher.

—Rebecca Wurzburger, PhD
Conference Convenor
Mayor Pro-Tem, City of Santa Fe

Mayor Pro-Tem and Conference Convenor Rebecca Wurzburger with Mayor David Coss at the opening reception for the conference. Photograph by Linda Carfagno.

Native American dancers and drum circle perform in the Convention Center courtyard. Photograph by Linda Carfagno.

INTRODUCTION TO THE SANTA FE &
UNESCO INTERNATIONAL CONFERENCE
A GLOBAL CONVERSATION ON BEST
PRACTICES AND NEW OPPORTUNITIES

by

Rebecca Wurzburger, PhD
Mayor Pro-Tem, City of Santa Fe, New Mexico

What is Creative Tourism? Why should creative cities worldwide, and specifically those in the UNESCO Creative Cities Network, collaborate about Creative Tourism? How can Creative Tourism be best organized to enhance economic benefits to cities and provinces and countries globally?

These questions were among those discussed in September 2008 during the first International Creative Tourism Conference, sponsored by the city of Santa Fe and other members of UNESCO's Creative Cities Network, including Aswan, Egypt; Bologna, Italy; Berlin, Germany; Buenos Aires, Argentina; Montreal, Canada; Popayan, Colombia; and Seville, Spain. At this conference delegates from 16 countries around the world convened to discuss emerging issues and best practices in the use of Creative Tourism as a powerful economic development tool for cities, provinces, states, and countries. Countries represented included Nigeria, the Bahamas, Spain, the People's Republic of China, Japan, England, Mexico, Canada, Pakistan, Russia, Scotland, Australia, France, Egypt, Germany, Italy, and the United States. Conference participants interacted with some of the world's renowned leaders in creativity, geotourism and cultural entrepreneurship. Through panel discussions led by UNESCO Creative Cities leaders, delegates had the opportunity to learn about best practices in a diverse range of creative industries represented by the UNESCO network, including culinary arts, folk art, music, and design. One of the highlights of the conference was the presentation of more than 50 Santa Fe creative experiences that showcased Santa Fe's unique historical, cultural, and creative industries. Also unique was the Open Space session that allowed participants to build a networking agenda around Creative Tourism interests and activities in their home cities.

This book was developed to further promote the provocative and informative global conversations that transpired at our Santa Fe conference. Intended audiences are not only conference participants but also creative individuals worldwide who are actively engaged in promoting creativity and Creative Tourism as both economic and cultural development.

The format of our book basically follows the conference design, showcasing articles from keynote and panel presentations from the "tracks," which were: UNESCO Creative Cities: The Road Ahead; Creative Entrepreneurs: How To; Creative Tourism and Economic Development; and Creative Tourism Experiences in Santa Fe.

This introduction highlights key questions, definitional concerns, and the history of Creative Tourism, short though it may be. The rationale for why we consider Creative Tourism as an important emerging issue globally is introduced, and preliminary ideas for Santa Fe's next steps in Creative Tourism are identified. We begin this introduction with a brief history of the conference to further clarify our intent and goals for this book.

Conference participants working with artist Heidi Loewen. Photograph by Seth Roffman.

The Creative Cities Network was launched by UNESCO in October 2004, to enhance the creative, social, and economic potential of local cultural industries as a means of promoting UNESCO's goals related to cultural diversity. The vision of the network was to create opportunities for cities to: "Showcase their cultural assets on a global platform; make creativity an essential element of their economic development; share knowledge across cultural clusters around the world; and cultivate innovation through the exchange of creative know-how, experiences, and technology." Early on, UNESCO designated seven cultural/creative themes around which creative cities could collaborate: literature, cinema, folk art, design, music, gastronomy, and media arts. By 2006, nine cities had been selected to participate in the network including: Aswan, Berlin, Buenos Aires, Bologna, Seville, Montreal, Edinburgh, Popayan, and Santa Fe.

From its inception, the UNESCO Creative Cities Network was envisioned as a global platform for local endeavor. As such the actual programming and collaboration opportunities were to be generated by network members. The first network member to propose such an international collaboration was the city of Santa Fe. In October 2006, Santa Fe convened a meeting of network members to explore the possibility of presenting an international conference on Creative Tourism. It was our belief that Creative Tourism could indeed bridge all seven of the cultural themes represented by the network. The design of the planning meeting was actually a test of the ultimate conference design in that hands-on experiences and active participation were the basis of the three-day meeting. One of the highlights of the meeting was the collective experience of roasting chile, making handmade tortillas and experientially learning about local ingredients, including red and green chile, posolé, and beans. Building upon extensive research conducted by Creative Santa Fe (see page 227), network members enthusiastically debated goals and objectives for the conference, and agreed upon a definition to guide the conference that underscored engagement in authentic experiences and conversation versus passive learning. And thus, the first International Conference on Creative Tourism, A Global Conversation was born.

CREATIVE TOURISM DEFINED

The definition developed by the conference planning committee was: "Creative Tourism is tourism directed toward an engaged and authentic experience, with participative learning in the arts, heritage or special character of a place."

This definition is consistent with that promoted by Crispin Raymond and Greg Richards, who first coined the term Creative Tourism in their seminal work in New Zealand, starting in 2000. Through the Atlas Newsletter of November 2000, Raymond and Richards first described Creative Tourism as: "Tourism which offers visitors the opportunity to develop their creative potential through active participation in courses and learning experiences that are characteristic of the holiday destination where they are undertaken."

Greg Richards and Crispin Raymond. Photograph by Linda Carfagno.

Central to both of these definitions are hands-on experiences that are culturally authentic. These defining principles are the primary variables that distinguish Creative Tourism from other forms, such as cultural tourism or ecotourism or agri-tourism. Rather than viewing these forms of tourism as competitive or mutually exclusive, Creative Tourism should be viewed as a positive enhancement of other forms of tourism.

Santa Fe musicians perform at an evening event. Photograph by Linda Carfagno.

Creative Tourism is an emerging idea whose time has come. Support for this argument was made by several of the keynote speakers at the International Conference on Creative Tourism, as briefly highlighted below:

- Geoffrey Godbey, Professor Emeritus at Pennsylvania State University, in his presentation entitled, "Ahead of the Curve, New Trends in Tourism, Leisure, and Creative Time," referenced three reasons that Creative Tourism may prosper: "The rise of the creative class, the emergence of the experience economy, and changes in the status of women." He further observed that, "The act of tourism for such travelers is always a moving toward something, rather than away from something. They seek the beautiful, the unique, and the authentic."

- Alex Pattakos, author of the internationally acclaimed, *Prisoners of Our Thoughts*, focused his address, "Discovering the Deeper Meaning of Tourism," upon his well-documented assertion that, "The search for meaning is a megatrend of the 21st century." In his summary, Pattakos argued, "This meaning-focused megatrend can also be applied to the cultivation of creative economies. In this connection, the tourism sector offers unlimited possibilities in the design and delivery to be authentically creative and meaningful."

- Eric Maisel, America's foremost creativity coach, added his unique perspective regarding the potential influence that "creativity for life" plays in the kinds of tourism experiences travelers select.

- Charles Landry, noted author of *The Creative City: A Toolkit for Urban Innovators,* spoke of the importance of breaking down the barriers of traditional culture—museums, galleries, theatres, and shopping—in order to engage a city's broad range of cultural and imaginative resources, including distinctive symbols, activities, and local products in crafts, manufacturing and services.

- Co-author of *Tourism, Creativity and Development,* Greg Richards argued that Creative Tourism, through "facilitating becoming" can, from a supply perspective, actually help a tourist become a different person. Noting that, "The synergy between tourism and culture has been one of the major themes in tourism development and marketing in recent years," Richards delineated the shift from culture development strategies to creative development and argued, "Creativity is also increasingly being applied to the tourism sphere."

- Crispin Raymond similarly observed, "As Abraham Maslow explained in 1943 in his hierarchy of needs, human motivations evolve as our core needs are satisfied. And so it is with tourism. Now that more and more people have stayed in attractive hotels, swum among beautiful beaches, have 'been there and done that,' holiday makers are looking for more imaginative ways to enjoy their holidays. By offering visitors interactive experiences that reflect the culture of their holiday destinations, Creative Tourism helps to develop bonds between the visited and the visitor, the host and the guest, and encourages what Maslow called "self-actualization."

The interactive trends of travelers looking for more than just observing or buying, while economic downturns abound worldwide means the competition for tourism dollars will become even greater. The competitive edge will increasingly go to destinations which offer pleasure travel that is more deliberate, more customized, more experiential and more authentically tied to the creative experiences unique to a place. The global conversation created by keynotes, panelists and participants repeatedly reinforced the emerging idea that Creative Tourism can indeed provide this edge.

CREATIVE CITIES CONFERENCE NETWORKING

A primary objective of the conference was to provide an opportunity to share experiences across creative cities, both within and outside the UNESCO Creative Cities Network. Toward this end three distinct conference tracks were designed to address this objective:

- Track #1: The UNESCO Creative Cities: The Road Ahead
- Track #2: Creative Entrepreneurs: How To
- Track #3: Creative Tourism & Economic Development

Photograph by Linda Carfagno.

Through guided discussions, designed as global conversations, conference participants had a chance to interact with creative, dynamic, experienced, international creative industries professionals, who presented pragmatic best practices and solicited new ideas for next practices.

Highlights of the UNESCO track included presentations that showcased the unique creative industry developments in Montreal and Buenos Aires (Cities of Design), Bologna and Seville (Cities of Music), Aswan and Santa Fe (Cities of Folk Art), and Edinburgh (City of Literature). In addition, representatives of The Creative City Network of Canada shared specific strategies they have employed to activate a most effective network. What was common to all the cities was passionate commitment and much documented success at promoting creativity as a viable economic tool. Detailed descriptions of the programs and strategies presented are found in Section 2 of this book: Creative Cities: Conversations About Best Practices.

Creative Cities Network meeting. Photograph by Seth Roffman.

Highlights of the creative entrepreneur and economic development tracks included "Artists Tours, International Art Markets, International Festivals; Leveraging Your Community's Art Resources," "The Creative Entrepreneurs of New Zealand," and "Local Gastronomy and Farmers Markets." Each provided practical how-to advice on using such tools to enhance the work of creative entrepreneurs. "Culinary Tourism; American Indian Arts Creative Industry Models," and "Attracting Visitors All-Year Long" are examples of the range of other topics covered. Certainly one of the outstanding conference keynotes was the conversation led by Becky Anderson, former director of HandMade in America, whose down-to-earth examples of how the organization of Appalachian artists turned around a regional economy. The title of her keynote perfectly describes what she revealed: "Yester-morrow: Using a region's heritage and culture for its economic future." This paper, along with others focusing upon Creative Tourism's economic relevance may be found in Section 3 of this book: "Creative Entrepreneurs: The Economic Connection."

Additional networking opportunities were offered at the conference through the Open Space session, where multiple interactive workshops were convened and facilitated by conference participants. This experience was appropriately titled "Creative Tourism: Your Stories/Your Ideas." Sample topics raised and addressed by participants included: "Prosumer Creative Tourism," "Mass Tourism to Quality Tourism," "How to Create Community Art Space," "Creating A Network of Creative

Cities USA," "Marketing Creative Tourism," and "Practitioner Models and Steps for Enhancing the Visitor Experience." From these workshops, literally, pages of ideas were generated around topics delegates wished to pursue in the future.

Wise Fool larger-than-life puppet at an afternoon conference break. Photograph by Linda Carfagno.

A WEALTH OF CREATIVE EXPERIENCES (CONTRIBUTED BY TOM MAGUIRE)

Some of Santa Fe's largest and finest arts and cultural organizations presented workshops during the conference, including: an amulet-making workshop held at the Museum of International Folk Art and watercolor and pastel workshops conducted at the Georgia O'Keeffe Museum. In a digital photography workshop, the world-renowned Santa Fe Photographic Workshops showed why the visual appeal of Santa Fe cannot be overstated. From evocative landscapes to weathered architecture to the living faces of its cultures—Santa Fe has moved inhabitants and visitors alike to capture the depth and breadth of its beauty.

Many workshops focused on the indigenous cultures of Santa Fe and the northern New Mexico region. Native Americans were the first fiber artists in northern New Mexico, followed by the Spanish who introduced wool and looms to the area. Both cultures carry on rich traditions of fiber arts to this day with examples seen throughout the area. The Española Fiber Arts Center offered a Rio Grande weaving and Spanish Colonial Colcha embroidery workshop that brought these historic art forms to life. Conference attendees also participated in a straw appliqué workshop led by Lenise Martinez, award-winning Santa Fe Spanish Market artist; a traditional adobe oven building workshop, where attendees experienced the magic of turning earth, sand, water, and straw into architecture; and finally, Native American cooking in the oven they built.

Clay pottery is one of the earliest art forms found in the deserted villages surrounding Santa Fe. The functional pieces are now considered priceless links to the city's history and are an avenue for understanding Santa Fe's beginnings. Internationally known porcelain artist and teacher Heidi Loewen taught the fundamentals of turning clay into art in her sunny Santa Fe studio in a well-received porcelain workshop. Micaceous clay is prized for the sparkling pottery created from it and has a long history of use by New Mexico's Pueblo artists. La Morena ArtWorks instructors helped participants create micaceous vessels of their own. Sculptor Lisa Gordon led participants on an outing to Tesuque Glassworks and Shidoni Foundry for a glass-blowing demonstration, sculpting class, and foundry tour.

A poetry workshop led by Santa Fe Poet Laureate Valerie Martinez examined the poetic tradition and helped participants realize the poet within, and visual artist Lisa de St. Croix showed participants how a travel journal is not just a memory book, but also a chance to delve deeper into the experience. Conference participants also found inspiration on the trails at the Audubon Center in the hills above our city and created their own visual nature journals by combining the written word with visuals. Finally, a writers' workshop by the organization WORDHARVEST rounded out the literary activities offered at the Conference.

Have you ever dreamed of running away with the circus? Wise Fool offered participants the opportunity to ignite their imaginations, not to mention stretch and strengthen their bodies, experiencing circus arts for adults, including puppetry, mask making, and more in a fun and safe atmosphere during the circus arts sampler they presented. The adventuresome attendees also experienced a physical theater workshop led by members of Theater Grottesco or experienced the power and community of African drumming and dance, learning drumming and dances from West Africa, the Congo and Haiti.

And, of course, there was food! At the Santa Fe School of Cooking, participants experienced a "Chile Amor" cooking class, including the techniques of master chefs, the lore of the region and, of course, fabulous food. Anyway you experience it, food speaks volumes about the history of a region, and some conference attendees experienced it all in the cooking demonstrations, at the Conference, where the food and cooking were exemplary.

Conference participant enjoying a break. Photograph by Linda Carfagno.

Conference participants at Santa Fe School of Cooking. Photograph by Seth Roffman.

NEXT STEPS

One of the most important next steps for Santa Fe in Creative Tourism is making the wonderful creative experiences we shared with Conference delegates available to travelers worldwide, who are interested in moving beyond mass tourism experiences. In conjunction with our 400th anniversary commemoration which commences in fall of 2009, we will be launching a new website: www.SantaFeCreativeTourism.org. This website will connect travelers with the authentic, hands-on experiences that Conference participants recognized as unique to Santa Fe. In addition, Santa Fe will continue to network with other members of our UNESCO network—now standing at 19 cities from around the world! As a result of the conference, many new collaborations are in process, including a visit of one of our outstanding Native American artists to Nagoya, Japan, to consult on authentic souvenirs.

As of July 2009, the members of the UNESCO Creative Cities Network are:

Aswan, Egypt — Craft and Folk Art
Berlin, Germany — Design
Bologna, Italy — Music
Bradford, UK — Film
Buenos Aires, Argentina — Design
Edinburgh, UK — Literature
Ghent, Belgium — Music
Glasgow, UK — Music
Iowa City, Iowa, USA — Literature
Kanazawa, Japan — Craft and Folk Art

Kobe, Japan — Design
Lyon, France — Media Arts
Melbourne, Australia — Literature
Montreal, Canada — Design
Nagoya, Japan — Design
Popayan, Colombia — Gastronomy
Santa Fe, New Mexico, USA — Craft
    and Folk Art, and Design
Seville, Spain — Music
Shenzhen, China — Design

Another exciting next step is the development of the International Creative Tourism Institute, whose primary objective will be to promote Creative Tourism throughout the world. We are pursuing this with several of our international keynote speakers and we expect the not-for-profit organization to be created in 2010.

This introduction concludes with an invitation for you to contact us with any new Creative Tourism ideas you may wish to share or any possibilities for new collaborations among our communities. Do so at: rebeccawrz@comcast.net or svpratt@santafenm.gov.

We have much we can creatively do together around this issue, by recognizing Creative Tourism as an emerging economic and cultural development tool that is, and will continue to be, to borrow author Donald Schon's expression, "an idea in good currency."

Rebecca Wurzburger

Rebecca Wurzburger, Mayor Pro-Tem, was first elected to the governing body of the city of Santa Fe in 2002, re-elected in March 2006, and is now serving her second term. Councilor Wurzburger has long held an active interest in her city and community and has held positions on and founded several distinguished community boards, including Founding Board Member, Cornerstones Community Partnership and Co-founder, Santa Fe Habitat for Humanity Women Build Program. In recognition of her contributions, she was the recipient of the 17th Annual Governor's Award for Outstanding Women in New Mexico. Councilor Wurzburger holds a PhD in Public Administration and has more than 30 years experience in strategic planning and managing complex projects at local, state, and national levels. Her many years of active civic involvement throughout northern New Mexico have demonstrated her outstanding abilities to work in different communities and with different cultural perspectives.

SECTION 1

KEYNOTES
AND
KEY CONCEPTS

INTRODUCTION AND COMMON THEMES
by
Alex Pattakos, PhD
Author, *Prisoners of Our Thoughts*

As suggested in the introduction to this book, Creative Tourism is as an idea whose time has come. The contributions to this section, each of which is based on a keynote presentation delivered at the Santa Fe International Conference on Creative Tourism, underscore and reinforce this contention, as well as seek to bring focus to its key, albeit still-evolving, attributes. As you read the contributions to this section, you'll notice a number of common themes: the deeper meaning and spirit of place; an emphasis on co-creating tourist experiences; the need for engagement between all members of the tourism community of stakeholders; the sense of community and connectedness among/between these stakeholders; a focus and emphasis on transformation and transformative experiences; authenticity in both processes and products; local hospitality as a key ingredient for meaningful engagement; and the search for meaning as the primary, intrinsic motivation of human beings. To be sure, each author displays a unique perspective and places a different emphasis on these themes, and it is up to the reader to discern the deeper meaning and practical significance of their varying points of view.

Author Charles Landry, in *Experiencing Imagination: Travel as a Creative Trigger*, warns that, within the context of the tourism experience, travel often times provides "too few chances to be creative, imaginative, inventive" and, concomitantly, does not touch the human spirit in meaningful ways. In his view, these unsuspecting tourists are therefore left shortchanged at best, and empty at worst, as a result of experiences that, for all practical and existential purposes, are disengaging—even hollow—in their bottom-line effects. Tourism experiences, under such a scenario, effectively and ultimately become encounters of the worst kind, not only for the tourist but also for the local economy that relies on them.

It is against this backdrop that Landry sees the emergence of Creative Tourism as an antidote to the malaise that threatens tourism in a postmodern world. Moreover, Landry contextualizes the concept of Creative Tourism by summarizing and weaving together a number of related and pre-existing concepts, such as the creative city, creative economy, and creative class. One common thread, proposes Landry, is the notion of empowerment, that is, the need to shape one's own destiny and, we could add, one's identity, throughout the entire human experience. And this form of empowerment, in each case, is dependent upon opening up opportunities for authentic, meaningful, and creative expression.

"Engaged detachment and distance, it seems, can clarify the mind," observes Landry. In other words, by visiting places other than where one lives and works, especially places that offer opportunities that are authentic, meaningful, and creative, the tourism experience becomes a laboratory and training ground for self-reflection and personal growth. Travel, in this way, becomes more than simply the act of visiting a place in a geographical sense; it becomes a pathway for exploring inner space as well.

Crispin Raymond, a Creative Tourism consultant from New Zealand, discusses the origins of the term, Creative Tourism, from his own, very unique, personal experience. Indeed, he describes how the name "popped up in his head" after reading emails from his elder daughter who had been traveling through Southeast Asia and Australia. In this regard, he learned that his daughter had experienced connections with people in ways that most visitors never get to do. These connections had deep meaning both for her and for her hosts, much more so than most tourists encounter in their travels. Raymond's "aha" moment came shortly after attending a lecture by Greg Richards, another keynote speaker at the Santa Fe International Conference on Creative Tourism and contributor to this volume, who shared concerns about what was being defined and practiced as cultural tourism. Besides beginning a collaboration and friendship with Richards, Raymond coined the term, Creative Tourism, as a way to describe what his daughter had experienced during her recent travels. In 2003, Raymond established a Creative Tourism business in New Zealand and Richards began to write about this emerging concept with the new name. They defined Creative Tourism as follows: "Tourism which offers visitors the opportunity to develop their creative potential through active participation in courses and learning experiences which are characteristic of the holiday destination where they are undertaken."

Building upon his keynote address, Jay Walljasper, a writer for *National*

Geographic Traveler, stresses a common theme, the importance of place, while seeking to integrate what he refers to as geotourism within the context of creative cities with our explicit focus on the concept of Creative Tourism. Rather than viewing tourists as a force that destroys the character of places, communities, and the environment, Walljasper, who is an experienced travel writer, chooses, instead, to believe that "travel could be something noble, born out of humans' natural instinct to see this fascinating world of ours."

Geotourism, according to Walljasper, refers to tourism that sustains or enhances the character of a place, its environment, culture, aesthetics, heritage, and the well being of its residents. In other words, he says, it is "tourism done right." And, importantly, when done right, tourism really can improve, instead of destroy, a place. Geotourism, in this connection, is closely related both to Creative Tourism and to cultural tourism. Moreover, like Creative Tourism and cultural tourism, geotourism is very much concerned about the soul or spirit of a place which, as mentioned, is another theme shared by each of the keynotes. Creative Tourism and geotourism, Walljasper argues, are ways "to protect the places we love, to prevent the homogenization and destruction of wonderfully unique places all over the world."

In "Discovering the Deeper Meaning of Tourism," I begin by asserting that the search for meaning is a megatrend of the 21st century and that it is the primary intrinsic motivation of human beings. As a motivational force, meaning drives engagement within a wide range of personal and work-related contexts and, in turn, drives and sustains worker/customer satisfaction, performance, creativity, and innovation at the individual and collective levels. The search for meaning megatrend can also be applied to the cultivation of creative and innovation economies. In this connection, I would argue that the tourism sector offers unlimited possibilities in design and delivery to be authentically creative and meaningful, as well as to be an integral part of a jurisdiction's innovation engine for community and economic development.

Moreover, by understanding how to leverage tourism from an innovation, not simply a creative perspective, another important dimension of the deeper meaning of tourism can be discovered and put to practical use. In my essay, I espouse a paradigm shift from creative economy to innovation economy, in which tourism is viewed as an integrated, meaning-focused strategy that adds maximum value and provides the highest return on investment for all stakeholders.

Then Crispin Raymond returns with a cautionary tale about the practical challenges of developing a Creative Tourism initiative, based on his experience in New Zealand, into a sustainable business. Among the lessons learned, Raymond found that it was easier to establish a supply of Creative Tourism experiences than it was to create a demand for them. In addition, he learned that Creative Tourism experiences are very rewarding for all involved, and this observation reflects and reinforces Creative Tourism's potential. Moreover, local traditions and skills are at the core of Creative Tourism experiences; in many countries, like New Zealand, these originate from the locale's indigenous people. Raymond also learned that authenticity is not a static concept and, in fact, is constantly evolving due to such things as immigration and globalization. Raymond ends his piece with a description of two alternative development approaches that were developed with the benefit of hindsight: a commercial tourism model and a community network model.

Robert McNulty outlines the history, vision, and mission of Partners for Livable Cities, a non-profit entity that he founded and serves as president. Partners utilizes a number of pathways—advocacy, information, leadership, and guidance—to help communities solve their problems. The organization believes in, and is committed to, public/private partnerships, and collaboration with the broadly-defined community of stakeholders. Civic engagement is viewed as the main pillar supporting such collaborative efforts. McNulty stresses that "tourism is a form of celebration of value. Tourism is a form of reinvestment in people." He also prefers not to call "tourists" tourists; instead, he likes to call them visitors. According to McNulty's definition, tourism involves visitors who, in successive stages of visitation, find something so enchanting that they become part of the fabric of the community, rather than a burden on the community. He also argues for including people 50-years and older as an integral part of the creative economy and as a key element of the Creative Tourism agenda and economic development engine. In his article, McNulty also describes other forces at work that will change the tourism landscape, and he suggests ways and offers examples of how to deal effectively with these change forces.

In his essay, tourism consultant and researcher, Greg Richards, contends that Creative Tourism "is a new form of tourism that has the potential to change existing models of tourism development and make a contribution to diversifying and innovating the tourist experience." He examines the background and development of the Creative Tourism concept, showing persuasively how the production and consumption of experiences have shifted from cultural tourism to Creative Tourism. He also presents a number of different models of Creative Tourism development and illustrates how the concept has been implemented in different ways around the world. After describing the growing importance of creativity and experience as personal preferences and as drivers for economic vitality and growth, Richards asserts that tourists are seeking more active, engaging experiences in the postmodern era. Importantly, he underscores that contemporary tourists are searching for "identity, meaning and roots," which impels many to seek experiences that give them the opportunity to interact with local communities, learning more about what makes them tick and how they relate to the world.

Experiencing Imagination: Travel as a Creative Trigger

by
Charles Landry
Director of Comedia
and author of *The Art of City Making*

Travel is the prism through which we will explore two words— creativity and experience. They constantly appear in brochures, books, and even headlines especially within the tourism world. They have emerged over the last decade with ever greater frequency. This indicates a problem. It appears we have too few chances to be creative, imaginative, inventive, and to express ourselves fully from within our deeper being. This leaves us feeling empty, as our spirit is not touched. For this reason, we are not feeling or triggering the full register or scale of experience we know we can have. Feelings of more profound, lasting meaning are too fleeting, rare and difficult to achieve. Travel often seems like an answer to capture special moments that then etch themselves into memory.

This process has deeper causes. Increasingly, experience is pre-packaged, created by someone else, targeted at you—a specific niche market with identified needs. You are boxed into a category. Chance encounter, discovery, exploration fall by the wayside. Many things we did in the past as part of everyday life are now turned into saleable products. They are monetized. They become themed products like taking a walk or seeing the locals. Through this process we are letting ourselves become un-free.

As these products, offers, and opportunities shout at us, we suffer from information overload. This makes many of us close in and shield ourselves, as we cannot absorb everything. Those selling to us then shout louder, they offer experiences that are more shrill, that are faster, more exciting.

Many react on the principle of "less is more." Less surface and more depth. Creative Tourism is one interesting response to a shallow world. Before we explore Creative Tourism and to provide a context, let us briefly summarize other creative concepts like creative city, creative economy, creative class. These emerged before Creative Tourism and yet we can now see how the idea neatly fits into a broader Zeitgeist—the desire to engage, to express oneself, to participate, and to be involved.

CREATIVE: A MANTRA OF THE AGE

Everything is creative today. Creativity is like a rash. A myriad of places and projects are calling themselves creative. There are creative cities (more than 80 at the last count), creative economies, that most countries are trying to strengthen, creative classes in hip cities the world over, and now Creative Tourism. What are some of the threads we can detect? One common theme and the most important is empowerment, using imagination, generating satisfactory experiences, and the idea of being a shaper of one's own destiny.

The Creative City

The creative city concept developed nearly 20 years ago in response to the dramatic economic, social, and cultural transformations then happening in Europe as cities restructured and rethought their roles and purposes.

When introduced, the concept was seen as aspirational, a clarion call to encourage open mindedness and imagination. It was intended to have a dramatic impact on organizational culture. Its philosophy was that more potential exists than we think. It posits that conditions should be created for people to think, plan, and act with imagination in harnessing opportunities or solving seemingly intractable urban problems. A positive concept, its assumption is that ordinary people can make the extraordinary happen if given the chance. It acknowledges that creativity is context-driven, and that not only artists and those involved in the creative economy are creative, although they play an important role. Creativity can come from any source, including anyone who addresses issues in an inventive way—a business person, social worker, scientist, or public administrator. Yet creativity, as legitimized in the arts and artistic creativity, has special qualities that chime well with the ideas-driven knowledge economy.

A Culture of Creativity

The creative city embeds a culture of creativity into how urban stakeholders operate. Encouraging creativity and legitimizing imagination within the public, private, and community spheres broadens the ideas bank of possibilities and potential solutions to any urban problem. Divergent, broad-ranging thinking generates multiple options. Convergent thinking narrows down possibilities, and urban innovations emerge once they have passed through the reality checker.

The creative city identifies, nurtures, attracts, and sustains its talent to mobilize ideas, talents, and creative organizations to keep and attract the gifted and the young. Within a creative city is wrapped the idea of the creative economy. This focuses on the media and entertainment industries, the arts and cultural heritage, and creative business-to-business services.

The people working within these areas are seen as key players in fostering innovation and as a source of economic growth and wealth creation. The latter sphere is perhaps the most important, since they can add value to every product or service. Design, advertising, and entertainment in particular act as drivers of innovation in the broader economy and shape the so-called experience economy. This spectacularizes the city, and artists are increasingly used to provide the imagination. For instance, major events, such as the opening of the Olympics or exhibitions and shows, have intensive artistic input.

The central concern of Richard Florida and his work on the creative class is on the quality of place. He asks rhetorically: "What's there: the combination of the built environment and the natural environment; a proper setting for pursuit of creative lives. Who's there: the diverse kinds of people, interacting and providing cues that anyone can plug into and make a life in that community. What's going on: the vibrancy of street life, café culture, arts, music and people engaging in outdoor activities— altogether, a lot of active, exciting, creative endeavors."

Richard Florida makes an important conceptual shift by focusing on the creative role of people in the creative age. He notes the emergence of a new social group or class—the creative class, that is a demographic segment of the population, and he develops indicators to measure the attributes of places that attract and retain the creative class, which in turn attracts companies.

It was assumed people moved to jobs, so regions should adopt investment attraction policies to attract companies. Florida reverses the argument, highlighting how companies, especially innovative companies offering high-value employment, are attracted to regions where creatives like to live and visit. From this follows the question: Who are these people and what are the key attributes of a region/place that attracts the creative class and finally, how can you encourage the creatives to cluster? Artists are one group at the core of this class, as are creative economy people, as well as brain workers such as scientists.

The philosophy behind creative tourism is to engender richer, more fulfilling experiences. Places like Santa Fe that provide this are usually deemed to be creative cites—places which attract artists, designers, creative economies types, and members of the so-called creative class.

Being Outside Helps You Look Inside

Let us now explore the creativity notion through the eyes of tourism. Travel can make you look inside, precisely because you are outside yourself. This allows you, in principle, to grow because you self-reflect. At its best this encounter with the other triggers other things too. You think of how lives are lived and therefore about your own; how individuals and groups connect across cultures, and how you might join with others too; how shared humanity could work and how you can foster common experience; how rituals emerge as common agreements to bind, bond, and broker community; and how your own place at home works at a deeper level.

Some while back, I undertook a survey of people involved in urban regeneration, and asked them what changed their mind most, what had the most transformative effect and caused them to learn and change themselves. The choices included reading a book, looking things up on the Internet, watching television, talking to friends or peers, visiting a site, or going somewhere with your peer group. The most profound effect was traveling together as a group, then experiencing a project that related to their concerns or life. The key was finding out how it worked, what made it tick, and then talking, eating and socializing with the local actors. What happened was that they reflected on their own work, their own circumstances, and their own home. Engaged detachment and distance, it seems, can clarify the mind.

What we see here is having a purpose, there being a promise of something as yet unknown, and the ability to learn. These ingredients contribute to a more rounded experience.

Not all forms of travel do this to you, of course. Let's take two examples. Traveling too much can mean you do not connect at all and there are vast swathes of the hyper-mobile. You are everywhere and nowhere at the same time. Things pass by too speedily. In this blur there is only the airport, the bus, the train, the car. The getting there and getting out is often all there is. And everything can look the same. When things are too speedy you often hold onto the familiar, the known, the safe. This can end you up in the ex-pat drinking den with other people like you, the globally branded hotel or seeing a musician you could have seen at home. The being in the moment, the being anchored, is lost. An anchored experience is usually slow; it takes time and some effort; it takes thought and thoughtfulness. It often goes step by step.

The second type of travel is the vast number of packaged, ordered, and pre-set trips. You can feel herded, timetabled, and structured. These trips are there to shut you off, to give you that two week window of letting go and having fun, to make you relax, be soporific so you can cope again with a life at home where many have little control of what they do. Too often it is a palliative for our lives that can feel as if they are insufficiently lived, self-conscious, and in the moment.

CREATIVE TOURISM

Creative Tourism tries to break a mould. At its best, it is an unmediated, direct, unfiltered experience that is not pre-digested and staged. There is no distant, detached observing; there is only living in the now. We can merge into a city's emotional landscape and get under its skin; we can understand how it functions day to day, and how its larger and smaller dramas unfold. It is not only about visiting heritage sites, icons, or cultural events. Much of the activity is ordinary, like seeing people go to work, waiting in a queue to catch a bus, standing outside the office and smoking, buying a drink or sandwich, chatting on the sidewalks, or watching young lovers canoodle on a bench. This is the lived experience of being there, rather than borrowing its landscape, sights, and delights, and keeping them to oneself. We call this authentic, and what we mean is that it is of itself and unsullied. The reality is that barely anything is so pure.

To make the most of being in a city or a rural area, we need to know someone who lives and works there. They are initially our guides, who take us deeper into the crevices and way of life of a place. These may include: how people earn a living, survive, are joyful or sad, how they celebrate their rituals, and matters that are important to them. In time as a creative tourist we co-create our experience with them; we share. It can be banal or profound. It can start with a conversation about their life and ours; we compare the way they and we do things. We discuss commonalities and differences. And as we know more, we want to get involved, we may perhaps imagine even living there and speculate what it would be like. We ask ourselves the question: "What could I do here? Is there a niche for me? What can I offer to them? Where would I live?"

Then, as a visitor we can turn into something more than we thought. Perhaps to feel like a welcome guest, even a temporary citizen, participating in the place we are visiting. By being involved and engaged in something relevant to the place, we have a chance to give back to the place we visit. This is because we are responding to it. Creative Tourism in this sense could be a jazz musician from afar improvising with a local band. It can be an advisor helping a city solve a problem; it can be a person learning a language or a student working as an au pair. It can also be learning to cook their cuisine, trying to learn their crafts, learning about their philosophy of life. But it can also be mundane, yet important, things like going out with the ambulance crew and finding out how they work, or hitching a lift with a delivery vehicle and finding you end up in odd places.

When we observe these experiences closely, we understand that they are the cultural resources, which are the raw materials of a place and its values. They are the value base, because people do things the way they do for their own special reasons. They are responding to their historical and locational circumstances. That is why we cook differently in different places, and ambulance crews might do their business differently than we do. In every culture, creativity is the method people use to exploit these resources and to help them grow.

The keen eye, aware of cultural resources, can see in every crevice of a city or rural area a hidden story or potential, just as locals do by taking a broad sweep of their cultural assets and trying to turn them to economic advantage. So if they have many trees, there are likely to be skills in carpentry. Cultural resources are embodied in peoples' skills and talents. They are not only things like buildings or heritage sites, but also symbols, activities, and the repertoire of local products in crafts, manufacturing and services, such as the intricate skills of sari makers in Indian cities, wood carvers of Bali, or dyers of Djenne in Mali. They are the historical, industrial, and artistic heritage of a place, representing assets including architecture, urban landscapes, or landmarks. They are local and indigenous traditions of public life, festivals, rituals, or stories, as well as hobbies and enthusiasms. Some are professional, and others are amateur. They also include resources like food and cooking, leisure activities, clothing, and sub-cultures that exist everywhere, but are often neglected. And, of course, cultural resources are the conventional range and quality of skills in the performing and visual arts, and the newer cultural industries. This culturally aware focus will go well beyond the tangible and also consider the senses from colour to sound, smell, and visual appearance.

So the traveling mind needs to ready itself to be open for a deeper experience. It needs intense curiosity, a love of detail and persistence, it needs a way of seeing, and the ability to interpret what it sees, feels, and does. One of the few travel books that helps us learn how to see is Philip Cornwel-Smith's *Very Thai: Everyday Popular Culture*.

MULTIPLE IDENTITIES

There is a new phenomenon, however, in that the more the world is mobile, and mass mobility is the order of the day, there are more people who for more reasons relate to many places. They have multiple attachments and identities to place. They might live there short term; they might visit regularly. In fact, they might decide that certain places are part of their identity, even though they are rarely there. This process is speeding up, conditioned largely by the changing nature of work and technological possibilities. Who are these people then? They are more than occasional visitors; are they tourists, guests, semi-residents, citizens? The distinction between the engaged outsider and the insider is changing and blurring. Who is more of a citizen, the committed outsider, or the unconcerned insider? Who has more rights to call themselves citizens? To be a citizen implies being a member of a community and carries the right to participation; it implies too some responsibilities and duties. What if a resident does not care?

In Essence: Experience

The idea of what tourism can be has gone along a trajectory that blurs insiders and outsiders. We had tourists, travelers, cultural tourists, and have now arrived at creative tourists. This is tourism, as defined by Greg Richards and Crispin Raymond, that involves the active participation of travelers in the culture of the host community through interactive workshops and informal learning experiences. This tourism seeks an engaged, unpackaged, authentic experience that promotes an active understanding of the specific cultural features of a place. The creative tourist is engaged.

The key distinction is between active and passive. This lies at the heart of the debate about tourists or travelers, and even citizens. The one, it is assumed, gazes and absorbs the pre-given, giving little back; the other seeks to understand, interpret, engage, to find significance.

Yet all forms of tourism in essence seek experience. The battle is between shallowness and depth, surface and substance, frenzied consumption as a palliative or quiet reflection, being a disconnected observer of the local, or seeking to understand it.

Is it tourism experienced from a safe, detached distance and catered for and organized? Is it, by contrast, self-made, and are encounters uncertain, open to chance, and serendipity? Are set pieces, spectacles, and events the sole object of the journey? Is the foreign culture considered an obstacle, an oddity, a nuisance? Are there chances to meet locals, or do we only meet others like us? Yet what we usually remember most is meeting a local on their own terms. That is why experimental tourism (see *The Lonely Planet Guide to Experimental Travel* by Rachael Anthony and Joel Henry) is so attractive. It takes us beyond the sites and scenes and encourages us to see a social security office, a suburb, a housing estate, the police station, the grocery store. Anyone who has lost their passport or had a mishap will know that, in spite of the travails, it is these encounters that are memorable. These are encounters that cannot be found within the guide book. It is a matter of direct contact that can become a transformative experience as you are open to being transformed.

City Safari

The ideas behind the City Safari Project in Rotterdam may be a new model.

They have invented a new sustainable approach to tourism development. The brand name City Safari has been stolen or copied by many, but not the core idea. The project has a list of more than 300 people or organizations that are willing to be visited. The visitor chooses the kind of people they want to meet. This could range from priests to imams, from urban planners and gardening enthusiasts to unusual shopkeepers, tattooists and collectors of the bizarre, like a man who owns over a thousand koi carp kept in tanks in a collective garden of a series of apartment blocks. They can choose places to go, from delicatessens to sex shops to a café employing recovering heroin addicts. The visitor gets an address and has to find their target by exploring and navigating the city. They encounter people a normal tourist would never meet. They hand over paid-for vouchers and in return they get a service—primarily a conversation about residents' lives and what they do. In addition, perhaps, they get a glass of wine, a tour of a building or a meal. Its power is that the tourist and the locals connect, and the benefits go directly to the local rather than an intermediary. City Safari was started as an economic development project by Kees de Gruiter and is now owned by Marjolijn Masselink, bringing more resources to local people rather than intermediaries.

SLOW CITIES AS A CREATIVE TOURISM METAPHOR

The slow cities movement is another movement with scope to change the tourism experience. It is a reaction to speed and based on ethos-driven development. Slow cities developed out of the slow food movement, which started in Italy in the 1980s. Slow food promotes the protection of local biodiversity, the right to taste through preserving local cooking and eating traditions, and highlights the folly of fast food and fast life. Slow cities is expanding the concept to be a way of life. It emphasizes the importance of local identity through preserving and maintaining the local natural and built environments: developing infrastructure in harmony with the natural landscape and its use; using technology to improve quality of life and the natural and urban environment; encouraging the use and production of local foodstuffs using eco-sensitive methods; supporting production based on cultural traditions in the local area; and promoting the quality of local hospitality.

The aim of the slow cities movement is to implement a program of civilized harmony and activity grounded in the serenity of everyday life by bringing together communities who share this ideal. The focus is on appreciation of the seasons and cycles of nature, the cultivation and growing of local produce, through slow, reflective living. Slow cities is not opposed to progress, but focuses on changes in technology and globalization as tools to make life better and easier, while protecting the uniqueness of towns' characters. To be a member of slow cities and to be able to display the movement's snail logo, a city must meet a range of requirements, including increasing pedestrian access, implementing recycling and reuse policies, and introducing an ecological transport system. Working with the Slow Food Network, the slow cities movement is spreading the word about its slow brand of community connectedness.

These are the kinds of projects that explain tangibly what sustainable tourism is. This manages resources to fulfill economic, social, and aesthetic needs and maintains cultural integrity, essential ecological processes, biological diversity, and life support systems.

The overarching theme though is experience of people and place, allowing exposure to circumstances, living through things with others, sharing, feeling, sensing, finding emotional significance and meaning in what happens and what you are doing.

The Search for Meaning

Underlying the desire to engage and experience deeply is finding significance, relevance, and meaning in what you do and are feeling. The will to achieve meaning is the purpose of life and what drives people, Viktor Frankl notes. As Sartre says, "Existence precedes essence," and so meaning is not given; it has to be achieved, either through deeds, by doing something important to oneself, by experiencing something of value such as a person, a place, a picture, or by suffering. Travel can be powerful, because it puts a mirror onto ourselves and so encourages us to self-reflect. Being outside helps you look inside. Travel, as F. Daniel Harbecke writes, is a metaphor for the meaningful experience of life.

To be ready for this transformative effect requires qualities of mind such as openness, the willingness to listen and to learn, or to want to be engaged or involved. It requires a mutual understanding with the insiders that you want to be a part of what they are about, as well as be a maker, shaper, or co-creator of your own experience. This might, at its simplest, be cooking a meal that you have learnt from a local, and it might extend over time to getting involved in a local project.

A Small Warning

Creative everything or experience has now become a catch-all phrase in danger of losing its bite and obliterating the reasons why the ideas of creative tourism, cities, economy, and class emerged in the first place. These are essentially about unleashing, harnessing, empowering people and potential from whatever source in a community. Overuse, hype, and the tendency for places and projects to adopt the term, creative, without thinking through its real consequences, could mean that the notion becomes hollowed out, chewed up, and thrown out until the next big slogan comes along. To be creative is about a journey of becoming, not a fixed state of affairs. It is a challenge, when taken seriously, to existing organizational structures, habitual ways of doing things, and power configurations. It is concerned with enabling potential and creation to unfold, so unleashing the ideas, imagination and implementation, and delivery capacities of individuals and communities. It means overcoming some more deeply entrenched obstacles, many of which are in the mind and mindset, including thinking and operating within silos, and operating hierarchically in departmental ghettoes, rather than horizontally across disciplines and fields.

Charles Landry. Photograph by Linda Carfagno.

Charles Landry helps cities reach their potential by triggering their imaginations. Working with local leaders as a critical friend, he facilitates and stimulates so cities can transform for the better. He helps find original solutions to seemingly intractable dilemmas, like marrying innovation and tradition, balancing wealth creation and social cohesiveness, or local distinctiveness and a global orientation. An authority on creativity and city futures, he focuses on how the unique culture of a place can invigorate economies, the sense of self and confidence.

He has published extensively, including *The Art of City Making* (2006); *The Intercultural City* (2007) with Phil Wood; *The Creative City: A Toolkit for Urban Innovators* (2000); *Riding the Rapids: Urban Life in an Age of Complexity* (2004) and, with Marc Pachter, *Culture @ the Crossroads* (2001). He has lectured all over the world and presented over 150 keynote addresses on topics including risk and creativity, creative cities and beyond, art in city life, complexity and city making, and diverse cultures, diverse creativities. Further details from www.charleslandry.com.

What's in a Name?
The Origins of the Term, Creative Tourism
by
Crispin Raymond
Creative Tourism Consultant

W hen parents name their children they usually choose an existing name from their family or a friend, from a character in a book or film, or perhaps a celebrity's name. But sometimes new names just pop into the head. And so it was with Creative Tourism.

At the end of 1999, my elder daughter was traveling through Southeast Asia and Australia on her way to New Zealand. Reading her emails at the breakfast table in England where we then lived, my wife and I were struck by what she was choosing to do on her journey. She enrolled in a week's introduction to Thai massage in Chiang Mai, spent a day learning vegetarian cookery in Bali, and then set off to the Australian outback for a course on how to be a jillaroo (the manager of a sheep or cattle station), before working as a volunteer on an outback property. She was excited to be learning new skills, but was getting even more satisfaction from learning about the lifestyles of local residents. She was interacting with a wide range of people in ways that most visitors never achieve. Her experiences had more meaning, both for her and her hosts, than most tourists encounter today. "Why isn't there a name for this sort of tourism?" my wife commented, before the conversation turned to the immediacies of the morning. "Pass the cornflakes," said I.

A few weeks later, on the morning of 24 January 2000 in Viana do Castelo, Portugal to be precise, I had the good fortune to attend a lecture from one of Europe's leading thinkers on cultural tourism. Greg Richards was speaking about the rapid growth of cultural tourism in Europe, but arguing that there was a danger of cultural tourists becoming disillusioned with the experiences on offer. Many of these were passive and dull, he felt, with too many old buildings (ABC, another bloody cathedral) and too many "so what?" historical factoids ("This is the room where the third count was married in August 1637"). "Cultural Tourism needs to become more interactive and creative if it is fully to engage and satisfy its growing number of consumers," he said.

This time a metaphorical light flashed. Creative Tourism, that would be a great name for what my daughter had been doing. I went up to Greg after his lecture, and a collaboration and friendship began that continue today. We decided that he would try to establish the term within academic circles through his lecturing and writing, while I tried to develop it in practice by setting up a Creative Tourism business in New Zealand when I migrated here in 2001 (www.creativetourism.co.nz).

We defined the term in the ATLAS Newsletter of November 2000 as: "Tourism which offers visitors the opportunity to develop their creative potential through active participation in courses and learning experiences which are characteristic of the holiday destination where they are undertaken."

As my daughter discovered, creative experiences are available in many countries if you have the time to seek them out. Names matter, however, and with its own name, this form of tourism has begun to be more widely appreciated and is becoming better established. This new tourism child now had a name that people remember easily and whose underlying concept is quickly understood and appreciated. The Santa Fe conference has been a significant step along the road towards the recognition and understanding of Creative Tourism.

Crispin Raymond

Crispin Raymond has a 25 year background in the arts, first as chief executive of the Theater Royal in Bath, England, and subsequently as the founder and leader of a consulting firm specializing in policy, management, building, and funding issues for charitable and arts organizations. Raymond and Greg Richards coined the term Creative Tourism, and launched Creative Tourism New Zealand in 2003.

WANT TO SEE A BETTER WORLD? HOW A NEW IDEA CALLED GEOTOURISM CAN IMPROVE THE PLACES YOU VISIT AS WELL AS YOUR VACATION

by

Jay Walljasper

Writer, Editor, Consultant

Contributing Editor, *National Geographic Traveler*

Executive Editor, *Ode*

(Mr. Walljasper's original presentation at the 2008 Conference included a Power Point presentation showing a number of geotourist destinations.)

The last several days have given me the chance to explore the heart and soul of Santa Fe—a community that is a beacon of what a creative city can be.

I can offer my own testimony for the power of creative cities. Two cities represented at this conference have had an immense impact on my own life. I attended college in Iowa City, with the idea of becoming a political science professor. But the town's literary culture exerted such a strong influence on me that I left, convinced that there was no greater mission for me in the whole world than to be a writer. And that's exactly what I have done. My favorite subject to write about is cities, a passion that was kindled during a visit to Montreal soon after completing college. Montreal, of course, is another of the cities taking part in this conference on Creative Tourism. From that point on, it was my life's dream to explore as many cities as I could.

As a relatively young man, I got what I thought was the perfect job, when I became a travel editor at *Better Homes and Gardens* magazine, with eight million subscribers. It was a great opportunity to travel and learn about magazines, but a lot of the time I felt as though I was promoting products sold by the travel industry more than I was writing about the special things that make places wonderful. I soon left the magazine, convinced that travel writing was not for me.

I became editor of a new magazine called *Utne Reader*, which left its mark on the world as an incubator of new ideas in the realm of politics, culture, and evolving lifestyles. I did have the opportunity to check back once in a while into the world of travel, since *Utne Reader* chronicled the rise of ecotourism and sustainable tourism. And it always surprised me how much tourism was seen as a baneful force in the world. Most observers seemed to view travelers as a force that destroyed the character of places, destroyed the fabric of communities, and destroyed the natural environment. I could see their point—the evidence of what's wrong with the travel industry was all around. Yet, in my heart, I felt that the impulse of most tourists was not to wreck places. I believed travel could be something noble, born out of humans' natural instinct to see this fascinating world of ours.

Luckily for me, I circled back to the world of travel writing when I picked up a copy of *National Geographic Traveler* magazine at a bookstore in Hayward, Wisconsin, on my way back from a vacation on the shores of Lake Superior a few years back. I immediately started reading an article about a new idea called geotourism, and realized then and there that geotourism was the reason I had originally wanted to write about travel.

Geotourism means, in short, tourism that sustains or enhances the character of a place, its environment, culture, aesthetics, heritage, and the well being of its residents. I like to think of geotourism as tourism done right. And when done right, tourism really can improve, instead of destroy, a place. The reason we visit places is because we love how unique and special they are.

Geotourism steps outside the travel industry's sometimes narrow focus on merely ringing up sales at the cash register, to look at the bigger picture—the music of a place, the dances of a place, the crafts of a place, the traditional architecture, the history, the arts, and everyone's favorite pastime, the food of a place. During the presentations the past two days, I have realized that the intersection between geotourism, Creative Tourism, and cultural tourism is quite large.

Geotourism allows you to seek out what's special and distinctive about a place, knowing there is nowhere else in the world exactly like the place you are visiting— whether the backstreets of Bangkok, beaches along the Aegean Sea, or even downtown Fargo, North Dakota. Don't laugh if you haven't been there—it's an interesting and lively place.

Geotourism is about soaking up the culture and the soul of a place. And it fosters a whole different view of development—development that is focused on making places vital and making them better places for people who live there, as well as for tourists.

I was excited by geotourism and like any self-respecting journalist, I used my press pass as a way to find out more about it. I contacted Jonathan Tourtellot, Geotourism Editor of *National Geographic Traveler,* as well as the founder of the Center for Sustainable Destinations, which is a project of the National Geographic Society. We had a great phone conversation, and made firm plans to meet up sometime in an interesting place, so that I could write an article about geotourism. It took awhile, but one day he called and said, "Can you come to Chile? I'm going there to do a geotouristic assessment." "Yes," I shouted back into the phone, and soon we met up in Santiago to embark on an exploration of the Andes, the vineyards, the seacoast, and all the things that make Chile.

As you can see, researching geotourism is a lot of fun, but it also is a very serious, important topic. Essentially, geotourism is the antidote for what Tourtellot calls, "Tourism on steroids." International tourism—the number of people who visit somewhere outside their country—doubled between 1990 and 2008. By next year, it is projected that a billion people will be traveling across the borders of other countries. And, by 2015, as more Chinese and Indians see the world, it is expected to be one and one-half billion. If we count domestic along with international travel, there will be seven billion tourists roaming the world.

Some people say that won't happen with the economic crisis and rising airfares. There have always been periodic dips in tourism, after 9/11 (few Americans thought they would ever visit another country after that), the SARS epidemic, the start of the Iraq war, and the dot.com bust. But none of those events had lasting effect on the number of people traveling around the globe. World travel is a powerful human instinct and people always find ways to do it, even when the economy isn't great.

Jonathan Tourtellot often declares that everybody in the world deserves a vacation. We can't denounce tourism as a rapacious industry, and tell all the people in the developing world they can't start traveling because it's bad for the environment.

But when seven billion people are roaming the globe, where will everyone go? We can love places to death. Machu Picchu in Peru probably is one of the most magnificent, amazing, interesting places on the planet. We've heard about it since we were small children and of course everybody wants to go visit. But what happens when everyone descends on Machu Picchu? One of the plans cooked up by the Peruvian government was to build a network of cable cars going up to the top of Machu Picchu, like a ski resort. Can you imagine what that could do to the experience of being in this sacred place that has been there for thousands and thousands of years? I am happy that this was eventually abandoned.

Many of the most remarkable places in the world are straining under the weight of visitors. The Galapagos Islands are facing an invasion of tourist boats that affect the unique ecosystem of that place. Spain's once lovely Costa del Sol is now widely known as the Costa del Concrete. It is looks like one long high-rise hotel, all along the Mediterranean Sea.

Creative Tourism and geotourism are ways to protect the places we love, to prevent the homogenization and destruction of wonderfully unique places all over the world. Geotourism can keep places distinctive, genuine and healthy. It is the cure for "tourism on steroids."

Maui is another of these places in danger of being loved to death. Everybody's heard about it, and wants to visit. But, as the cliché goes, there is still a Maui that tourists seldom see. A man who loves Maui has created a business taking travelers "out into the back country." He's an interpretive guide, telling people about the ecosystems, the local stories, and lore. He instills in visitors a respect for taking care of the place. This is a perfect example of geotourism.

An interpretive guide is a key element of geotourism. Geotourism and Creative Tourism are about creating a relationship with a place and hiring someone who's knowledgeable to show you around is a great way to do that.

I don't want to paint too dark a picture of the tourist industry, because there are a number of places around the world that handle large volumes of tourists and do it well with minimum damage. The first places that leap to mind are Vermont and Tuscany, which are very popular tourist destinations and yet, when you're there, you don't feel the experience has been degraded. The reason for this is that people, when they travel to Vermont, want to see the rolling hills and town commons and general stores and country inns and downtown diners. They are not demanding chain restaurants and motels. In Tuscany, they want to experience Tuscan food and wine and scenery, not what they usually have back home.

This is the core of geotourism and it helps protect those places. When you are seeking the authenticity of a place as a traveler, then you don't want to participate in activities that ultimately trash the place. You are not going to insist on having the same food and beer and high level of plumbing that you are used to.

When people hear about geotourism, ecotourism, sustainable tourism, they think this applies only to some untouched place in the countryside, some pristine natural environment. But actually, cities are quite central to the idea and practice of geotourism.

There are simple reasons for this. For one, cities are used to absorbing a lot of people. On any day in the world's large cities, you are sharing the streets with thousands or tens of thousands of other tourists, but it doesn't feel as if you are in some overcrowded urban theme park. These places were created to accommodate large numbers of people.

The other reason is that urban tourism doesn't stress the environment in the same way as travel to remote destinations. No one is building a new landing strip in the middle of a pristine forest so more people can visit New York City or Cairo or Copenhagen. The infrastructure is already there and tourists are icing on the cake.

One of the great things about cities as a geotouristic destination is that they have such a wealth of things to do. Not everyone who goes to Paris is going to insist on seeing the Mona Lisa. I have yet to see the Mona Lisa during my half dozen visits over the past 20 years.

But what would happen if everyone did want to see the Mona Lisa? There are 1.5 billion global tourists each year, and let's suppose they are all hell-bent on seeing the Mona Lisa? How would it work? Jonathan Tourtellot calculates that even with tourists allowed to see da Vinci's famous painting for only one minute in groups of 25, with the Louvre open 24 hours a day, it would still take more than 115 years for all of them to see the Mona Lisa. That's not only unsustainable, it's a lousy tourist experience. Geotourism is about improving the traveler's enjoyment just as much as preserving the places we all cherish.

One focus of geotourism is getting people away from just visiting the famous sites. It's fine to see the Eiffel Tower or even the Mona Lisa if that's a longtime dream, but the most memorable, wonderful elements of a trip often come from discovering little, out-of-the-way spots on your own. My wife and I first went to Paris on our honeymoon, and saw a lot of the famous sites. But what we talk about most today is buying bread and cheese and wine at a street market and carrying it up the seven flights of stairs at our one-star hotel to eat out on the terrace amid the rooftops of Paris. Then there was dinner at a wonderful little Thai restaurant that I still count as one of the best meals I ever ate. And the funny miniature black poodle stationed in front of a sidewalk café on an obscure side street who fiercely and effectively claimed the whole sidewalk as his territory whenever any larger dog walked down the sidewalk. We still laugh about him.

Geotourism can also guide new development, as well as protect existing treasures. A great example is Monterrey, California, the setting of John Steinbeck's great novel *Cannery Row*, which several decades ago was full of rusting, abandoned canneries. A woman named Julie Packard suggested creating an aquarium and a museum there to celebrate the ecosystem and the culture of Monterrey Bay. It has been a huge success and attracted many tourists by giving them an authentic experience. Celebrating what is unique about a place is the heart of geotourism.

Minneapolis, Minnesota, my hometown, is not a place high on most international travelers' lists of places to visit, unless they're great fans of the musician Prince, who lives there. But Minneapolis has the Mississippi River, which most people around the world do want to see. Minneapolis turned its back on the river for most of its history. Railyards and highways were constructed along the riverfront. Finally, people realized the river is one of our great assets. A stone railroad bridge, fenced off since the 1980s, was turned into a pedestrian bridge that has become the favorite meeting place and new symbol of Minneapolis. The project was done to enhance city life for local residents, not boost tourist development, but tourists now flock there because it captures the spirit of the place.

There is an old railroad trench running through the middle of Minneapolis's south side that recently was converted to a bicycle path. Grunge rock was invented in Minneapolis, before it came to fame in Seattle with Kurt Cobain, and one of the pioneering grunge bands, the Replacements, was photographed sitting on an old couch someone had thrown into the middle of the railroad trench. It was truly a grungy place. But the bicycle path has been a great success and often when I ride along it, I hear other bikers speaking French or Swedish or Japanese. Minneapolis, despite its cold weather, is one of the biking capitals of the U.S., and exploring it on two wheels is a great way to discover its geotouristic essence.

Geotourism also means getting out of downtown or the suburban strip by the airport to explore fascinating spots hidden away in neighborhoods. You can be an explorer discovering treasures in an out-of-the-way neighborhood. Jonathan Tourtellot, founder of National Geographic's Center for Sustainable Destinations and the originator of geotourism, taught me this lesson as we traveled through Chile. As I mentioned earlier, I met up with him in Santiago, Chile, at the bar of the Sheraton Hotel to be precise, where he was speaking at a conference of the Society of American Travel Writers.

To be honest, I was quite disappointed with my first impression of Santiago, which looked like a pale imitation of Los Angeles—all the sprawl with none of the glamour. I was desperate to get out of town right away, so that we could see the real Chile. But Jonathan was not so quick to give up on the city. He had heard about a lively neighborhood called Bellavista—a bohemian district where the artists, mavericks, and radicals lived. There had been a plan to build a freeway through the middle of Bellavista. You have to remember there was a brutal dictatorship in Chile for many years, and even after democracy returned, there was absolutely no tradition of protest or civic activism. But the neighbors of Bellavista rose up to stop the highway and saved their neighborhood. Now, it is a gem of a place full of sidewalk cafes and hopping music clubs. We had a great time there, and it was as hip as any corner in San Francisco or Brooklyn or Austin. Definitely worth a visit if you are ever in Chile.

But the highlight of the trip for me—more than hiking the Andes, or combing the beaches, or staying at an exquisitely elegant old country estate—was visiting a poor neighborhood, also remarkably called Bellavista, in the charmingly shabby port town of Valparaiso. This city is a combination of San Francisco and New Orleans, steep hills and fading elegance. There are a dozen funicular railways chugging passengers up and down the hillsides. Valparaiso has been named a UNESCO World Heritage Site for its historical ambience. The entire Bellavista neighborhood has been designated as an outdoor sculpture garden, and many of the old houses have been painted in wild, bright colors. It's a fascinating place to stroll around. A home once owned by Nobel Prize-winning poet Pablo Neruda has been turned into a museum. Bed and breakfasts have been opened in many old mansions. The neighborhood is still poor, but this small-scale, geotouristic development is making a difference.

If you do geotourism right, it enhances the community and helps both the character of the place and the prospects of the people who live there. It also benefits to the traveler.

Geotourism is not just for ardent activists and the politically pure. *National Geographic Traveler* commissioned the Travel Industry Association of America to do a study of Americans who travel abroad, asking why they liked to travel, what they hoped to find on their vacations, and which were their greatest experiences. Seventy-four percent of Americans traveling abroad listed some sort of geotouristic goal as one of the reasons they were traveling.

Many, even most, people out there planning their vacations are looking for geotourist opportunities. National Geographic Society's Center for Sustainable Destinations is trying to make that happen. Jonathan Tourtellot and his colleagues have drafted a geotourism charter where a country, province, or city agrees to adhere to the principles of geotourism, which a number of places from Norway to Montreal to the Mexican state of Sonora have signed. The organization is also creating local councils where the tourist industry and local leaders come together to create more geotouristic opportunities for travelers. They create many geotouristic maps, which highlight the most interesting things to do in any given locale. There is a column in *National Geographic Traveler* called "Destination Watch," which looks at places around the world that are harmed or enhanced by tourist development.

For information on geotourism, people can go to the website of *The National Geographic Society*.

Many people ask how geotourism differs from sustainable tourism and plain old tourism as usual. Let me try to explain from my own perspective.

For all of us who travel, eating is one of the favorite pastimes. Under tourism as usual, that often means going to McDonalds or Chili's. Under sustainable tourism, it's indigenous cuisine, just like it's always been cooked. Under geotourism, it's traditional dishes, using local ingredients, but often jazzed up through the creativity of chefs. Scandinavia, for instance, has long been considered a wasteland in terms of cuisine, but a new generation of cooks is winning world competitions by taking traditional fare like reindeer meat and cloudberries and serving them in new ways, such as spicy reindeer sausage and cloudberry chutney.

In terms of accommodations, tourism as usual is an all-inclusive resort owned by an out-of-town company with sixty percent of the profits going to a corporate headquarters somewhere else rather than being re-circulated through the community. Sustainable tourism is a bunkhouse in an eco-preserve. Geotourism is an interesting old house fashioned into a bed and breakfast where you can join the owners for a meal and then retreat to the privacy and comfort of your own room.

For sightseeing, tourism as usual means gazing out the window of a tour bus that stops only at the big sites for about 11.6 seconds each. Sustainable tourism is a much better tour with a bus that runs on biofuel. Geotourism means you're on your own part of the time, wandering the side streets, hiking the local trails, and looking for things that interest you. But you also can hire a knowledgeable guide who gets you into places no tourist could penetrate.

For shopping, tourism as usual is hitting the gift store at the Hard Rock Café and the duty-free shop at the airport. In sustainable tourism, you make a donation instead to a local charity. In geotourism, you seek out work from local artisans and local artists, but save something for the charity.

Partying, tourism-as-usual-style, is lots of fun until you wind up in jail for throwing rum bottles from the balcony of your hotel. With sustainable tourism, you're uncertain whether partying is in keeping with the noble intentions of the socially responsible tour, so you drink your rum discreetly from a juice container and take the bottles home in your luggage for recycling. With geotourism, you buy the rum at the corner store and sit and drink with the shop owner who tells you where to recycle the bottles and lots else about the place.

The philosophy behind tourism as usual is anything goes, you're on vacation. The philosophy for sustainable tourism is taken from the medical profession: first, do no harm. The principle of geotourism is: first celebrate the place and, second, think of every dollar in your pocket as a vote. When you spend it, you're voting for what you want to see more of in that place.

Jay Walljasper.
Photograph by Linda Carfagno.

Jay Walljasper is a writer for *National Geographic Traveler*'s "Destination Watch" column as well as editor of OnTheCommons.org, Senior Fellow at Project for Public Spaces, and editor-at-large of *Ode* magazine. He is author of *The Great Neighborhood Book*. For 15 years, he was the editor of *Utne Reader* magazine. Walljasper speaks and writes frequently about travel, cities, contemporary culture, and sustainable issues. Much of his work can be found at www.JayWalljasper.com.

DISCOVERING THE DEEPER MEANING OF TOURISM

by
Alex Pattakos, PhD
Author, *Prisoners of Our Thoughts*

The search for meaning is a megatrend of the 21st century. It also has been well established, both conceptually and empirically, that the search for meaning is the primary intrinsic motivation of human beings. As a motivational force, meaning has been found to drive engagement within a wide range of personal and work-related contexts. In turn, the power of meaningful engagement drives and sustains worker/customer satisfaction, performance, creativity, and innovation at the individual and collective levels.

Across industries and sectors, there is growing interest among organizations and jurisdictions in providing meaningful work, creating meaningful workplaces, and delivering meaningful results (in terms of experiences, products, and services) to their broadly defined community of stakeholders. This meaning-focused megatrend can also be applied to the cultivation of creative and innovation economies. In this connection, the tourism sector offers unlimited possibilities in design and delivery to be authentically creative and meaningful, as well as to be an integral part of a jurisdiction's innovation engine for community and economic development.

By understanding how to effectively harness and leverage the search for meaning as a motivational force among both tourism service providers and tourists, the seeds of tourism are more likely to take root and flourish in creative, engaging, and sustainable ways. Moreover, by understanding how to leverage tourism from an innovation, not simply a creative perspective, another important dimension of the deeper meaning of tourism can be discovered and put to practical use. In this essay, a paradigm shift is espoused, that is, from creative economy to innovation economy, in which tourism is viewed as an integrated, meaning-focused strategy that adds maximum value and provides the highest return on investment for all stakeholders.

The Search for Meaning

In the book, *Megatrends 2010: The Rise of Conscious Capitalism*, by Patricia Aburdene, one of the foremost trend trackers in the United States, the search for meaning is evident in every chapter and provides a platform for what essentially is a new consciousness about how we live and work in the postmodern era. Like Aburdene, I have also observed a shift in consciousness, or new awareness, about what really matters to people in their lives. More and more people are expecting and searching for meaning in their lives, both in their personal circumstances and in their work-related situations.

Viktor Frankl, a psychiatrist who suffered through imprisonment in Nazi concentration camps during World War II, found meaning because of, and in spite of, the suffering all around him. His life's work resulted in the therapeutic approach called Logotherapy, which paved the way for us to know meaning as a foundation of our existence (among his many publications, he is the author of the classic bestseller, *Man's Search for Meaning*, which was named one of the ten most influential books in America by the Library of Congress). Logotherapy, in short, seeks to make us aware of our freedom of response to all aspects of our destiny, and strengthens trust in the unconditional meaningfulness of life and the dignity of the person. By applying this philosophy to the job, at home, and within our entire human experience, we can more deeply humanize our lives and bring deeper meaning to life itself.

Like my mentor, Dr. Frankl, I believe that the search for meaning in life is the primary, intrinsic motivation of all human beings, and that it is not a secondary rationalization of instinctual drives, which effectively serve to reduce and marginalize human potential and experiences. When we live and work with meaning, we can choose to discover meaning, to see meaning, and to share meaning. We can choose our attitudes about life and work. We can choose how to respond to others, how to respond to our jobs, how to respond to different life experiences, and how to make the very best of difficult circumstances. We can transcend ourselves and be transformed by meaning. We can find connection to meaning in the most unusual places and with the most unexpected people. We can become meaningfully engaged in whatever we do and experience. Indeed, meaning is full of surprises. It defies our expectations and heightens our awareness. And as Viktor Frankl liked to say, "I am convinced that in the final analysis, there is no situation that does not contain within it the seed of a meaning."

The Tourism Context

The search for meaning in tourism, broadly defined, occurs on multiple levels. On an intra-personal level, it involves both individual tourists and tourism service providers in terms of their personal motivations and predispositions. Of course, we have all been tourists at some point and, whether we recognize it or not, we are all tourists of life. In this regard, each of us has a yearning for experiencing an authentic, meaning-full life, which, as I have pointed out, is a primary, intrinsic motivation of all human beings.

Our lives present us with a labyrinth of meaning even though it is not always evident. Life and relationships unfold; they change; we change; sometimes we embrace the process; sometimes we change our circumstances and start over. Indeed, if you want things to stay the same, then something is going to have to change! This is true in our private lives as well as in our work. Again, it is part of the labyrinth of our life. As tourists of life, we are on one path and it takes us through many turns of fate and fortune, pain and pleasure, loss and gain. It is a path that shapes us, that uncovers our fears, that tests our courage, and that leads us to this very moment. It is a sacred path of individuality and no one walks it but us. Yes, we are the real accidental tourists, to borrow from the 1988 Oscar-winning movie by this name!

Importantly, the providers of tourism services must recognize that no matter what their specific job might be, it is the work that they do that represents who they are. To be sure, this basic tenet applies to all jobs, be they full-time or part-time, paid or volunteer, white-collar, blue-collar, or no-collar. When we meet our work with enthusiasm, appreciation, generosity, and integrity, we meet it with meaning. And no matter how mundane a job might seem at the time, we can transform it with meaning. Meaning is life's legacy, and it is available to us at work as it is available to us in our deepest spiritual quests. It is no wonder, then, that the search for meaning is a megatrend of the 21st century. Our quest for meaning, in our everyday lives and in our work, is ours right now, at this very moment.

Against this backdrop, tourism providers have an obligation, as do all workers, to continuously search for and discover the deeper meaning in their work. By so doing, they become fully engaged in their work, increase their enthusiasm and passion for what they do, and drive higher levels of personal performance, including creativity, as a result. By exercising the freedom to choose their attitude (for more on this meaning-centered principle and other practical applications of Viktor Frankl's Logotherapy, see my book, *Prisoners of Our Thoughts*), tourism service providers build their capacity for achieving their highest potential in the pursuit of excellence. Moreover, they are more likely to find fulfillment in and from their work regardless of the particular circumstances that they may be facing (e.g., an economic downturn, increasing competition, and the like).

A similar set of meaning-centered principles operates for the so-called traditional tourist. Intra-personally, some tourists fully expect to be meaningfully engaged and will not venture out unless they are assured that such will be the case. These folks consciously look for opportunities that will enable them to realize their "will to meaning" (another Logotherapeutic principle that is introduced in my book, *Prisoners of Our Thoughts*). In this connection, tourism experiences that are not meaningful, that is, they do not offer authentic pathways for personal learning, growth, and development, are not likely to be attractive or represent targets for investment in time, money, and energy among this particular group of tourists. They are hungry for experiences that truly matter to them, experiences that feed their soul.

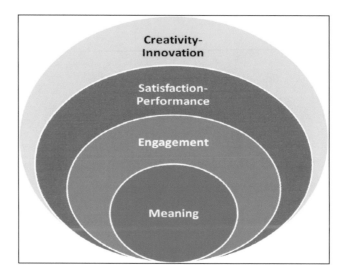

Figure 1. Meaning at the Core

Meaning, from this perspective, comprises both the primary intrinsic motivation for viewing tourism as a life goal or objective to be achieved, and the key driver behind the level of engagement that the tourist will enjoy. Once again, this is particularly important because, as a motivational force, meaning has been found to drive engagement which, in turn, drives and sustains worker/customer satisfaction, performance, creativity, and innovation. (See Figure 1.) The levels of engagement, moreover, can be viewed along a continuum, from those individuals, be they tourists or tourism providers, who are actively disengaged from the tourism experience to those who are pro-actively engaged. That is, they actually help to co-produce or co-create the experience in tandem with their tourism counterpart. (See Figure 2.)

Actively Disengaged   Pro-Actively Engaged

Figure 2. Continuum of Engagement

Let me underscore that understanding intrinsic human motivations is very important for building and leveraging the power of meaningful engagement along this continuum. Among the foundational building blocks of Frankl's existential philosophy and therapeutic system is the commitment to meaningful values and goals—the will to meaning. In brief, Frankl identified three categories of values that, when actualized, provide sources of authentic meaning: (1) Creative values, that is, "by doing or creating something"; (2) experiential values, that is, "by experiencing something or encountering someone"; and (3) attitudinal values, that is, "by choosing one's attitude toward suffering or hardship."

Actualizing such values, individually or in combination, is not only the quid pro quo of the human quest for personal meaning but also, in large part, helps to determine where on the engagement continuum a person might find her/himself at any given point in time. From a distinctly tourism perspective, it should not be difficult to imagine how both tourists and tourism service providers may actualize these particular values as sources of personal meaning in their own quests.

Moving now to an inter-personal level, both tourists and tourism service providers also have their respective obligations and responsibilities for discovering meaning. In effect, the tourism experience is co-created by them, even if they are not consciously pro-actively engaged, whereby the whole is greater than the sum of its parts. Tourism, in other words, is a two-way street, and no matter how much someone may want to remain strictly or only a passive observer, even the act of observing something, such as viewing a museum artifact, becomes part of the co-creation process. Of course, there are some tourists who just may have a negative or bad attitude about a particular place or experience, and therefore will never be satisfied or fulfilled, no matter how hard a tourism provider tries to remedy or change the situation.

Many of these people, whom I call prisoners of their thoughts, have no justifiable reason to be dissatisfied—they just are so! This said, their attitude, for better or worse, plays an influential role in co-creating the tourism experience as a process and its ultimate product or end result. One's choice of attitude may even become a self-fulfilling prophecy. Consider this scenario: as a tourist (or tourism service provider), you don't expect to have a positive experience. Guess what? You don't. The same thing, of course, can happen the other way around. Besides referring you back to the notion of actualizing attitudinal values as a source of meaning, let me also suggest that, since you can't escape the fact that you are part of the co-creation equation, you might as well become pro-actively engaged in the process and seek to increase your return on investment. Or you could choose, either consciously or subconsciously, a negative attitude toward the situation and complain about it.

Indeed, we all know complainers. At one time or another, we've all been one. Sometimes we like them because they do our complaining for us, and allow us to vent our frustrations without risk. Other times complainers weight us down with their misery, and we can feel our own mood and energy take a dive. When we get locked into our own complaining shadow and focus on all the bad stuff, we immediately lose sight of the good stuff. Ironically, blaming and complaining get us nowhere, even if we really do have someone to blame or something to complain about.

When we make complaining a habit, as many people (including both tourists and tourism providers) do, we make meaninglessness a habit. Before long, we are invested in our complaining so deeply that all opportunity to see experience as a rich part of our lives vanishes. Instead of taking the time to find meaning, we take the time to find and focus on meaninglessness. And, ultimately, complaining undermines the integrity of our experience. It takes the meaning out of our work or personal experiences, and out of our relationships to our work or our personal experiences. This doesn't mean that it's not necessary to complain once in awhile. (For example, I'm reminded of places where tourism is a major, if not the primary, source of economic sustenance, but where a love-hate relationship with tourists is also evident). What it means is that we need to be aware of when and why we are complaining. Is it to bring about a simple moment of relief? Or, have we started to define our work and experiences by habitually negative perceptions? So, from now on, ask yourself why you complain and, perhaps more important, what's the payoff from your complaining?

Innovating with Meaning

The search for the deeper meaning of tourism also takes place at a macro or collective level. By this I mean at some level of aggregation, such as a community or other politically defined jurisdiction. Meaning at this level typically reflects the need to cultivate those conditions that add value by contributing to the quality of life and economic base of the jurisdiction. Such changes also must reflect, as best as possible, the core values of the community of stakeholders involved.

In this regard, there needs to be a purpose that drives (or pulls) change so that it adds value. This often comes from the vision or mission. However, even a compelling vision or strategy may not be enough, if we do not learn and grow from the change that accompanies it. Change for change's sake will not necessarily allow us to achieve either our personal or collective aims. Reflect for a moment on the following assertion: you can change without growing but you can't grow without changing. Truly meaningful change, in other words, must involve some kind of development (e.g., disconfirming that the old ways work) and must make a positive difference (e.g., add value). Put differently, truly meaningful change is, by its very nature, innovative.

Fostering and sustaining innovation is a hot topic these days, especially in light of the current economic climate. Having led and participated in the emergence of this important field over the last two decades, I have witnessed the transition from viewing innovation as simply the commercialization of new technology to a much broader perspective, one that encompasses innovation in products, services, processes, and overall business strategies. Indeed, never before has there been a greater need for strong leadership in the field of innovation.

So what is true innovation? In her book, *The Seeds of Innovation*, Elaine Dundon offers the following comprehensive and integrated definition: "the profitable implementation of strategic creativity." Although this may sound like a mouthful, it actually is simpler to grasp than it may seem at first. Dundon's definition combines four key components:

- **Creativity**—the discovery of a new idea.
- **Strategy**—determining whether it is a new and useful idea.
- **Implementation**—putting this new and useful idea into action.
- **Profitability**—maximizing the added value from the implementation of this new idea.

Let's repeat the definition of innovation: "the profitable implementation of strategic creativity." Significantly, this definition goes beyond simply referring to the act of creativity or the identification of new ideas. To be sure, innovation is grounded in creative expression, but creative expression is not sufficient for the seeds of innovation to take root and grow. Creativity, in this connection, needs to be on strategy (i.e., useful), be actionable, and importantly, be profitable (i.e., add value). It is the added value component of innovation that most closely aligns with our focus on meaning.

Across industries and sectors, many leaders are struggling to advance their organization's or jurisdiction's innovation agendas. Like the pursuit of change for change's sake, there are also leaders who are pursuing innovation for the sake of innovation, just because it is a hot topic these days. And then there are those leaders who espouse innovation, but then launch new products and services that really aren't adding anything to the world, or even to the bottom line.

The missing element in each of these scenarios, that strikes at the very foundation of authentic leadership, once again, is meaning. That is, authentic leaders must lead with and to meaning. With this meaning centered value orientation in mind, let me offer a new mental model for those who have been entrusted with an innovation mandate, innovating with meaning.

As I have already mentioned, if everyone connected with the deeper meaning of their work, they would have the opportunity to be more fully engaged and contribute to the organization, reaching its (and their) highest potential. Without meaning, on the other hand, employees become disengaged, lose their passion, and stop offering new ideas, all of which ultimately lead to lost productivity, as well as effectively stalling the organization's innovation engine.

Meaning gets at the true essence of what an organizational entity and its products and services are all about. Why, in other words, do we do what we do? Are we doing all we can do to help our customers/citizens and truly add value to our community and the world? Are we making a positive difference? What is our legacy? What is the true meaning of our work, both individually and collectively? As a tourist, tourism professional, or person charged with articulating and advancing a tourism strategy of some kind, please reflect seriously upon these existential questions about the nature of tourism as you see and experience it.

Authentic leaders at all levels can help others connect with the meaning of their work in everyday situations. There is meaning in identifying new ways of doing things; there is meaning in the way co-workers and customers/citizens interact with each other; there is meaning in choosing a positive attitude instead of complaining that things are always changing or are not working right. We must understand that when we ourselves bring meaning to work, we bring with us the possibility of meaningful change in our work, in our workplace, and in the results of our work.

To be sure, being successful at advancing and sustaining innovation, especially all the lines espoused by Elaine Dundon, requires a transformation of culture. It requires strong leadership that is authentically committed to encouraging employees to engage with each other (and with their work) in more meaningful ways. It also requires strong leadership that is authentically committed to encouraging and allowing customers and citizens (e.g. tourists) to relate to their organization in new and meaningful ways. Without a focus on meaning, innovation activities are just that, activities. Busy work. A waste of resources. It's time to take innovation to the next level. It's time to truly lead and innovate with meaning.

Cultivating the Innovation Economy

It is a basic thesis of this essay that a focus on the search for meaning as a motivational force among tourism service providers and tourists will allow the seeds of tourism to take root and flourish in creative, engaging, and sustainable ways. Furthermore, by leveraging tourism from an innovation, not simply a creative, perspective, its potential for supporting and advancing community and economic development, including workforce development, will be enhanced. In other words, this essay calls for a paradigm shift from a creative economy to an innovation economy in which tourism is viewed as a comprehensive, integrated, meaning-focused strategy that adds maximum value and provides the highest return on investment for all stakeholders.

Furthermore, the so-called creative industries are being asked to join this new tourism mindset by supporting not just the creative economy, but the innovation economy, whereby the common definition of innovation is "the profitable implementation of strategic creativity." In other words, being creative is not enough to fuel community and economic development effectively, efficiently, and equitably. Good intentions notwithstanding, a new emphasis on driving innovation within the tourism industry or domain is necessary. This emphasis, moreover, must seek to integrate a wide variety of human systems under the tourism banner. Integration, in this connection, involves four key dimensions (See Figure 3): policy, organization and management, linkages, and service delivery.

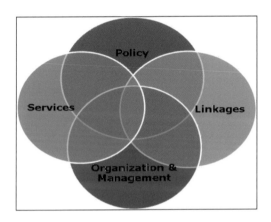

Figure 3. Dimensions of an Integrated Tourism Strategy

Policy refers to the public policy statements and actions by the jurisdictional authority responsible for coordinating and advancing tourism initiatives in relation to community and economic development. All manifestations of public policy related to tourism, ideally, should be consistent, based on meaningful values, and aligned with the jurisdiction's strategic intent. Organization and management refers to the operating apparatus within the jurisdiction that is responsible for carrying out the policy pronouncements related to tourism. Again, this apparatus and all standard operating policies and procedures should be consistent, based on meaningful values, and aligned with the jurisdiction's strategic intent. Moreover, as with the policy dimension, the organization and management dimension should be highly visible and transparent in order to reflect authentically the centerpiece role that tourism plays within the innovation economy.

Linkages refers to the various connections between tourism players within the jurisdiction. Here, for instance, is where attention should be paid to building viable networks between tourism professionals and service providers in order to offer tourists (or visitors) as many seamless opportunities as possible for meaningful engagement with the tourism community. Again, such linkages should be consistent, based on meaningful values, and aligned with the jurisdiction's strategic intent, so that these connections don't become just encounters of the worst kind for either the providers of tourism services or the tourists.

Finally, services refers to the actual mix and delivery of tourism opportunities within the jurisdiction. Such services should be as authentic as possible, reflecting the meaningful values embedded within the jurisdiction, and should seek to be as engaging as possible. In this regard, the mix of tourism opportunities should be designed to include continua of experiences, from passive to active, from instructive to interactive/experiential, etc.

From a jurisdiction-wide perspective, the tourism challenge, especially if it involves advancing community and economic development, is to integrate (or at least coordinate) these four dimensions as much as possible. Only in this way will tourism as an industry sector reach its full potential as part of the engine that drives the innovation economy. Only in this way will the seeds of innovation advanced by Elaine Dundon have a real chance of taking root and flourishing within such a robust economy. And only in this way will the search for meaning, a megatrend of the 21st century, see its practical application in the tourism sector become a reality.

Alex Pattakos

Alex Pattakos, PhD, is an author, affectionately nicknamed Dr. Meaning. He is the founder of the Center for Meaning, and author of the international best-selling book, *Prisoners of Our Thoughts: Viktor Frankl's Principles for Discovering Meaning in Life and Work*. He is a former therapist and mental health administrator, political campaign organizer, and full-time university professor (and graduate program head) of public and business administration. He has worked closely with several presidential administrations on social and economic policy matters, and served as an adviser to the Commissioner of the U.S. Food and Drug Administration. Dr. Pattakos was also one of the initial faculty evaluators for the Innovations In American Government Awards Program at the John F. Kennedy School of Government, Harvard University, and has been a faculty member at The Brookings Institution. He consults internationally with individuals, teams, and organizations in all sectors and industries with an explicit focus on designing innovation systems, processes, products, and policies that make a positive difference and that are truly meaningful.

THE PRACTICAL CHALLENGES OF DEVELOPING CREATIVE TOURISM

A CAUTIONARY TALE FROM NEW ZEALAND

by

Crispin Raymond

Creative Tourism Consultant

Over the last few years, an initiative has been taking place in New Zealand that aims to develop Creative Tourism into a sustainable business. This is the story of that initiative, its progressions and regressions, and the lessons that have been learnt. It concludes with some suggestions for others who wish to establish Creative Tourism in their communities and proposes two alternative development models.

PHASE 1: PILOT PROJECT

Creative Tourism in New Zealand has gone through three phases. It started in May 2003 with a pilot project that was managed by an arts' marketing trust based in Nelson, a city at the top of the South Island, which is the heart of a region known for its arts and creativity. The trust was attracted by the Creative Tourism concept as a way to add a new income stream for the artists it represented. Mainly through the trust's existing contacts, 23 tutors were persuaded to join the Creative Tourism initiative as founding members, and they offered a mix of informal workshops covering 29 topics. A supply of Creative Tourism experiences was thus established.

The tutors were all local Kiwis and ranged from Mike, whose Maori ancestry went back 47 generations, to Stephan who had migrated a decade before. The workshop topics reflected many aspects of local culture and included bone carving and bronze casting, harakeke (New Zealand flax) weaving, and seafood cookery.

During this pilot period, tutors decided the frequency with which they presented their workshops, from as many as six per week to flexible provision to meet demand and set their workshop prices. Tutors also took their own bookings. Workshops took place in the tutors' homes and workplaces and ranged in length from half a day to four days. The two target markets were baby boomers and backpackers, both of whom seemed likely to be interested in learning more about local culture.

Eighteen-thousand dollars New Zealand (approximately US $10,000) was raised to finance the pilot from grants, sponsors, tutor subscriptions, and accommodation providers. Most of this income was spent on the development of the website, www.creativetourism.co.nz and on the print and display of promotional leaflets. The trust provided staff time at no cost.

The pilot lasted 12 months, but in spite of much hard work only 23 people paid to take part in workshops. In retrospect, it was easier to establish a supply of Creative Tourism experiences than a demand for them. While disappointing, however, a great deal had been learnt and enthusiasm for the Creative Tourism idea continued. After some agonizing, the decision was made to set up Creative Tourism New Zealand (CTNZ) as a business in June 2004 and to build on the lessons of the pilot.

PHASE 2: WORKSHOP PROMOTIONAL AGENCY

The new company had four shareholder/directors and a start-up capital of NZ $50,000 (US $28,000); one of the new directors became the full-time, paid chief executive. The number of tutors and workshop topics on offer were reduced to concentrate on those with the greatest potential; workshops that lasted longer than a day were dropped. The workshops that were retained had to be available consistently on the same days each week. A free phone number was introduced and bookings were taken directly by CTNZ to provide a more professional service.

Demand responded to these improvements to supply—but not by enough. While the number of paying workshop participants grew to 147 in the year, Creative Tourism had still not taken off and the company had used up more than half its available cash. Again, the Creative Tourism initiative came close to ending but whether through admirable determination or foolish pride the shareholders decided to try another approach and to keep going. Phase 3 began in June 2005.

PHASE 3: TUTOR DEVELOPMENT AGENCY

Creative Tourism New Zealand's role was redefined to focus on helping tutors develop and promote their workshops effectively to visitors. In other words, tutors became CTNZ's primary customers rather than workshop participants. A handbook was written for tutors, outlining what had been learnt about best practice in workshop provision, and CTNZ began to promote itself to potential tutors throughout New Zealand as a cost-effective way of promoting their workshops in a cluster. The aim was to become the main promotional agency for creative workshops in the country.

Initially, the geographical spread of workshops increased as more tutors joined. But CTNZ's deteriorating cash position meant that it was no longer able to pay its chief executive, and it was now run by its directors, working part time and without pay, supported by international volunteers. Money was a constant concern and finances became so tight that the organization's ability to promote workshops, beyond providing the website and seeking free press coverage, shrank. As less was offered to tutors, their annual subscriptions were reduced. CTNZ became more financially stable but at an ever-reducing turnover.

This third phase still continues. The irony is that while the company now believes it knows how to develop Creative Tourism successfully, it no longer has the resources to do so itself. As the Creative Tourism concept receives increasing international recognition (e.g. through the UNESCO Creative Cities Network and the Santa Fe Conference), here in New Zealand, some six years after the initiative started, Creative Tourism is close to running out of steam. New partners will be necessary to take it forward.

KEY LESSONS

So what has been learnt from this often painful tale? There are eight key lessons:

- **Workshop participants are often ecstatic about their experiences**. Although CTNZ has had far too few workshop participants, those who have taken part have always enjoyed their experiences, and have frequently hailed them as "the best thing I did in New Zealand" or even life-changing. Creative Tourism experiences are very rewarding for all involved and this underlines belief in Creative Tourism's potential.
- **The most popular topics reflect the established image of the workshop location**. Cities and regions have images that have been developed over time through their history and/or deliberate promotion. Workshop topics that reflect these images are easier to sell than those based on the random enthusiasms of tutors.
- **Short workshops are more popular than long ones**. Most visitors do not have time to take part in workshops that last longer than a day. Unless

a particular workshop topic has become so well established that it is a primary reason for a visitor's holiday and something that other plans will be organized around, this is unlikely to change.

- **Many tutors need support and training**. The best tutors, namely those who provide informal and informed, friendly and professional experiences, take time to develop their workshops successfully and appreciate help in learning how to do this.

- **It is difficult to market workshops to both backpackers and baby boomers simultaneously**. While CTNZ has found that both backpackers and baby boomers are attracted to Creative Tourism experiences, they are different market segments. The former are generally time-rich but cash-poor while the latter are the opposite, cash rich but time poor. Trying to promote a mix of workshops successfully to both groups is something that CTNZ has not resolved.

- **Be sensitive to the traditions of indigenous people**. Local traditions and skills are at the core of Creative Tourism experiences, and in many countries these originate from the region's indigenous people: indeed some traditions may still be felt to belong to them. Sensitivity is thus necessary when others wish to base creative workshops and experiences on these traditions.

- **Globalization means that authenticity is constantly evolving**. While CTNZ believes that Creative Tourism experiences should always be authentic, it recognizes that authenticity is not a static concept. Immigration adds new dimensions to local cultures; those returning from holidays abroad bring ideas and enthusiasms with them too. One of the challenges in developing authentic Creative Tourism experiences is thus to find a balance between a location's historic culture and the realities of its culture today.

- **The words, *tutors* and *workshops*, are not ideal**. CTNZ recognized early on that it needed a vocabulary for the key elements of Creative Tourism and settled on tutors leading workshops for participants. However, the first two words can sound overly formal, particularly to North Americans. Partners may be better than tutors; creative experiences better than workshops.

ALTERNATIVE DEVELOPMENT MODELS

So with the benefit of hindsight, what should CTNZ have done differently and how can Creative Tourism be developed successfully elsewhere? CTNZ now believes that there are two alternative development approaches and that a choice needs to be made between them.

The Commercial Tourism Model

This first model is suitable for an existing business or entrepreneur who wants to develop Creative Tourism commercially. The key features of this approach are to:

- **View Creative Tourism experiences as tourist products**. Workshops need to compete with other tourist products and be available through tourism marketing channels using the commission structures that other tourism products use.
- **Partner with a tourism business that has an established client base**. In most cases, it is likely to take too long and therefore cost too much, to build demand for Creative Tourism experiences from scratch. Better to start by tapping into an existing demand (e.g. by partnering with an accommodation provider(s), by including workshops in local festivals, by selling workshops alongside other tourist products or perhaps a mix of these).
- **Choose workshop topics to meet this established client demand and then find tutors to teach them**. In other words, work outwards by selecting experiences that the partners' clients want, and then finding interesting, skilled, reliable, local people to teach and lead these experiences. The sort of partner chosen should therefore influence the sort of workshops provided. For example, partnering with a five-star hotel will mean offering a different experience mix and different prices than partnering with backpacker accommodation.
- **Ensure sufficient finance to cover the start-up period**. This is obvious, of course, but CTNZ, like many small businesses, has been undercapitalized. Consequently, because tutors were an immediate source of income, CTNZ has always chosen to charge them to promote their workshops rather than pay them to provide workshops for CTNZ.
- **View workshop participants as customers and tutors as suppliers/ partners**. Under this approach, workshop participants provide the main source of business income, while tutors are paid by the Creative Tourism business for providing experiences to its customers.

This first approach is a demand led, commercially focused development model.

The Community Network Model

This second model is suitable for a community that wishes to develop its creative image by showcasing its creativity. The key features of this approach are to:

- **Invite potential tutors to join a Creative Tourism network.** Using local media and other channels, contact local artisans and other creative individuals and small businesses, and encourage them to offer creative experiences to visitors.
- **Promote tutors' workshops as a cluster.** This will involve developing a good website and using traditional and web-based promotion (e.g. blogs, Internet forums etc.). It could also involve encouraging local festivals to include some of the tutors' workshops.
- **Establish the network as a not-for-profit.** Some external funding is likely to be needed to support this model, and in most cases it will be easier to attract this to a not-for-profit organization than to a commercially structured one. Public funding may come from local government that wishes to develop the community's creative image. Support may also come from trusts that fund new job opportunities for artists and crafts people. Sponsors may be willing to support a worthwhile community initiative.
- **Minimize the use of the word tourism in promotion.** In most countries tourism is seen as a profitable business venture that stands or falls on its own merits. If external funding is to be sought for developing Creative Tourism, it is prudent to emphasize the creative element of the experiences and downplay the tourism element.
- **View workshop participants as the tutors' customers and tutors as the network's customers**.

This second approach is a supply led, community-inspired development model.

Conclusion

As can be seen, CTNZ has elements of both these development models, but rather than achieving the best of both worlds, it has tended to fall between two stools. Our future now is either to refocus as a commercial tourism business that will need a new partner with an established tourist demand and new capital, or to become a trust and seek public/charitable money to develop a wider community network. Given the objectives and beliefs of the four shareholder/directors, who are community focused and not tourism professionals, the latter is more likely.

For others seeking to develop Creative Tourism in their communities, the New Zealand experience suggests that the deceptively simple question, "Why do I want to develop Creative Tourism?" should be the starting point. In spite of the challenges described here, CTNZ continues to believe in Creative Tourism and suspects that it will develop faster in countries whose culture is a core aspect of their tourism offering.

New Zealand's clean, green, outdoor image—the country is promoted internationally under the phrase "100 percent Pure New Zealand"—does not contribute to the promotion of creative cultural experiences here.

Others should also find it easier to establish Creative Tourism now that both the concept and the term are more widely recognized. Good luck and if New Zealand can help, please get in touch: www.creativetourism.co.nz.

CREATIVE TOURISM AND LIVABLE CITIES
by
Robert McNulty
Founder and Director, Partners for Livable Cities

There is an interconnected world of people who are concerned with a creative economy, economic development, tourism and cultural heritage tourism, discovery tourism, and Creative Tourism.

Partners for Livable Cities grew out of the energy of Nancy Hanks, Chairman of the National Endowment for the Arts (Endowment). She believed that culture is an asset which should relate to everyone's life and make everyone's life better. She thought the only difficulty with the enabling legislation of the Endowment was that one of the great American art forms was the circus. She wanted to support circus arts throughout America, but Congress frowned on that. She did support, though, architecture, urban design, historic preservation, land use planning, and neighborhood conservation. For eight years, I was the assistant director of a granting program, giving out funds to support local people who, with a small amount of money, made a difference in looking at the future of their community.

The roots of Partners grew from Nancy saying there's always too much to do and too little money. She urged me to create a non-profit of the best and brightest people I met during my eight years of granting, to set up a cooperative to help others. Ms. Hanks said the Endowment would then fund it. We received thirteen years of support from the Endowment. Ms. Hanks, who passed away in

1983, is remembered as a person who brought the Endowment to a higher budget than it has ever had—26 years ago. The Endowment has, regrettably, gone downhill, because no other chairman has embraced her broad definition of what culture can be—an asset in affecting everyone's lives.

We tend to look at livability as a relationship to the issues that you have to face within your community, whether you are the mayor or a citizen. It has to relate to jobs. The number one definition of a livable community is to be able to support your family. It has to relate to people. There is a large category of people in America who haven't been given a fair shake. Some people have been discriminated against and marginalized. A community has to have upward mobility. Finance is important so you can pay the bills. There have to be adequate revenues coming in that can support the needs of government and provide services. The community has to have places that denote uniqueness and value. It has to take a look at some of the issues of sprawl that we're not dealing with.

A community needs leadership, and not just the mayor. Partners believes it takes the public and private sector, the angry citizen, the volunteer, the soccer mom— a variety of players that make up a community, to set a vision for the future. The vision lasts for twenty years, and most mayors don't stay in office for twenty years. We basically say, as a philosophy, you must shift the vision to a civic group that reminds every incoming mayor of the agenda.

It takes twenty years to change a troubled city into a livable city. Chattanooga, Tennessee became the poster child for change. It had the most polluted air quality in America; it had a declining economy; a leadership body that discriminated against African-Americans; it refused to have women involved. When it was finally opened to a process of public participation, Chattanooga was nominated and accepted by the United Nations (UN) as the model for sustainable development in the world. Think: twenty years, a fair team, restructuring leadership, quality of life, boosterism, and hard work. This is what it takes to make a livable community.

Dr. Harvey Perloff, a professor of planning at UCLA, as well as the economist who designed Operation Bootstrap for Puerto Rico, was a founding board member of Partners. Dr. Perloff told me in 1977, the first year of Partners, "Bob, there's a whole new field out there. It's called cultural economics and cultural planning." Dr. Perloff, more than any other person, invented the field of economic leveraging of culture, as a relationship to the service sector economy, as we were going through the transition from manufacturing to service.

Partners has continued Dr. Perloff's legacy over the past thirty years to try to tweak the relationship between quality of life and economics, as we keep morphing into different forms of economic structure. We are now into the creative economy and the world of e-commerce.

In 1977, with the help of Dr. Perloff and others, Partners did a forum on tourism in Paterson, New Jersey. Paterson is an old mill town where Alexander Hamilton and

Aaron Burr had their debate as to what would be the future of America, an agrarian society or an industrial society. Paterson is where the waters of the great falls of the Passaic River were used to power the mills; where Samuel Colt first based his arms manufacturing before moving to Hartford, Connecticut; where Rogers Locomotive made the engines which spanned America via the transcontinental railroad. However, in 1977, Paterson was dormant and derelict.

In our first tourism forum in Paterson, we declared opening day an amnesty for all those who were embarrassed to say they were from Paterson and we welcomed them home. Two thousand people attended the amnesty party. We began to talk about what tourism could do that would give value, pride, and slowly build a sense of, "I'm not ashamed of my community." You now see this concept in the Ruhr, in the industrial heartland throughout Europe—industrial gritty-city communities that are restructured. Their factories, their mines, their civic spaces, their mills are heritage tourism attractions. Pittsburgh no longer makes steel, but some of those steel spaces, preserved by Arthur Ziegler of the Pittsburgh History & Landmarks Foundation, and one of our founders, has turned them back to contemporary use.

My slogan is, "Tourism is too important to be left to the tourism professional." Tourism is a form of celebration of value. Tourism is a form of reinvestment in people. Tourism is a form of raising resources from visitors (we don't like to call them tourists, we like to call them visitors). And those resources, if invested back in the community, can help the community build that museum; help have that superb library; have that convention center; have a medical facility.

Tourism brings in seasonal revenue from outsiders, or regular year-round revenue that helps pay the bills for amenities and values that you year-round citizens need to have in a livable community. A city needs to decide how many visitors it wants and the impact on the community, for that revenue stream that benefits the year-long person who lives in the community.

In seasonal economies, such as in the Outback of Australia or Newfoundland, tourism is what allows Outback communities to have a recreation center with an indoor air conditioned volleyball or basketball court. It is the events that are held in the summer that provide the funds for the year-round facilities in those places. This is true as well for some health care and recreational facilities along the coast of Newfoundland. We should think of tourism as a critical resource that can help support the citizen who lives there, and not solely for the amusement of the visitor.

Thirty years ago, Fred Bosserman wrote *In the Wake of the Tourist*, saying that it is a management strategy that needs to be put in place that facilitates your visitors, so it doesn't erode your use of your own community. Unfortunately, managing is difficult. The profits are to be maximized by having as many tourists as possible; visitor management is not very popular.

Some forms of tourism, such as the advent of English bachelor parties going to Eastern Europe and getting drunk and fighting, are not a good form of cultural tourism. I think we want to discourage that. Hanging out in Hong Kong and Singapore with all of your friends on Thursday night, taking over the streets, is probably not a good form of what we call cultural or Creative Tourism. Cultural or Creative Tourism should be where you immerse yourself in a community as a visitor, enrich your life and find values.

A first time visitor discovers a community, meets people, sees institutions and traditions, and is enchanted enough to wish to return, but not to tell all their friends to return, because they don't want it to be spoiled. A second time visit brings a deeper association, perhaps a desire to move there, to buy a second home, to send your kids to school there, so you'll have an excuse to visit more often, and perhaps become associated by taking the local newspaper so you can keep up with current affairs. A third association comes on retirement, when you move there, open a new business, become involved in the chamber of commerce, become a volunteer, or a docent in the museum. A fourth association is when you pass away and leave your resources to the new town. This is my definition of tourism; it is the definition of a visitor who finds something so enchanting that they become part of the fabric of the community, rather than a burden on the sanitation department of that community.

What about the social, capital concerns of the creative economy and the whole issue of creative tourism? When Richard Florida produced his book on the creative economy, he focused primarily on individuals aged 18-34, the high flyers who would go to Argentina for a year, then to Prague for two years, then move to Shanghai, and perhaps return to Santa Fe. This is a valid market. However, Mr. Florida left out the most important part of the creative economy—the older person—wealthier, healthier, wiser than most of the young people. I'm going to live longer, have greater net worth and disposable income—far more than they will. The 50-plus generation, led by the boomers, were completely left out of the creative economy. Don't leave us out of the Creative Tourism agenda, because we are the people that can really power your tourism engine.

AARP, people 50 years and older, in four years will reach a $2 billion-a-year industry with 50 million members. These people are looking for lifestyle issues, and they have hired Partners to define what is a livable community for all, so there are no barriers to the older person to participate in every aspect of life—political, social, economic, volunteerism, travel, discovery, and lifelong learning. Atlanta has passed accessibility zoning for new housing that says that the ground floor of new housing should be accessible by wheelchair; the door width should be large enough to get a wheelchair into the bathroom. Are you focusing, in any way, upon accessibility issues for an older visitor who may be just a superb consumer of the heritage and culture and resources that you have? This is a huge growth market.

Today, airports are slightly congested. Imagine what it will be like in 15 years when more people will need ambulatory assistance to get on a plane. I have no idea how we will reach the gates in time when there are 30 to 40 wheelchairs going down the corridor. We're not thinking ahead. We need to retrofit and rethink our communities, including the tourism resources, to accommodate, nurture, and support older individuals.

Allegheny County, Pennsylvania, has invited Elder Hostel to move into the county, to facilitate, through transportation, the access of older people to city parks, libraries, museums, and cultural centers. It is a wonderful concept of socialization—providing transportation, particularly if there is a bereavement or loss, getting people out of their homes into a social and cultural setting. Do you need Elder Hostel here as a permanent infrastructure to ensure that everyone has access to these resources?

In the case of Pittsburgh, it is funded through a combination of medical facilities and Jewish charities—no public money at all. Health tourism for older people is an important issue. What relationship do you have with some of the expert facilities on health and wellness that might be a form of cultural or Creative Tourism?

In the next 30 years, we will add some 40 million people to the United States. Forty percent of those will not have been born in this country, and 60 percent of all new small businesses will be formed by people who were not born in this country. The backbone of small business in America will be newcomers. These newcomers should be very active in your hospitality industry. Who will help them when they arrive in Santa Fe, not speaking English? Why not the library system, the museum? Cultural institutions might be the best hospitality of welcoming newcomers into a community, and helping them learn the language, do a business plan, and gain access to financing. The Urban Libraries Council in Chicago, believes that the library is the quintessential institution that should be the welcoming gateway of immigrants and welcome them into the opportunity of participating and profiting from being in this country.

How will your tourism portfolio vary as we become a nation of minorities? Will you reach out to me as an African-American, or an Asian Pacific person or a Latino or a person from a different background? Will you have different offerings? Houston has decided for its strategic future to link its port and oil technology to Asia. Thus, the Asian Pacific community did a strategic program with Rice University to explore how to raise the visibility of Asian Pacific leadership in Greater Houston in order to show its new business partners in Asia that it is serious about equal opportunity. The Asia Society in New York is opening its third headquarters in Houston as a sign that Houston cares about Asia. The Houston Fine Arts Museum has just opened its first Korean wing.

Perhaps America's leadership will change as you see immigrants and people from different countries as key assets. St. Louis is negotiating for the landing rights at its airport to be the major hub of all trans-shipment of goods and services from China back and forth to America. They see the loss of Anheuser-Busch as a small issue compared to the opportunity of gaining a key China hub in St. Louis. How will this vary the tourism offering?

Let us talk about sustainability. We are in a wonderful time of constraint—

financial, water and energy. Nothing creative occurs from times of plenty, but great activity occurs from times of challenges. There is a whole host of people that might now come together to talk about water, energy, transportation, and sprawl. How does this relate to your visitation planning for that cultural experience? Is there some opportunity to get the development community and the environmental community to break common bread? Is there an opportunity to change some of your building design and zoning policies? What will the light rail system do to the rental car business? There are major opportunities. One pundit said that with the change of our climate, the Four Corners area of this country and the Arctic will be the most impacted in the whole Western Hemisphere. You will be under dramatic change.

How will all of this affect labor force skills and training? The hub of the creative economy is having a skilled labor force. There are vacant jobs in Iowa because they can't get people to fill the jobs. How are you bootstrapping the labor force? Are there institutions that would prepare people, who dropped out of schools and need special help, to be a part of the creative economy?

Young Aspirations/Young Artists is one of the best youth development programs in America. It has been honored by Oprah Winfrey. These are young kids from some of the lowest census income tracts in America who are now making $100,000 a year as master artists. Do you have a YA/YA that can take your school dropouts, people who are difficult, and make them part of your creative economy? There are other organizations that use culture as a labor force mentoring device, teaching citizenship or reliability, team work, and the ability of earning a living. Put your cultural resources to work helping with that labor force you need for the future.

People of color really haven't had an equal opportunity in many cases in the U.S. Can we say that cultural tourism will lift all boats in your community? Are there any bootstraps for minority entrepreneurs that are available? Years ago the Napa Valley Vintners created a venture fund for primarily Hispanic, Mexican-American agriculture workers who got citizenship and showed entrepreneurship and promise. There are now five vineyards in Napa Valley that are owned by former farm workers. This is social investment in an industry that is a huge cultural tourism industry, allowing for upward mobility and minority ownership of the production.

The National Trust for Historic Preservation in its Main Street Program three years ago, hired a diversity officer, a woman from Guatemala, to deal with the growth of the Hispanic and Latino communities on Main Streets in states across the country. They found that they couldn't speak the language of the new constituency, that they weren't understanding the culture. It took 30 years to recognize the diversity of our historic Main Streets' merchants. We shouldn't wait too long to recognize the opportunities we have. Santa Fe and the other cities attending the meeting, are rich in cultural institutions.

My organization has worked with the Ford Foundation for the last six years under its asset-based community development program. It has a program dealing with how to take the cultural institutions that ennoble, empower, and provide resources to this creative economy, and put them on the street in low-income neighborhoods. Partners worked with the Queens Museum of New York City to hire a community organizer to make a connection to people who don't speak English. The neighborhood organizer said the first thing we needed to do was have a cleanup because the area was besot with pigeon waste and debris. So, they mobilized the museum staff and volunteers to clean up a plaza that needed to be beautified and renovated two miles away from the museum. They learned about half the people were undocumented, so they were concerned their health might be suffering, and convinced the museum to develop a health agenda and bring in screening for diabetes, heart, AIDS and more. The museum had a health festival in the cleaned up plaza that worked well. The museum then took out a group health care policy so they could give out free memberships to the museum and provide health care coverage to 2,000 citizens. Suddenly the Queens Museum went from being a museum to a health care provider for a low income neighborhood of about 50 percent immigrants. Could your museums do the same?

A garage in Honolulu became an art center adjacent to 90 percent of all the public housing in the state of Hawaii—Laotian, Vietnamese, and Cambodians. They used the art program to entice children and their parents to attend, and then to articulate their complaints about the lack of police protection. The art facility became the vehicle for these people to use for parades, festivals, and events, saying that we deserve a better slice of life in Honolulu.

Ajo, Arizona, is an open-pit mining town near the Mexican border. The mine was closed during a strike. The mine owned the town and started selling the houses for $25,000 each. A glass artist moved in who had been head of the Neighborhood Reinvestment Training Institute at Neighborhood Works, bought a house, started mobilizing resources, and using connections for capital. An old school has been refurnished as 88 units of artists' housing with artists from around the world coming to this town. The artists have to, in their art, stress the common humanity of the Native American, the Hispanic American, and the Anglo American—it's an equal opportunity agenda using arts and culture to take away the hostility of the mining era when there were segregated schools and communities. They are now expecting 100,000 tourists a year.

In Holyoke, Massachusetts, Nueces Raiesas is a Puerto Rican group. They spoke to the mayor about raising fresh produce, and the mayor said, "The only things we're going to grow in Holyoke are welfare checks." A young man from Puerto Rico worked with a local convent and the nuns opened a farm. They have pig roasts, cultural events, grow vegetables, and mentor 250 kids. They just got a grant from the Massachusetts Council on the Arts for $1.7 million to create a Puerto Rican Heritage Farm for tourism in the northeastern United States. One person changed the perception of a town where the mayor said they only grow welfare checks.

Jackson Hole, Wyoming, has a rich tourism heritage and a rich population with the highest average income of any county in America. They found that all of the service workers in tourism came from two small villages in central Mexico. In developing a community art center, they said Jackson Hole was becoming bifurcated as a society. "There's us and the service workers. We don't know much about them; they don't know much about us." So, the arts council sent a poet, a cook, and a photographer to live with the families of their service workers for two months in these two small towns in central Mexico. They then came back and had a celebration of poetry, photography, and food for all the citizens. This might be something that you could do—celebrate the culture of a worker by giving respect and dignity to them as part of the community.

I reiterate: Tourism is too important to be left to the tourism planner. It's a civic agenda. Creative Tourism needs to have equity, upward mobility, and bootstrap values. The world is changing. Take advantage of it, and look for the long haul for what you want your own community to be for you, your family, and your family's family, not for the tourist.

Robert McNulty

Robert McNulty is the founder and president of Partners for Livable Communities, a twenty-year old non-profit organization and a national leader on issues of livability in American cities. Partners utilizes a number of pathways—advocacy, information, leadership, and guidance—to help communities solve their problems. As the founder and head of the organization, McNulty is known for his ability to forge effective public/ private partnerships that can transform cities. Prior to founding Partners, McNulty had a distinguished career in federal agencies, and as a professor at the Columbia University School of Architecture. He is a frequent writer, editor, and lecturer on urban issues. He holds an undergraduate degree in business, a law degree, and was a Loeb Fellow at the Harvard Graduate School of Design.

CREATIVE TOURISM AND LOCAL DEVELOPMENT
by
Greg Richards
Tourism Consultant

Creative Tourism is a new form of tourism that has the potential to change existing models of tourism development and to make a contribution to diversifying and innovating the tourist experience. By doing so, Creative Tourism can help stimulate local economic, social, and cultural development. This paper examines the background and development of the Creative Tourism concept, showing how the production and consumption of experiences have shifted from cultural tourism to Creative Tourism. In conclusion, a number of different models of Creative Tourism development are presented, illustrating how the concept has been implemented in different ways around the world.

THE ORIGINS OF THE CREATIVE TOURISM CONCEPT

The roots of the Creative Tourism concept go back to the mid-1990s, when a group of researchers and practitioners were looking at ways to enhance the sales of craft products to tourists (Richards 2005). The basic aim of the EUROTEX project was to help conserve craft production by marketing local products more effectively to tourists, developing new outlets for craft sales, and securing local jobs. It quickly became clear that one of the biggest challenges for craft producers was distinguishing their high value, handmade products from the cheaper mass-produced items. Unless the tourists can appreciate the work and skill that goes into making handcrafted products, they are unlikely to want to pay more for them.

Through discussions with craft producers and interviews with tourists, we quickly realised that many visitors were interested in seeing how craft products were made, and many wanted to learn craft skills for themselves. As a result, we decided to develop craft experiences which allowed the visitors to get involved with the production process, either by seeing craft producers at work or by learning particular textile production techniques.

These basic ideas became the inspiration for what would later be called Creative Tourism.

WHY CREATIVE TOURISM IS BECOMING MORE IMPORTANT

Many tourists are becoming increasingly bored with the packaged, sanitised products currently on offer in the tourism market. Even cultural tourism, seen by many destinations as the antidote to low quality, mass tourism (Richards 2007; 2009), has become so ubiquitous and large scale that it has taken on many traits of conventional tourism. Almost every major city now has a bus tour linking all the must-see cultural sites, and the cultural tourists dutifully troop in and out of the bus, taking photos of the same (preferably tourist-free) vistas as everybody else.

The desire to creatively engage with tourism has spawned initiatives, such as experimental tourism, in which travel is determined by chance and whim, rather than by the tourist industry. For example, the *Lonely Planet Guide to Experimental Travel* (www.lonelyplanet.com/experimentaltravel) includes strategies such as "A-Z-travel: choose a town to visit from A to Z. Find the first road beginning with A and the last beginning with Z and draw a line between the two. Walk the length of this line and discover the city alphabetically."

Creative Tourism is becoming more important, not just because the tourists are bored, but also because the cultural sector and destination managers are looking for new ways to interact with tourists. It is becoming increasingly important not just to sell the culture of a place, but also to use tourism to support the identity of the destination and to stimulate the consumption of local culture and creativity (Richards and Wilson 2007).

Creative Tourism is therefore driven by factors emanating from the sphere of consumption and from the production side. These include the increasingly skilled nature of consumption, the growing importance of experiences, and the greater role for intangible and everyday culture in tourism.

The Rise of Skilled Consumption

Initially, the basic drivers of human behaviour in developed societies shifted from meeting basic needs (such as food and shelter) towards outer directed consumption, such as the acquisition of status goods (TVs, cars, a sun tan in winter). Such forms of outer directed consumption require money, rather than specific skills, and Scitovsky (1976) therefore labelled these unskilled consumption. In contrast, the current movement in society is towards skilled consumption, including education, self-development, and creative activities that depend on developing individual skill and creativity. Whereas unskilled consumption tends to become boring with repetition, skilled consumption actually becomes more interesting the more it is practiced. By developing a skill, people can also increase their level of challenge and therefore the excitement of the activity.

The development of skills through consumption is also linked with a high level of involvement and absorption in the experience, which has resonance with the ideas of Mihály Csíkszentmihályi (1990) about flow. Creativity offers much more stimulating experiences, as well as enabling the participants to develop themselves through those experiences.

The attractiveness of creativity is also highlighted by the growing numbers of people with creative professions. In the United States, Ray and Anderson (2000) describe the emergence of the cultural creatives as an identifiable group, and Florida (2002) points to the emergence of a creative class in cities worldwide. Florida argues that creative people are attracted by places that are diverse and lively, usually as the result of a thriving creative sector. Although this argument is fairly circular, there does seem to be a correlation between creativity and the attractiveness of places.

The Experience Economy

The growing importance of the creative sector is also a result of what Pine and Gilmore (1998) have called the experience economy, where competition based on producing goods or services has been replaced by competition to produce experiences. They argue that goods and services can be easily copied, which drives prices down, reducing profitability. In contrast, experiences are unique and cannot be copied, because they are produced for and directly involve individual consumers.

But it is clear to everybody that experiences are also being copied, and that competition is increasing, even for master experience crafters such as Disney. For example, Disney has taken action against a number of Chinese theme parks for their alleged copying of Disney characters, rides, and attractions. A banner over the entrance to Shijingshan Amusement Park in Beijing recently made this emulation obvious to visitors, "Disney is too far, so please come to Shijingshan." The Beijing park already has its own versions of Snow White, Cinderella, Dumbo, and Winnie the Pooh, so why travel to California?

Pine and Gilmore have also recognised that experiences themselves may become subject to replication, and therefore may ultimately lose their value. They postulated that a further stage of economic development would place the emphasis on transformations—experiences that actually change the person consuming them. Activities such as yoga, learning a language, or developing a craft skill give the consumer far more value than any single experience, however entertaining and engaging. For many producers, therefore, adding value to experiences will mean allowing consumers to use their own creativity in interacting with the experience. This is already evident in the world of computer games, which are increasingly shifting towards multi-player virtual environments.

SHIFT FROM TANGIBLE TO INTANGIBLE TOURISM RESOURCES

The increasing importance of experiences as part of the tourism product is also marked by a growing deployment of intangible cultural resources in the tourism product. Increasingly, tourism depends on intangible elements such as the image or atmosphere of places. The media is also increasingly important for distributing and forming such images. Narratives are also more important, creating stories about people and places that make specific destinations attractive. For example, the Dutch city of Den Bosch, birthplace of the medieval surrealist Hieronymus Bosch, has no tangible evidence of its links with the painter. His works are spread around museums in Europe, America and Asia, but nothing remains in the city itself. So when Den Bosch decided to capitalise on its famous son, it had to do so by using intangible resources: heaven and hell boat trips along the underground river in the medieval heart of the city, accompanied by a storytelling guide and interrupted by an impromptu theatre performance; an interactive Hieronymus Bosch experience telling the story of his life; and projections of Bosch-like scenes onto the facades of buildings. It is clear that creativity is needed to deploy intangible resources and turn these into experiences and products for tourists.

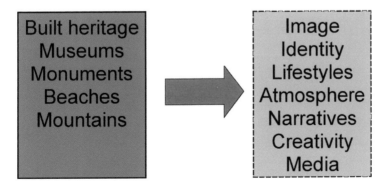

Figure 1: The shift from tangible to intangible resources in tourism

Shift From High Culture to Everyday Culture

The growing importance of intangible culture also means that the type of cultural content is changing. In the past, cultural tourism was dominated by high culture, the museums, art galleries, and monuments that constitute the must-see sites for many destinations. Increasingly, these mass cultural sites are places to be avoided for the discerning tourist, who prefers to seek out small scale, out-of-the-way places that other cultural tourists have not yet found. The local bar or café, the intimate restaurant serving local food eaten by local people, the market selling fresh regional produce—these are the types of places where tourists hope to encounter authentic culture. High culture may attract mass cultural tourism, but everyday culture is increasingly the refuge of the knowledgeable cultural tourist and the creative tourist.

Desire for More Active, Engaging Experiences

What the tourist is seeking in these local places is more contact with real people and engagement with the local culture and creative practices. The post-modern search for identity, meaning, and roots impels many to seek experiences that give them the opportunity to interact with local communities, learning more about what makes them tick and how they relate to the world. This drive also explains why volunteer travel has become so important, and why more and more young people are spending long periods studying and working abroad (Richards 2008). What people increasingly seem to want is an experience that makes them feel part of the community, rather than a passive observer.

The Need for Places to Make Themselves More Distinctive

At the same time tourists are looking for new experiences, therefore more and more places are transforming themselves into tourist destinations. The problem is increasingly: How can we make ourselves stand out from the crowd? Of course, some cities have gone down the route of building new cultural monuments to make their name on the global stage, such as the Spanish city of Bilbao with its Guggenheim Museum. However, there are few communities that can afford these sorts of investments, particularly as the cost of making a real impact spirals. Using creative resources to develop intangible events and attractions may therefore provide a viable alternative for many communities. For example, the city of Providence, Rhode Island, has utilised fire installations to revitalise the riverfront and attract visitors. Creative use can be made of all sorts of resources, such as recycled materials (Festes de Gràcia, Barcelona), tomatoes (La Tomatina in Buñol in Spain), and water (the waterfalls of a New York art installation) to make places attractive to residents and visitors alike and to make them stand out from other places.

The changes we have noted in the production and consumption of tourist experiences lead us to believe that there is a double shift occurring in the basis of cultural tourism. On the consumption side, tourists are engaging more actively with the culture and creativity of places and increasingly turning their backs on products which reduce them to mere observers of culture. On the production side, communities are beginning to utilise the full range of cultural and creative resources available to them, which include not just the high culture highlights, such as national museums and monuments, but also incorporate popular and everyday culture as elements of the tourist product, since these are often the factors that allow a destination to differentiate itself (the Irish craic, the vibrant arts community in Santa Fe, Carnival in Rio).

In summary, all these different elements combine in what Richards and Raymond (2000) first identified as Creative Tourism: Tourism that offers visitors the opportunity to develop their creative potential through active participation in courses and learning experiences that are characteristic of the holiday destination where they are undertaken.

There are some reasons for supposing that Creative Tourism offers an alternative to the serial reproduction of culture, while also fitting in with the consumer for self-development and authentic experiences. Leaving creative space for the consumer to be creative avoids the "McGuggenheimisation" of cultural experiences, while the emphasis on intangible resources reduces production costs and increases flexibility for the destination.

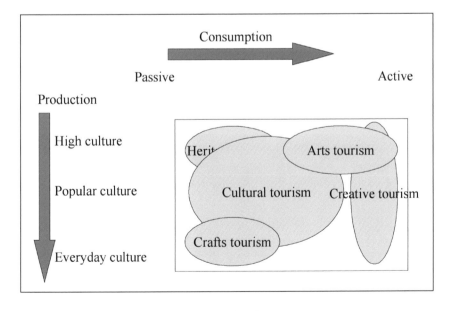

Figure 2: The shift from cultural to Creative Tourism

Creative Tourism is becoming more important because: cultural tourism is becoming mass tourism; cultural tourists are becoming more experienced and demanding more engaging experiences; and destinations are looking for alternatives to traditional tourism products. Creativity is important in tourism because: it creates atmosphere; it feeds on people's need for self-development; it creates a direct link between the culture of the tourist and the host population; and it avoids problems of heritage burnout and serial reproduction.

Although creativity is being recognised by many destinations as being important to tourism activity, Creative Tourism does not just happen—it must be actively created through interaction between tourists and the places they visit. One of the most important elements of the definition of Creative Tourism is that the experiences developed should be characteristic of the place in which they happen. In order to develop such experiences, communities need to make creative use of a wide variety of creative assets (inherited, created, and creative assets) in order to provide creative experiences for tourists. The crucial thing is to develop a specific reason for tourists to engage in creative activities in your particular destination.

This requirement implies that destination managers need to become more creative. In particular, they need to stop thinking about their roles as simply supplying tourist products, services or experiences and to start thinking about their roles as enablers of tourist creativity. They need to find ways to actively involve tourists as the co-creators of the experiences that their community offers. (Binkhorst 2007)

FORMS OF CREATIVE TOURISM

Creative Tourism is nothing new. People have been engaging in creative, educational, and learning experiences on holiday for a long time. The difference now is that this type of tourism has become so common it can be identified under a new label—Creative Tourism. The rapid strides made in the few years between the definition of the concept and the staging of the first International Conference on Creative Tourism in Santa Fe are testaments to the dynamic growth of the sector.

The last few years have seen the emergence of a wide range of Creative Tourism development strategies and the advent of a wide range of Creative Tourism experiences. In our view, Creative Tourism is not a single model of tourism development, but rather a broad range of different possible approaches to engaging tourists with creative experiences.

In general, there are two basic modes of implementation of Creative Tourism:

1) Using creativity as a tourist activity.
2) Using creativity as backdrop for tourism.

The first is a more classic model of Creative Tourism, since it emphasises the active engagement of tourists in creative activities in the destination. However, increasingly communities are realising that their creative lives can make a place attractive to be in, even if the tourists don't do anything creative themselves. Santa Fe is a good example of this; the artistic and creative community of Santa Fe produces a particular atmosphere or vibe that makes the city attractive to be in, even for visitors who don't visit the opera or buy a painting.

There are also many different types of experiences and products which can be offered to the creative tourist. Again, these experiences range from more active forms of involvement, such as learning a specific skill, to browsing galleries and shops looking at creative products.

Basis of activity	Type of experience
Learning	Workshops
Tasting	Experiences
	Open ateliers
Seeing	Itineraries
Buying	Galleries, Shop windows

Table 1: A typology of Creative Tourism experiences

These different types of creative experiences are also linked to various forms of delivery and organisation structure. Many new networks are springing up that link together creative producers in order to engage in collaborative marketing and to increase the visibility of creative activities. Destinations are also beginning to form partnerships of creative enterprises, as well as linking the creative and tourism sectors in order to develop new creative experiences. The following section provides a number of different examples of how creativity is being injected into tourism around the world.

EXAMPLES OF CREATIVE TOURISM DEVELOPMENT

Creative Tourism Networks

The most developed Creative Tourism network can be found in the city of Nelson, New Zealand, where Creative Tourism New Zealand has been established as a network of creative businesses offering products to tourists (www.creativetourism. co.nz). The network provides a wide range of creative experiences, including bone carving, Maori language classes, weaving, felting, woodwork, and New Zealand gastronomy. The focus is very much on learning experiences, with a range of hands-on workshops being run by local tutors. (Raymond 2007. Also see Raymond's chapter in the current volume)

Creative Tourism Barcelona (www.barcelonacreativa.info) takes a slightly different approach, acting as an intermediary to link creative producers in the city with people from other parts of the world who want to engage in creative activities there. Their website allows potential creative tourists to indicate the types of creative activities they are interested in, and they are then put in touch with local creative sector actors who can provide the facilities or resources to make it happen.

Spaces

Creativity needs space, and creative destinations make innovative use of their spaces to facilitate Creative Tourism. This also applies to the area of accommodation, which is usually one of the least creative aspects of the tourism product. In Barcelona, different forms of accommodation have tapped into the creative sector to develop new experiences. The Chic and Basic Hotel has staged fashion shows, using its individually designed bedrooms to showcase the products of young local designers. The Equity Point Hostels group (www.equity-point.com/hostelart/index_es.html) runs a hostel art programme, giving young artists an opportunity to exhibit their work in hostel rooms and introducing young travellers to the creative sector in Barcelona. The Camping House Barcelona (www.barcelona-house.com/CHcast/arquitectostxtC.html) is a new concept in tourist accommodation, providing guests with the sensation of camping in the middle of the city and adding design value to their stays.

Particular spaces have also been developed to offer creative learning experiences to visitors in different parts of the world. For example the Italian coffee producer Illy's Università del Caffè provides courses on all aspects of coffee and coffee making at eleven different locations (www.illy.com/wps/wcm/connect/us/illy/the-world-of-coffee/universita-del-caffe/). Since 1999, approximately 22,000 students have graduated from this institution.

Events

Ceolas is a week-long music school that was established on the island, South Uist in Scotland, in 1996 by the Gaelic Arts Agency (http://www.ceolas.co.uk/). The objectives of Ceolas are:

- To provide opportunities for high quality tuition in the Gaelic arts and a memorable cultural tourism experience.
- To encourage community celebration of the indigenous Gaelic arts and culture of the area.
- To raise local awareness of the socio-economic development potential of the arts as well as their educational and cultural value.
- To promote the Gaelic arts as a unique and vital cornerstone of Scottish cultural identity.

- To stimulate community confidence and prompt new ideas and new local developments.

During the week-long programme, a wide range of events, concerts, and activities are organised and the number of people attending Ceolas events has varied between 2,000 and 3,500, almost as many as the total population of the island of 4,000. The event fills all the available beds in South Uist for a week, boosts visitor spending, and helps to develop interest in local culture. The festival has increased pride in local culture among residents and raised social cohesion.

In spite of the isolated location of the island, many of the participants come from abroad. The development of social events and the house ceilidhs (informal social gatherings) have integrated the visitors into the life of the island and cleverly transformed the visitors, who may think of themselves as outsiders, into part of the life of the island—even if it is only for one week in the year. In particular Ceolas is a good example of the way in which traditional cultural tourism based on museums and monuments is being transformed into new modes of experience, such as Creative Tourism. Tourists and residents essentially become partners in the production of a cultural experience that is based on tradition as a source of inspiration for contemporary creativity.

The Festes de Gràcia is a local festival in a district of Barcelona that has developed into a major celebration for the whole city. The key element of this event is the decoration of local streets by residents, using recycled materials. Each street is themed and there is a high level of creativity involved in creating a totally new space from discarded items such as water bottles and milk cartons.

Cultural Itineraries

Cultural itineraries can also be a means of linking together creative enterprises and events, stimulating visitors to see a number of different activities in a specific region. The Craft Route of the Alto Minho in Northern Portugal includes a large number of crafts producers, most of whom work from home. The brochure and website give tourists the possibility of visiting these producers, but the lack of any form of contact, apart from telephone, makes it difficult for non-Portuguese speakers. As a practical solution to the problem of dealing with foreign tourists, the tourist board has now begun to sell craft products in its information centres. Sales are supported by demonstrations from crafts producers during the high season.

The results of this initiative have been positive, with a rapid increase in craft sales. Producers said they were happy with the increased sales and with the extra marketing efforts by the tourist board. The main problem was that the project-based funding finished after three years, leading to a lower level of marketing activity and lower sales.

As a new approach to the cultural itinerary concept, the Council of Europe is developing a cultural corridor scheme, initially in southeast Europe. The Council of Europe defines cultural corridors as: "Networks of interaction and economic exchange based on culture and creativity, incorporating principles of sustainability, fairness and inclusion, based on wide stakeholder partnerships which are rooted in solid institutional frameworks that stimulate regional socio-economic development.

The basic idea is to create networks that move beyond physical routes linking cultural sites to include the full range of creative assets in a region (Richards, Russo and Grossman 2008).

Creative Backdrops

Many cities have a reputation of being creative in one way or another, just as Santa Fe does. In many cases, this creativity is experienced by the visitor not so much in the direct consumption of creative activities, but rather through the general atmosphere or buzz of the place as a whole, which is generated by the creative sector.

Not only is the creative buzz of a place important in attracting people, but it can also be turned into a specific attraction as well. In Barcelona cuisine is a major attraction, particularly as Catalunya has a growing reputation as a major area of culinary innovation. One advertisement for Catalan cooking courses emphasises the active involvement of participants, who can, "Learn about the variety and quality of Catalan food in a guided visit to the famous La Boqueria market, after which Jaume, our active and experienced cooking teacher, will cook with the help of the group, two main dishes and a dessert based on some of the most famous recipes of regional Catalan cuisine." Barcelona has also discovered the creative sector as attraction in its own right, as one tour operator now runs a Creative Talent excursion in Barcelona that, "Takes you directly to the artists and craftspeople, giving you an insight into the creative process and providing an opportunity to buy at advantageous prices, before their creators become too famous." The creative backdrop provided by Barcelona is also utilised by a number of people to run courses in creativity.

Creative Tourism Even for Package Tourists?

Creative Tourism doesn't only have to be about small, exclusive groups of tourists. The same philosophy can arguably be applied even to packaged holidays. For example, Grecotel is the largest hotel chain in Greece, but it applies many of the principles of Creative Tourism through its cultural programme. Grecotel has established the Agreco Farm in Crete, where hotel guests can enjoy, "An innovative display of environmentally friendly methods for traditional and modern cultivation and breeding. The overall objective is to give visitors a first-hand experience of the traditional production methods of traditional Greek products."

Grecotel also supports a monastery near some of its hotels in Crete, and helps the nuns to display their craft skills and sell craft products to tourists. Although the level of interaction may be lower than in some of the smaller scale Creative Tourism experiences, it does bring package tourists a lot closer to the local culture than they would normally get.

OPPORTUNITIES FOR CREATIVE TOURISM

In conclusion, it seems that Creative Tourism can offer many advantages to destinations wishing to develop new forms of tourism activity. Arguably, it has a number of important advantages over many more conventional forms of tourism, including cultural tourism:

- Creativity can provide a source of tourism activity, as well as an attractive backdrop for general tourism activity.
- Creative development of tourism can help sustain the atmosphere of the destination.
- Creative Tourism can become a means of business development for crafts producers and other small creative enterprises.
- Creative Tourism enables local people to use their own creativity (and puts them in control of the process).
- Creative Tourism is a renewable resource.

We look forward to seeing how destinations around the world innovate and develop on the basic Creative Tourism concept to produce new forms and models of culturally-sensitive, sustainable tourism in the future.

Greg Richards. Photograph by Linda Carfagno.

Keynotes and Key Concepts

89

Greg Richards is a partner in the company Tourism Research and Marketing and has worked with many governments. He has extensive experience in tourism research and has held positions at universities in Spain, the Netherlands, and England. He is also the author of well-known publications on creative and cultural tourism and is a co-founder of Creative Tourism New Zealand along with Crispin Raymond. As a European executive member of the Association for Tourism and Leisure Education (ATLAS), he has directed projects on topics including cultural tourism, crafts tourism, sustainable tourism, tourism education, and labor mobility in the tourism industry. He has worked extensively on developing Creative Tourism in Barcelona and Burgos, Spain; Manchester, Newcastle, London, and Edinburgh, United Kingdom; Amsterdam, Rotterdam and Den Bosch, Netherlands; Sibiu, Romania; Amman, Jordan; and Macao, China. At the time this book was published, he was working with the Dutch city of Den Bosch to develop a series of events celebrating the 500th anniversary of painter Heironymus Bosch.

REFERENCES

Binkhorst, E. (2007) *Creativity in Tourism Experiences; The case of Sitges.* In Richards G. and Wilson, J. (Eds) *Tourism, Creativity and Development.* London: Routledge, pp. 125-144.

Creative City Network of Canada (2005) *Creative Tourism Bolsters Cultural Community in Rural Ontario.* www.creativecity.ca/resources/project-profiles/Strathroy-Baskets.html

Csíkszentmihályi, Mihály (1990). *Flow: The Psychology of Optimal Experience.* New York: Harper and Row.

Florida, R. (2002) *The Rise of the Creative Class: And How It Is Transforming Work, Leisure, Community and Everyday Life.* New York: Basic Books.

Pine, B.J. and Gilmore, J.H. (1999) *The Experience Economy.* Boston: Harvard University Press.

Ray, P.H. and Anderson, S.R. (2000) *The Cultural Creatives.* New York: Three Rivers Press.

Raymond, C. (2007) *Creative Tourism New Zealand: The practical challenges of developing Creative Tourism.* In Richards G. and Wilson, J. (Eds) *Tourism, Creativity and Development.* London: Routledge, pp. 145-157.

Richards, G. (2005) *Textile Tourists in the European Periphery: New Markets for Disadvantaged Areas? Tourism Review International*, Volume 8, no. 4, pp. 323-338.

Richards, G. (2007, ed.) Cultural Tourism: Global and local perspectives. New York: Haworth Press.

Richards, G. (2008) Youth Travel Matters: *Understanding the global phenomenon of youth travel.* Madrid: World Tourism Organisation/WYSE Travel Confederation.

Richards, G. (2009) *The Impact of Culture on Tourism.* Paris: OECD.

Richards, G. and Raymond, C. (2000) Creative Tourism. ATLAS News, no. 23, 16-20.

Richards, G., Russo, A.P. and Grossman, M. (2008) *Cultural Corridors in South East Europe: Refinement of concept and development of pilot projects.* Strasbourg: Council of Europe.

Richards G. and Wilson, J. (2007) *Tourism, Creativity and Development.* London: Routledge.

Scitovsky, T. (1976) *The Joyless Economy.* Oxford: Oxford University Press.

THE SPIRIT OF PLACE
by
Jack Loeffler
Historian, Writer, Radio Producer and Sound Collage Artist

When Tom Maguire and I were talking about what it would be fun to address, he suggested we talk about the spirit of Santa Fe, New Mexico that has inspired so many artists. Many states and countries are represented at this conference.

Thinking about Santa Fe and the Southwest has dominated my cultural point of view for many, many years. It comes to mind that Santa Fe is in various ways, a nexus. It's a place where many different things come together. For example, this is one of two places in the contiguous 48 states where three distinct physiographic divisions of the continent coincide—The Rocky Mountains, the Great Plains, and the Intermountain West, which itself contains the Basin and Range province, the Colorado Plateau, and the Columbia Plateau. I understand that Santa Fe Mayor David Coss is very interested in the Santa Fe River. Indeed, the notion of watershed thinking takes place big time in Santa Fe. It has to, because we live in one of the most arid parts of the North American continent.

In thinking about this, 12,000 to 15,000 years ago, people came trailing in here following big game during the Pleistocene Epoch, the last Ice Age, and settled in over a long period of time. Many, many different cultures have lived here and thus this area has become a cultural nexus approached from every direction. Several hundred years ago, there was a pueblo situated on the site of the current convention center, a community that preceded Santa Fe as we know it. In 1598, the first of many great roads or trails of European provenance entered into this region. It was then that Juan de Oñate led a group of colonists up what is now known as El Camino Real de Tierra Adentro—the road to the interior—that extended from Mexico City to Santa Fe. In the 19th century, the Old Spanish Trail took off from Santa Fe for the West Coast. During the same relative period, the Santa Fe Trail extended from St. Louis and parts east to Santa Fe.

John Baxter, who is an authority on much of the history of livestock in the American Southwest, calls Santa Fe "The Queen City of the Southwest." It was the Southwest's first major city and has thus remained one of the most wonderful. Various roads and trails came into Santa Fe from every direction, converging here in an area already inhabited by cultures that could trace their ancestries into deep antiquity through oral tradition and rock art. This area is known by people who live along the Northern Rio Grande in several different pueblos, including Santa Clara, San Ildefonso, San Juan, Tesuque, and other pueblos—as the Tewa World. The Tewa World was contained within four great peaks—to the west the peak of the Jemez Mountains, the peak to the north known as Canjilon, Truchas Peak in the Sangre de Cristos to the east, and Sandia or Turtle Mountain to the south.

I am fascinated by the notion of geo-mythic mapping that identifies important landforms and gives them mythic significance. The stories and legends that recall historic and mythic events of antiquity that occurred throughout the landscape constitute the foundation of the mythic processes that give meaning to human cultures that exist here. The mythic process contributes to the way we intuitively define our cultural relationship to homeland.

One of my great ongoing adventures over the past 45 years—I turned on my first tape recorder 51 years ago—is traveling throughout the American West, Mexico, even as far as the Tropic of Capricorn, and the Cook Islands, recording the sounds of habitats and the words and songs of the peoples who live in these different habitats.

My friend, Tomas Martinez Saldañá, a scholar from Mexico City, forwarded the idea that a group of Tlaxcalan Indians came northward with Juan de Oñate in 1598. These Indians had earlier joined the Spaniards in their war against the Aztecs in Mexico, and as a reward, the Tlaxcalans were given high relevance among the Spanish people. According to Dr. Saldañá, there is a strong likelihood that the city of Santa Fe was laid out initially by Tlaxcalan Indians. This is a geomantic kind of thing, where they were sensing the spirit of this landscape, and the town that they were supposed to be laying out had to comply with certain characteristics or fundamentals vital to a community's success. Obviously, whatever the Tlaxcalans did really worked, because it is now more than 400-years later and Santa Fe is a thriving place. Much of it had to do with proximity to the Santa Fe River.

On the other side of the Santa Fe River from where we are meeting in this convention center are adobe structures known as the Oldest House and the Oldest

Church. One of the characteristics of the church is that at the moment of sunset on the day of the winter solstice, by opening the front doors of the church, the sun shines its beam right on the altar. It is an amazing solstice marker, and that really raises the spirits of everyone who's watched it. There are many solstice markers in the American Southwest.

The Southwest is known for an enormous amount of rock art. One of my favorite places, south of here, is Comanche Gap in the Galisteo Basin. Unfortunately, we can't go there anymore because it's been bought and is privately held. But, it remains one of the most evocative places in that it taps into archetypal motifs from deep within human consciousness.

My friend, Roy Kady, is a Navajo weaver who takes much of his inspiration from the flow of nature, from the landscape where he was born. When Roy Kady told me this story, he had taken me in his four-wheel drive vehicle over 25 miles of really tough road to the "hooghan," or traditional Navajo home where he had grown up as a boy. The hooghan was beginning to show signs of deterioration, but we went inside and sat on some stumps. Roy pulled out his medicine pouch, and took out Indian tobacco and an Indian pipe. He lighted the pipe, blew the smoke, and thus blessed me, my microphones, my recorder, himself, and the inside of the hooghan. He then started to speak:

"So in our offerings, in our prayer, we always start with our beautiful language—may it always be beautiful. And that's why you name the four mountains, the four directional mountains, because that's where we acquired the language. That's why we go to these mountains, and we make offerings to them on a yearly basis.

"To the east we have "Tsisnaasjini,'" Blanca Peak, and when you say the mountains and your offerings early morning, when you say "Tsisnaasjini,'" you're saying 'In beauty may you surround me with a protection of a rainbow belt to protect me on my track, my daily track or in life.' When you say "Tsoodzil," which is the south mountain, Mount Taylor, you're saying 'Also give me the beautiful language of turquoise to give me the ability to communicate what I have to communicate today. May my words be all beautiful.' And then our west mountain is "Dook'o'oosliid," and when you say "Dook'o'oosliid," you say 'From the tip of the peak of San Francisco, may you always have this beam of light to light where I'm going, whether it be day or night. May that beam always be bright for me so that I know my path, where I'm headed.' And then when you say "Dibe Nitsaa," which is the northern mountain, Mount Hesperus, you're talking about the sacred sheep that we all know is the backbone of the Navajo society. That is a very sacred animal and that's why our fourth sacred mountain is named "Dibe Nitsaa." With that, we're strong, and the reason why sheep is so important—in a lot of our traditional stories that are told with all the monsters, it was the sheep, the bighorn sheep, that was the sole survivor of all poverty. The bighorn sheep withstood every test, even with the lightning gods. They've tried to strike him down, to cease him. But the bighorn sheep always survived and was the only animal to do that. And that's why the northern mountain stands for that mountain. It's the mountain that gives us strength. It's the mountain that is our protecting mountain. It has a lot of strength, and then that's why it's called Bighorn Sheep Mountain."

A sense of habitat can't be over emphasized, especially in the minds of the indigenous peoples who live here. Santa Fe is a place that in my own mind doesn't have political boundaries. It is part of a huge region of beauty, incredible landscapes. There is no place in the American Southwest where I don't feel totally at home and able to throw out a sleeping bag and be a happy camper. It's the most wonderful place I know. This huge region that we think of as the American Southwest only became part of the United States about 160 years ago. Before that, it was Mexico, and before that, it was New Spain, and before that it was Indian Country. It still is Indian Country, big time.

I have been fortunate to have actually lived with many different groups over the last 50 years. For a time in 1964, I lived in an old forked stick hooghan, what they call the male hooghan. I lived there for about seven months and herded sheep. It turns out I was herding Churro sheep, but I didn't know it. The Churro sheep are the very sheep that came north with Juan de Oñate in 1598. Somehow, some of those sheep were "liberated" by some of the Navajos. It was the Churro wool that became absolutely vital to Navajo weaving. The next time you look at Navajo weaving, there is a chance that some of the weavings may be of Churro wool.

I want to mention that all of the traditional Native American people that I know have a real proclivity for seeing themselves as part of the biotic community, and not separate from it.

One of the most important rivers to us is the San Juan River. In the 1970s, we committed an unnatural act by getting water from that watershed to pass beneath the Continental Divide and empty into Heron Lake, which is part of the Rio Chama watershed that empties into the Rio Grande from whence Santa Fe and Albuquerque get a lot of our water. If we didn't have the San Juan/Chama diversion, we might be in real trouble—we might be anyway. This is arid country.

One of the really neat things about what I do for a living—actually it's the way I spend much of my life having as much fun as I can possibly have—is to go out into the wilds with a good digital recorder and excellent microphones and then listen a few hundred percent better than you can with the naked ear. You can really hear the way a lot of our fellow creatures hear. About 15 to 18 years ago, I was down in the Kuakatch Wash in the Sonoran Desert that is the most luxuriant desert in North America and possibly in the world. It is excruciatingly beautiful. I camped there for a week, all by myself in a part of this desert, recording wildlife. Early one morning before sunrise, when there was still light in the eastern sky, I set up my recording apparatus. I made a cup of coffee on my Coleman stove. I had my headphones on, and I started hearing distant alarm calls from birds, going south to north. When you're listening in stereo, you are hearing spatially. I got out my binoculars and saw a low flying hawk at the place of the alarm calls. The calls continued as the hawk continued to fly north. It was an epiphinistic moment when I realized I was hearing inter-species communication that had nothing to do with me. It sort of puts you in your place. There was no evidence of a human in 200 square miles. It was a good feeling to hear this—this biophany of inter-species communication.

One of my very special friends from the Tewa world is Rina Swentzell who is an amazing woman. She understands both her Tewa heritage and the ways of modern western culture. Here she speaks of her sense of community:

"What I have been thinking is that we have too small a definition of community. I go back to the pueblo thinking, because their community was not just the human community. It included the place within which we lived, so that the mountains were part of community. The water was part of community. Trees, rock, plants, animals. You couldn't have moved through any day in that Old World, even when I was growing up, without knowing that you were part of that whole community of trees, rocks, people. Today, what we do is just talk about human community. It gets to be such a small thing within the larger scope of things. And I think that that is the demise of our modern lives today. We keep making the world smaller and smaller until it is nothing but us, just human beings out of our natural context, out of our cosmological context. We have become so small in our view of the world as simply us human beings. And it is crucial that we get beyond that and move back again to seeing ourselves within context."

One of the things that I think is really important about the message that can be delivered from this wonderful region is that it is a place where many cultures have contributed to the spirit of this place. And a lot of that is reflected in the art that comes from Santa Fe, and much of that art is a meld of myriad points of view. I have many artist friends, and musician friends, and writer friends. We've had some tremendous writers who've passed through New Mexico, including Paul Horgan who wrote one of the great history books of all times, *Great River: The Río Grande in North American History*.

I spent time with Paul Horgan about twenty years ago, and he talked about the coming of the many cultures to the American Southwest. Also, my living friend, John Nichols, wrote wonderful things about New Mexico. Frank Waters, D. H. Lawrence, Leslie Marmon Silko, Simon Ortiz, Arthur Sze, and many other great writers have taken much of their inspiration from this land. My late compañero was a writer who spent a lot of time in Santa Fe, a fellow by the name of Edward Abbey. This is the 40th anniversary of the publication of his book *Desert Solitaire*, one of the great classics in American literature.

I would like to mention one other thing about Santa Fe that is very important, and that is the presence of the new bioregional movement over the past 30 years, which is alive and well around Santa Fe. Santa Fe has one of the most thriving farmers markets in the United States. It is amazing when you think that Santa Fe is located in one of the most arid regions in the United States with only 12 to 13 inches of precipitation annually, if we're lucky. Ten inches or less constitutes a desert. I think of this as high desert with piñon and juniper trees and grass.

We live in the Rio Grande watershed that is fed by a few tiny tributaries. Farmers of all persuasions—Native Americans, Hispanos, Anglos, and others—are growing crops in this watershed, in large measure thanks to a collaborative effort, and they contribute a large amount of food to the region.

In the minds of a lot of the artists, writers and vendors, at least those I know, Santa Fe represents a social area where we have decentralized from the bigger picture in America and are diligently striving to pursue our own collective destiny here in a mutually collaborative fashion. The great turn-of-the-twentieth-century Russian philosopher Peter Kropotkin expressed his major idea that cultural evolution owes far more to mutual cooperation than to mutual antagonism.

Santa Fe is far more than an ancient city shaped by many cultures. It is a place of pilgrimage for those who wish to hone their intuitions to the spirit of place.

Jack Loeffler.
Photograph by Linda Carfagno.

Jack Loeffler has produced nearly 300 radio programs, including the thirteen-part series, *The Spirit of Place* and the six-part series, *Moving Waters: The Colorado River and the West*. His books include *Adventures with Ed: A Portrait of Abbey, La Musica de los Viejitos: The Hispanic Folk Music of the Rio Grande del Norte*, and *Interviews with Iconoclasts*. He is currently on a four-year grant from the Ford Foundation to document the relationships of indigenous cultures to their habitats, a project that will result in a radio series and a book. Loeffler is an advocate of grass roots activism in reshaping communities' futures. Loeffler is a 2008 recipient of the Governor's Arts Award from the state of New Mexico.

SECTION 2

CREATIVE CITIES:
CONVERSATIONS
ABOUT BEST PRACTICES

INTRODUCTION AND COMMON THEMES
by
Sabrina V. Pratt
Executive Director, City of Santa Fe Arts Commission

Members of the Creative Cities Network and others arrived at the 2008 conference in Santa Fe excited about sharing their work and learning about programs and projects happening in other cities. Exchange of information happened through many different types of interactions, some of which are documented in this section.

As Sonya Carreau of Montreal, Canada, says in her article, "It is always exciting to meet with representatives of the other cities in the network, who, like us, are driven by a willingness to find new ways of making and thinking about their cities, to build for the future in a context of creativity, and to motivate each other so that each of their actions have structure enhancing impacts over the long term." Conference conversations from this track underscored the dedication and passion of members of the Creative Cities Network.

At the opening plenary session of the conference, Georges Poussin, Chief of the UNESCO Section of Creative Industries for Development, which oversees the Creative Cities Network, discussed UNESCO's work in cultural and Creative Tourism, introduced the concept of the Creative Cities Network and discussed possible opportunities for social and economic benefits. Creative partnerships among network members have the possibility of not only local, but global level results.

Conversations described by the contributors to this section represent the network disciplines of design, literature, music, gastronomy, and crafts and folk art. The conversations were led by people working on behalf of cities to promote projects and programs through their membership in the network. These same people served as panel moderators and presenters on other topics. Reflections on the discussions, presentations, and work in the field are included in this section.

Also included are case studies of very interesting work being done by cities that are not part of the UNESCO Creative Cities Network. For example, the presentation made about Barcelona Creative Tourism showcased that city's effort to organize Creative Tourism activities that not only involve the local culture, but also the interaction of cultures through visiting creative types. Another very proactive organization, the Creative City Network of Canada, is also profiled.

Themes that run across these articles and some of the initiatives of this group of very diverse cities include the following:

PARTNERSHIPS AND SUPPORT AMONG CITIES

Georges Poussin's article describes UNESCO's networks that encourage the interaction and partnership of cities across the world. Many of the Creative Cities Network members address work they have done and thoughts on how to pursue more partnerships both within a field or between fields. Elizabeth Keurvorst of the Creative City Network of Canada describes how the municipal "creative bureaucrats" who are members of this organization function in their city environments and support one another.

UNESCO CREATIVE CITIES NETWORK PROMOTION

Presenters who are involved in day-to-day work connected to their city's Creative Cities network designation comment on how the UNESCO network can be used to position a city to stand out as a result of its creativity. Shenzhen, China was hoping at the time of the conference to be appointed to the network and indeed is now the 14th network city. One of the nine members of the Shenzhen delegation wrote an interesting paper on the 28-year history of their city and what they found in Santa Fe to build upon.

ACTIVITIES IN SELECTED UNESCO CREATIVE CITIES DISCIPLINES

Information on projects and programs from cities designated in the fields of literature, crafts and folk art, music, and design is further detailed in this section. One example is Edinburgh, Scotland's story of how they came to be the first city in the network and what they have done over the past four years to promote literature through successful local and nationwide programs. Other practical examples come from Montreal, Canada, that describe the role that festivals play in their city, where many festivals contribute to exciting cultural tourism and include Creative Tourism elements. In addition the Montreal article discusses a new initiative titled *Building Montreal* in which network members are invited to participate.

TOURISM—CREATIVE, ECO, AND CULTURAL

Barcelona's Creative Tourism program overview gives the reader some interesting and inspiring ideas about the city's creativity and its interest in hosting visitors who want to experience something about Barcelona, or get assistance with bringing a creative presentation to Barcelona. Ossama Meguid describes the challenges of community based eco-tourism in Aswan, Egypt where visitors can experience traditional village life in Nubian villages.

SUMMARY

Partnerships, promotion, cultural program models, and artist exchanges are just a few of the hands-on, best practices readers can learn about in this section. Reflections of municipal leaders on international relations, specific examples of engaging communities and visitors, and thoughts on how a city can stand out in the world based on its creativity make this group of articles inspiring.

THE CREATIVE TOURISM MOVEMENT
by
Georges Poussin
Chief, UNESCO Section of Creative Industries for Development

One time more, I express my great privilege to be present here in Santa Fe, and UNESCO's gratitude to the city of Santa Fe and all the organizers of this International Conference on Creative Tourism, held following the wish of the UNESCO's Creative Cities Network expressed here two years ago.

In the framework of this first roundtable, I would like to present to you UNESCO's concept of cultural tourism and its perspective on Creative Tourism.

In the United Nations family, the UNWTO (World Tourism Organization) is responsible for all aspects of tourism. UNESCO's role is in relation to this with its goals of protection and promotion of cultural diversity, and cultural dialogue and sustainable development.

Tourism demand is increasingly shifting toward experiential modes of consumption, with a growing importance of the role of image, atmosphere, and quality of experience. Travelers search for authenticity and unique experiences and hope to achieve a better understanding of the country visited and its development, or to connect in some way with the cultural identity of the local population.

Cultural and natural resources, tangible and intangible heritage, and all aspects of history and identity of a region have always played an important role in economic development as part of overall tourism strategies. Culture and tourism both aim at conservation and economic value enhancement, but managing sustainable development of tourism is certainly not an easy task, yet is quite a critical issue, as it holds potential to preserve cultural resources for future generations.

Reflecting on culture and creativity as major resources of tourism, UNESCO has developed cultural tourism and development projects in the framework of the Millennium Development Goals. Cultural tourism is considered as a tool for economic and social development, for fostering heritage, and developing cultural industries. Creative and cultural industries are often associated with cultural tourism, for example the index established by UNESCO in the field of craft, tourism, and development, indicating the relationship between tourism and the development of local quality craft.

According to UNWTO, cultural tourism increases more than global tourism (+5 percent a year and +8 percent for LDC) and represents in 2007, 40 percent of global tourism.

There are many benefits to cultural tourism. It is recognized as providing opportunities to: preserve cultural resources; support cultural heritage conservation and management; promote community-based tourism products and services; and develop local employment.

Now, UNESCO is very much in favour of this new form of tourism that is seizing the place of sustainable tourism development—Creative Tourism. Creative Tourism could be considered as a variation on previous models of educational tourism and cultural tourism or even ecotourism that focuses on protecting local cultures and the natural environment. Furthermore, we understand it in principle as a community-based tourism. It aims to share the host community's culture with visitors, offering an experience or activities related to creative learning in collaboration with the local community. We also appreciate its comprehensive approach to culture, including not just physical heritage, but also intangible cultural heritage, contemporary artistic creativity, creative industries, and lifestyle and the atmosphere of the destination.

UNESCO fully supports the idea of linking tourism and creativity, especially through the Creative Cities Network programme, which has endorsed Creative Tourism as a cross-cultural engagement of sharing and exchanging unique cultural offerings in respect to the diversity of cultural expressions.

UNESCO's Creative Cities Network is a network of cities, structured around seven creative industry fields—literature, crafts/folk arts, music, design, cinema, gastronomy and media arts—so that cities can establish social, economic, and cultural development at local and global levels through forging creative partnerships.

As I have already indicated, the first global gathering of the UNESCO Creative Cities Network on the subject of Creative Tourism was convened here in Santa Fe, New Mexico, from October 25 to 27, 2006. And during this meeting, the Creative

Cities Network agreed on the following working definition of Creative Tourism: "Creative Tourism is travel directed toward an engaged and authentic experience, with participative learning in the arts, heritage, or special character of a place, and it provides a connection with those who reside in this place and create this living culture."

I believe this aspect of connection with those who reside in this place is the most essential element to its sustainability. The local communities and visitors will have an educational, emotional, social, and personal interaction with the place and the local culture, as well as share an experience of exchange with the local population. It is a chance to build up a relationship based on mutual respect, rather than on pure commerce.

Therefore, Creative Tourism shows potential to become a true laboratory of intercultural dialogue. It can continue to embody, develop, and implement the key principles of one of the major, international, normative frameworks of UNESCO in preservation and promotion of creative diversity, the 2005 Convention on the Protection and Promotion of the Diversity of Cultural Expression.

In this respect, we highly encourage developed countries and those in the developing world to undertake sustainable tourism plans, taking into account local objectives, and understanding the importance of establishing a policy framework to create and strengthen their means of cultural expression through Creative Tourism initiatives.

On the other hand, Creative Tourism also aims to build local capacities by empowering local communities and their cultures, as well as enhancing local socio-economic development. As local populations are directly involved in promoting their own cultural resources, it revitalizes their cultural identity and enables them to be actively engaged in cultural preservation and transmission. It can also offer a major opportunity to develop new income streams, enhance the skills of local practitioners, and provide a local solution to poverty. Therefore, it gives possibilities to identify local economic opportunities and develop socio-cultural and economic assets in the home communities, especially in the developing world.

For example, let me just briefly share with you the experience of one of our members, Popayan, Colombia. As part of the gastronomic cities network, Popayan seeks to expand its gastronomic culture and open up new forms of cooperation in food and tourism industries. In this context, it has made an effort to enhance the skills of people working in local restaurants by developing gastronomic tourism programmes. As a result, Popayan has become the first gastronomic destination in southwest Colombia, enhancing gastronomy's economic impact.

UNESCO's Creative Cities Network aims to assign creativity a strong position in the context of globalization. In recognizing that Creative Tourism can become a source of human encounter, multi-cultural exchange, intercultural dialogue, and a new means of cultural preservation, human development, and social reconciliation, the Creative Cities Network heartily supports the diversity of Creative Tourism initiatives.

Our network is equally committed to pooling together various cultural resources from different cities, thus making new links and connections so that Creative Tourism can be further explored to a new level—experiencing the network's entire spectrum of cross-sectoral partnerships.

Georges Poussin.
Photograph by Linda Carfagno.

Georges Poussin has been a staff member of UNESCO's Secretariat since 1998. At present, he is chief of the Section of the Creative Industries for Development, which is one of the two sections of the Division of Cultural Expressions and Creative Industries of the Culture Sector. His section is especially in charge of strengthening national and regional policies, partnerships, and projects in the field of books, translation, music, cinema, crafts, design, and creative industries, in general. The section especially manages such programmes as UNESCO's Creative Cities Network, Award of Excellence in Crafts, Design 21 and Design Social 21 programmes (see www.UNESCO.org). Before he joined UNESCO, Georges Poussin was secretary-general of the French National Commission for UNESCO. He is a post-graduate in Law and Political Sciences and a former broadcast journalist.

Montréal's Presence in Santa Fe

by
Sonya Carreau
Cultural Organization Management Consultant
Design Montréal

W e very enthusiastically responded to the city of Santa Fe's invitation to take part in the inaugural International Conference on Creative Tourism, held in conjunction with the annual meeting of members of the UNESCO Creative Cities Network, of which Montréal is a member. As a cultural metropolis and a UNESCO City of Design, it was important for Montréal to be present at, and indeed actively participate in, this event, on the one hand, to promote its cultural and Creative Tourism assets internationally, and on the other, to be part of dialogue and discussions aimed at nurturing a reflection on novel practices and strategies for cities seeking to achieve economic growth through Creative Tourism. Since the concept of Creative Tourism in a creative cities context is a fairly new one, our participation in this forum for exchange proved to be an opportunity to acquire more in-depth knowledge of the subject. The Design Montréal office created a delegation with representatives of two key players in the city's tourism industry: Tourisme Montréal and the Transat Chair in Tourism at the Université du Québec à Montréal (UQAM) School of Management, via its Tourism Intelligence Network (TIN).

Open House Design Montréal. Exhibition of projects of the graphic design firm Paprika.
Location: Commissaires. Photograph by Arturo Velazquez.

In view of Montréal's positioning as an exceptional cultural tourism destination, our objective, besides that of sharing best practices with the international delegates, was to strengthen our links with other member cities of the network, to share the experience Montréal has gained in the field of design, and to stimulate creation of projects that are conducive to exchanges between designers from here and abroad. The Design Montréal office also took advantage of the meeting to present its project, Building Montréal, the goal of which is to initiate discussions on ways of continuing dialogue among elected officials, citizens, experts, and project promoters with an eye to making the designation, Montréal, UNESCO City of Design, vital and tangible, and to rally the members of the network, in all disciplines combined, around creative, structure enhancing projects for each of the cities.

"In terms of the contribution of our city, Building Montréal is meant to reinforce the bonds between us, to develop our professional friendship, to promote co-operation among us, to bring together our creativity, and to interlace our networks," explains Marie-Josée Lacroix, Montréal's Design Commissioner and Director of Design Montréal.

Pecha Kucha Night for elected officials, Mr. Gérald Tremblay, Mayor of Montréal.
Photograph by Mathieur Rivard.

Imagining Place D'Armes *UNESCO Urban Design Workshop, Designers from Berlin, Buenos Aires and Montréal. Location: La Fabrique de la paroisse Notre-Dame.*
Photograph by Design Montréal.

In my capacity as cultural organization management consultant, I was tasked by the Design Montréal office to coordinate and accompany the Montréal delegation, consisting of Martine Lizotte, cultural tourism specialist with Tourisme Montréal and Claude Péloquin, analyst with the Tourism Intelligence Network (TIN) of the Transat Chair in Tourism at the Université du Québec à Montréal (UQAM) School of Management.

In addition to presenting the Building Montréal project to the members of the Creative Cities Network and conference delegates during the discussion UNESCO Creative Cities Network: Design Conversation, I took part in the panel, Creating an International Festival in Your City.

Building Montréal is a project aimed at stimulating, energizing, and consolidating links between the member cities of the network. We were very pleased to see that the project presentation generated keen interest on the part of members, who demonstrated their willingness to be part of it. We now know that this project has relevance within the network, given the motivation and interest shown by our international counterparts.

In my capacity as an expert consultant in the management of international arts organizations (including funding, tourism development, and international promotion) and as a member of the board of directors of MUTEK, I also took part in the panel Creating an International Festival in Your City, sharing my experience and giving a presentation on one of Montréal's outstanding cultural assets—the city's strong concentration of international festivals and events, as well as the know-how of their management teams. These include the Festival International de Jazz de Montréal, the Montréal High Lights Festival, MUTEK, the Festival TransAmériques, Festival Juste pour Rire / Just for Laughs, the World Film Festival, and the Festival du Nouveau Cinéma et des Nouveaux Médias, to name only a few.

One thing that emerged from the panel and generated a lot of interest from participants was the importance that is ascribed to the concept of hospitality when organizing international events. Host services are a hugely important aspect of successfully running a world-class event and standing out from the other major cultural gatherings that take place in big cities, especially when one works in the arts and culture milieu.

A stimulating context must be implemented to promote high quality gatherings and efficient networking among artists, audiences, industry professionals, partners, and the media in order to facilitate future international collaborations.

With the many festivals that make up its cultural calendar all year long, Montréal has developed solid expertise in the organization of international-calibre events and in developing promotional and presentation strategies for cultural events. Most of these events' organizing committees benefit from financial assistance from the

Government of Québec, Tourisme Montréal, Conseil des Arts de Montréal, and the Ville de Montréal. These institutions invest in the development of the city's festivals because they acknowledge the role that they play in positioning Montréal as a cultural metropolis, along with their massive appeal as tourist attractions and the significant economic benefits that go with it. Festivals are also important in a creative city like Montréal because they function as catalysts for creative expression and as platforms for international meetings, which are vital to the evolution of the full range of arts disciplines.

MUTEK

A non-profit organization, MUTEK, produces an annual festival devoted to performance and development of digital creativity in sound, music, and audio-visual art. The organization has won several prestigious awards in recognition of the quality of its programming, its outstanding contribution to the digital creative community, and its important role as a driver of tourism (more than half of the festival's audiences are visitors to the city). MUTEK is in the image of its host city—connected and open to the world. MUTEK also organizes events abroad and is a committed, active player on the international scene. It is a member of I.C.A.S, a new support network for international festivals that are run by independent non-profit organizations dedicated to advancing sound cultures, music, and related arts. Since its inception, MUTEK has implemented opportunities for meetings and dialogue between audiences and the artists, including master classes and the creation of venues for them.

MURCOF @ MUTEK 2008. Photograph by Caroline Hayeur.

In my presentation, I also cited the example of the Montréal High Lights Festival, which is a private, non-profit organization, administrated by a 16-member board whose members come from Montréal's arts, business, and tourism communities. The festival invites Montréal audiences, visitors as well as tourists, to take in activities focused mainly on three themes—light, the performing arts, and fine dining. Along with its program of special events and live performances, the festival gives members of the public a chance to take cooking classes with renowned local chefs and to sample dishes made from local products, prepared in creative, innovative ways. What is most notable about this festival is that it takes place in the middle of winter, a challenging season for tourism development in Montréal—and yet, the event now attracts record audiences and enjoys a growing local, regional, national, and international reputation and influence.

Montréal High Lights Festival 2007. Photograph by Jean-François Leblanc.

Montréal High Lights Festival 2007. Photograph by Jean-François Leblanc.

These discussions and dialogue with my peers were extremely stimulating and inspiring. In addition to gaining a better overall picture of the issues involved in Creative Tourism, I was able to note that support for artists and artisans is still fragile and that we must build on their development.

As for Tourisme Montréal and the Tourism Intelligence Network (TIN), they have continued their discussions and cultural tourism intelligence gathering and now have a greater awareness of the concept of Creative Tourism. On this subject, TIN analyst Claude Péloquin has written a summary of the conference presentation given by Charles Landry, which can be viewed on the TIN website (French only).

"Culture provides a way of living in spaces—when they are animated in this way, they open up to the world and allow a city to re-create itself through its artists and creators. That is a true measure of its success as a tourism destination!" says Michel Archambault, holder of the Transat Chair in Tourism at the Université du Québec à Montréal (UQAM) School of Management.

It would be interesting to see whether in the future the TIN could serve the UNESCO Creative Cities Network by performing studies or intelligence gathering so as to further discussions and, especially, explore how creative cities can maximize their potential over time while working closely with creators, designers, and artists.

It is always exciting to meet with representatives of the other cities in the network, who, like us, are driven by a willingness to find new ways of making and thinking about their cities, to build for the future in a context of creativity, and to motivate each other so that each of our actions have structure enhancing impacts over the long term. These annual meetings are essential for enlivening the network.

Lastly, it was truly a pleasure to take advantage of this opportunity to experience Creative Tourism first-hand in Santa Fe and a great privilege to meet the event organizers, who so warmly welcomed us. Santa Fe now ranks as a world-class destination and it accomplished its mission with aplomb, meeting international standards. We all came back delighted and dazzled by the work of the organizers, who really know how to do their job. Merci, Santa Fe, for this memorable get-together!

MONTRÉAL, CREATIVE CITY AND CULTURAL METROPOLIS

Culture, heritage, and design are issues fundamental to Montréal, its vitality and its reputation. The Montréal, Cultural Metropolis—Rendez-vous November 2007 event, held in Montréal, marked an outstanding opportunity to bring together representatives of the arts and culture community, government, the city administration, and other civil society stakeholders with an eye to accelerating the deployment and consolidation of the vision of Montréal as an international-calibre cultural metropolis. The notion of design received particular attention and was incorporated into the Action Plan, 2000 – 2017—Montréal, Cultural Metropolis. The partners in the Rendez-vous agreed on the importance of making sustained efforts to enrich the cultural quality of Montréalers' living environment. To this end, they made a firm commitment to promoting excellence in architecture and design. With regard to the city's international status, they committed to promoting recognition of Montréal as a cultural metropolis among major international cultural development organizations. More specifically, this involves highlighting Montréal's designation as a UNESCO City of Design.

For Montréal, design is defined in its broader sense, including all the creative disciplines that shape and have the power to qualify and enrich our living environment. We are building a creative environment—landscape, architecture, urban design, interior design, industrial design, graphic design, and fashion design. Ever since Montréal was designated a UNESCO City of Design, the Design Montréal office has made considerable efforts to position the city on the national and international scenes, as a young design centre.

The Design Montréal Office

Created in January 2006 by the Ville de Montréal, the Design Montréal office pursues the mission of improving design throughout the city and positioning Montréal as a city of design. Its actions are implemented through three main services—guidance, communications, and networking.

Since 1991, through the actions of its Commissariat au design, the Ville de Montréal has been making private- and public-sector players aware of the benefits of quality in design and architecture. Following a major awareness-raising effort from 1995 to 2004 targeting merchants and the general public via the Commerce Design Montréal program—which it initiated and which has now been adopted by other cities around the world—the city announced its new integrated action plan Montréal, Design of the City / City of Design in September, 2005. It aims at introducing the concept of design innovation into all decisions and activities affecting the built environment and intensifying promotional and educational initiatives as well as international networking of made-in-Montréal design.

The Tourism Intelligence Network of the Transat Chair in Tourism at the Université du Québec à Montréal (UQAM) School of Management.

The Tourism Intelligence Network (TIN) is an organization specializing in strategic intelligence gathering in the field of tourism. It was created by the Transat Chair in Tourism at the Université du Québec à Montréal (UQAM) School of Management. The mission of this organization is to locate, gather, analyze, and distribute value-added information to enhance the Québec tourism industry's competitiveness and help its decision-makers develop forward looking strategies. Staff researchers actively monitor the evolution of the tourism industry around the globe, earning this innovative service a number of awards since its inception. Visit www.tourismintelligence.ca for more information.

Tourisme Montréal

Tourisme Montréal is a private, non-profit organization, founded in 1919 and incorporated in 1924. It comprises more than 750 members and partners from Montréal's tourism industry, who share the common goal of promoting the city as a premier travel destination to non-local markets. Tourisme Montréal has adopted a marketing thrust mainly focused on using the city's cultural attractions to sell it as a destination in international markets. It also builds on the burgeoning cultural scene, whereby Montréal best expressed its vitality and creativity. Visit www.tourisme-montreal.org for more information.

WEBSITES:

Design Montréal: www.designmontreal.com
MUTEK: www.mutek.org
I.C.A.S.: www.icas.us
Chaire de tourisme Transat: www.chairedetourisme.uqam.ca
Montréal High Lights Festival: www.montrealenlumiere.com

Sonya Carreau. Photograph by Miguel Legault.

Sonya Carreau. Since 1995, Sonya Carreau has been deeply involved in the cultural sector as a communications and marketing professional. She counts among her wealth of experience 15 international events, for which she directed and consulted teams in the fields of research and financial development, tourism development, and international development. Her career has been underlined by distinction and eloquence; most notably, she has undertaken mandates of direction and coordination for the MUTEK Festival, the ESG Transat Chair of Tourism at UQAM, the IKT 2008/PARACHUTE Congress, the International Festival of New Cinema and New Media, the International Festival of New Dance, and the Canada Dance Festival. From 2000 to 2007, she served as director of Communications and Strategic Development for the founding of MUTEK and its consequent development at a regional, national and international level, efforts that earned the festival numerous prestigious awards. In addition, she is regularly solicited as an expert consultant, with the Canada Arts Council, the Dancer Transition Resource Centre, and the offices of Design Montréal (City of Montréal) regularly drawing upon her services. Always wholeheartedly integrated in the cultural scene, she currently sits on MUTEK's Board of Directors.

She is renowned for her dynamism, her integrity, her devotion to the cultural domain, her expertise in the development of organizational partnerships, her vast knowledge in the management of cultural organizations, and the breadth of her professional network.

BARCELONA CREATIVE TOURISM
by
Caroline Couret
Barcelona Creative Tourism

We have been asked to talk about the Barcelona Creative Tourism program as a case study of tourist promotion at a city level. Indeed, our approach to Creative Tourism is a transverse one, by which we give support to people willing to run an artistic and creative activity in our city. Be they members of a youth orchestra, amateur swing dancers, aspiring photography artists, art craftsmen, or other creative people, visitors do appreciate Barcelona as an ideal place to express themselves creatively.

We will first of all review those characteristics of Barcelona that are attractive for creative visitors and then, proceed to explain how we manage the program.

CREATIVE TOURISM: BARCELONA'S ASSETS

Today, Barcelona's attraction to creative tourists is based on three components: its creativity as a cultural fact; its appeal to tourists generally; and the launch of a program dedicated to Creative Tourism.

Creativity as a Cultural Fact

Barcelona is a creative city. This idea has been expressed by generations of artists—be they amateurs or professionals—as well as by businessmen from all sectors that recognize the city's ability to stimulate creative minds and to generate synergies.

However, it can seem difficult to define or describe what a creative city is, since creativity is a process that can take place in a very wide range of sectors. But it's generally easy to differentiate a creative city from one that is not, and also to observe among cities said to be creative the attributes they have in common and their differences. Indeed, they defy description; the city's creativity has to be felt or lived. What are easier to talk about are the geographic, historic, and social backgrounds that are the foundation of this creative ability. Barcelona's creativity is not a marketing gimmick, but the result of deeply rooted elements the city has known how to maintain and, most importantly, how to renovate and adapt. Barcelona has always been a talent pool for artists, be they native or not, all attracted by the bohemian and creative atmosphere of the city. The reasons for this are numerous:

The Participatory Tradition of the Citizenry

In Barcelona and in Catalonia more generally, the voluntary organizations have always been a major factor in society. Whether to overcome the lack of material resources or to elude the obstacles imposed by the long years of dictatorship, civil society has demonstrated its enterprise and resourcefulness in various circumstances. The layout and activities of the city are there to prove it: from the Santa Maria del Mar Gothic church, built over a period of fifty years by the citizens themselves with the help of craftsmen, to the Palace of Catalan Music, the construction of which has been funded by donations from citizens, through the numerous neighbourhood festivals organised all year long by their inhabitants. The list goes on. Peoples' willingness to take part in the city's events has remained the same throughout the decades, and their artistic expressions are a major feature of the city's identity and culture.

The Upholding of Traditions

On the other hand, the people have maintained traditions. Among them are the applied arts that have adorned the city during Modernism. Today, there are many Barcelonans who train in artistic glass, ironworks, jewelry, enamels, etc, just as a hobby. But traditions also thrive in other areas, like the performing arts, that are seen as a reference at the international level.

A Melting Pot for the Arts

Barcelona is known as a great melting pot in which arts and cultures fruitfully merge. Many foreign artists collaborate with local ones during their stays in the city.

In these collaborative projects, various artistic branches often mesh. This livens up and enriches the culture.

To sum up: savoir faire, open mindedness, enthusiasm, and daring combine to foster all the steps of the creative process, from training to mastery and improvement.

That Barcelona is a creative city is obviously a key to the development of Creative Tourism. Obviously, another one is the ability to offer tourist services.

BARCELONA: HOW TO BECOME A TOURIST HOTSPOT?

In 2008, the attraction of Barcelona to tourists is obvious. Nevertheless, it hasn't always been the case. Though Barcelona ranks high among tourists' preferences, it was not always that way. We just have to remember what a stricken city it was two decades ago, after suffering long years of dictatorship. At that time, visitors were mostly business travellers who came to the city for professional reasons. A turning point in the city's revival occured in 1992. In that year, Barcelona hosted the Olympic games, and wanted to offer the world the image of a modern, open, and friendly metropolis. The organization of the Olympics went hand-in-hand with a wide-ranging urban transformation. Buildings were brightened up, infrastructures were created, new squares and avenues were developed, and above all—beaches. The city opened up to the sea. This redevelopment both strongly highlighted and strengthened the citizens' drive and self-confidence. This event gave them the opportunity to make their jovial and welcoming nature known all over the world. The city was thus ready to rank high in tourist destinations. During the following years, the media reported the increasing number of visitors.

With offers targeted to the most diverse travel purposes—from cultural tourism to medical services, through sport to the accommodation of people attracted by low cost flights—Barcelona has quickly reached and even exceeded the tourist volumes of other European capitals, putting itself at risk of losing its friendliness.

The Barcelona Creative Tourism program was designed to counterbalance this trend. It proposes to humanize the relationships between visitors and inhabitants by using creativity, a universal attribute, as the motive for collaborations between travellers and locals.

The Creation of the Program

It should not be a surprise that the Fundacío Societat i Cultura (FUSIC) foundation had taken the initiative to create this program. This had to be appropriated by the cultural sector and with a strong participative element. And it's precisely on these lines that FUSIC has been operating for thirty years. Indeed, the foundation was created thirty years ago, after the end of the dictatorship, to give people the opportunity to actively take part in cultural life by arousing their creativity. All the projects led by FUSIC to this day include this participative component. Creative Tourism is in keeping with this.

Greg Richards' and Crispin Raymond's illuminating works on Creative Tourism helped us proceed in this direction. As a new promotion tool for the city, it has the support of Consorci Turisme de Barcelona, Barcelona's tourism promoting body. The program was officially launched during the summer of 2006.

WHAT DOES BARCELONA CREATIVE TOURISM PROGRAM CONSIST OF AND WHAT DO WE OFFER?

Let's review briefly the program's philosophy, what kind of visitors it is attracting and what services sustain it.

The Philosophy of the Program

Designed by Martí Ribas.

The picture on page 121 represents the city of Barcelona. It's possible to recognize monuments and hallmarks of the city, like the chimneys of Gaudí's house La Pedrera, the front of houses of Plaça Reial, the Olympic torch, the Joan Miró monument, etc. And yet, it is not a traditional sight but a vision that invites creative visitors to have a personal relationship with the city. This picture contains the philosophy of our program that proposes a singular approach to visitors searching for artistic involvement with the city. Our approach to Creative Tourism is a two-way relationship: on the one hand the opportunity for visitors to discover a wide rage of cultural fields through educational activities and exchanges with local artists, and on the other hand, the hosting of creative tourists who are primarily interested in performing or exhibiting in our city.

Our approach to Creative Tourism is a two-way relationship; on the one hand, the opportunity for visitors to discover a wide range of cultural fields through educational activities and exchanges with local artists, and on the other hand, the hosting of creative tourists who are primarily interested in performing or exhibiting in our city. Let's see examples of both.

Who are the Creative Tourists Who Come to Barcelona?

Most creative tourists visit Barcelona with an educational project. Please, let us introduce you to some of those interesting visitors:

- Ayako, a young Japanese pianist who, won over by Alicia de Larrocha's musical interpretation, came to Barcelona in order to study under her direction.
- Leah, a young Canadian businesswoman, came from New York, where she lives, in order to attend a life-drawing course and sketch Barcelona street life.
- Alysson and Sarah came respectively from Colorado and Saudi Arabia in order to learn Catalan traditional painting from a local artist.
- Marc, a French professional guitarist, regularly comes to Barcelona in order to learn different music styles with local musicians.
- Sussana, a young citizen from the Bahamas, spent five days of her week in Barcelona taking part in a ceramic workshop.
- Jimmy, a Swedish student, came to Barcelona with some friends to take part in an artistic glass workshop and thus to discover Catalan modernist art by experiencing it.

With different profiles and aspirations, these artists-to-be and creative visitors share a common interest in Barcelona as a city where visitors can learn, experiment, or exhibit their art.

Artistic glass workshop.

Besides a wide choice of dedicated courses,
some art centers offer premises which visitors can rent by the hour.

Many international choirs and orchestras come to Barcelona to perform in singular venues of the city. Photograph by Mercè Benet.

Tap dance workshop at the beach.

An important part of our work is to offer our support to creative tourists' projects. Which kind of support? We offer customized solutions to the specific requests we receive from creative tourists. They contact us because they have an artistic project in mind—from learning or improving artistic skills to more sophisticated projects— but they are ignorant of the artistic resources of the city. As their trip is focused on its artistic purpose, they do want to guarantee its quality. As the case may be, we offer advice or information—sources, contacts, or services that may range from event design to technical production, including communication, press relations, and translation, as well as tailor-made stays.

About Tailor-made Stays

We could cite the case of a French music band that wanted to learn the Catalana rumba music style in Barcelona, as it's the city where this music was born. But rumba is, above all a way of life, and it would have been illogical to limit the experience to a two-day workshop. Thanks to our knowledge of the sector, we could partner the training with a local group, but we also created a program that included jam sessions, performances, interviews, thematic sightseeing, and other activities that offered the French musicians the opportunity to fully live the rumba, a rich experience, both artistically and in human terms. They might not have had access to this specific information without an entity like ours acting as a go-between.

The inquirers are often tour operators who turn to us for the implementation of their projects. In this way, they can be sure to meet their customers' demands in terms of artistic content and devote themselves to the logistics. We have recently designed a stay for a tour operator whose customers were art students interested in experiencing the creative atmosphere that is typical of the Raval neighbourhood. We organized workshops with different artists and residents of this area, who usually don't work in front of the public, as well as activities aimed at fostering the students' creative potential, interviews with local personalities and opportunities to exhibit the works they created during their stay. To manage this kind of project, we draw on our knowledge of the creative, as well as of the human resources of the city.

About On-demand Services

In some cases, we get only partially involved in the execution of a project. For instance, we will search for the ideal venue for an event or handle technical production or communication campaigns, etc. Many orchestras commission us to deliver such support services, which both contribute to the success of their concerts and free them to enjoy more of the city. That's why we also have to be creative ourselves to meet all the requests. It wouldn't make sense for us just to provide data on an auditorium or another conventional venue (although we do it if we are asked). If it's the best answer to the request, we will organize a concert in an art gallery, an exhibition in a clothing store, or a screening session at a hairdresser's.

A Factor of Economic Development

In this way, we also support entities that collaborate with cultural projects only occasionally. In some cases, we act for cultural entities wanting to open their core activities to the reception of creative tourists. A case in point could be that of an art school that wanted to develop its activities by offering courses aimed at foreign people. We helped them to design the courses, to communicate about them, and even with translation. All these examples show how Creative Tourism is a factor of creative development.

The Tourist Promotion of the City

Another important part of our work is the promotion of the program itself. By gathering all these different initiatives on a common platform, we aim to promote the city as an ideal place to spend creative holidays.

Our main promotion tool is our website, www.barcelonacreativa.info, that is available in four languages—Spanish, Catalan, English, and French—and works as an interface between people from Barcelona and foreign visitors. The Catalan version is the one browsed by local people in which they can find inquiries from creative tourists (once we have translated them), whereas the three other versions—Spanish, English, and French—give creative tourists access to course announcements, calls for artistic projects, etc.

CONCLUSION

In conclusion, we would like to recount the elements that are essential for our program to achieve its goals:

- The city's assets; its geographical situation, its history and culture, its people and creativity.
- The fruitful collaboration between artistic and tourist sectors.
- An exhaustive knowledge of artistic resources of the city, and a cultural know-how to offer visitors personalized attention and tailor-made proposals.
- A two-way traffic of artists and creative people in constant movement, and to receive foreign input as much as to share local productions with visitors.

Caroline Couret

Caroline Couret was born in France in 1977, where she graduated with a degree in management of culture, and collaborated with festival organizations including Festival International de Cinéma de Cannes and Festival de Théâtre d'Avignon. Afterwards she carried out postgraduate studies in cultural policies, investigating the French Culture International Network. That led her to collaborate with various projects in Louisiana, Mexico, and Morocco. Since 2001 she has worked at FUSIC (Fundació Societat i Cultura), a non-profit cultural foundation in Barcelona, Spain. She has been in charge of a wide range of projects like Barcelona Street Arts Festival and Orquestrades of Catalonia, all related to art and international networks. She is currently responsible for Barcelona Creative Tourism, a program of FUSIC whose objective is to foster Creative Tourism.

COMMUNITY-BASED ECOTOURISM: CONCEPT, CHARACTERISTICS AND DIRECTIONS

GHARB-SEHEL VILLAGE, ASWAN, PILOT PROJECT

by

Ossama A.W. Abdel Meguid
Director, Nubia Museum

Tourism has now become the world's most important civil industry, representing economic activity of US $3.5 trillion. The travel and tourism industry employs 127 million workers; this is one in fifteen workers worldwide.

The segment of tourism undergoing the fastest growth is community-based tourism, which includes ecotourism. Community-based ecotourism has been estimated to account for between ten and fifteen percent of all international travel expenditures, and that figure seems to be increasing rapidly. It is quite clear that unless this growth receives careful and professional guidance, serious negative consequences, some of which may have terminal effects, could occur.

Community-based ecotourism, as defined by the World Conservation Union (WCN), is "environmentally responsible travel to natural areas, in order to enjoy and appreciate nature (and accompanying cultural features, both past and present), that promote conservation, have a low visitor impact, and provide for beneficially active socio-economic involvement of local peoples."

Community-based ecotourism can bring numerous socio-economic benefits to a country or a locality, in terms of generating foreign exchange, creating local employment, stimulating national and local economies, and fostering international peace and increased environmental awareness and education. But appropriate management structures, as well as adequate planning, design and building guidelines for tourism facilities, are required to ensure that tourism enhances, rather than detracts, from the natural setting. Further, carrying capacity needs to be assessed relative to the management objectives of each area, and appropriate management and physical structures must be designed to keep the number of visitors and the visitation mode within each area's carrying capacity.

If uncontrolled mass tourism is allowed to continue with the overuse of many areas of natural and cultural significance, irreversible damage will occur. Many of these areas throughout the world are rich repositories of biological and cultural diversity, as well as important sources of income and well-being. It is then a matter of global interest to foster the symbiotic relationship between tourism, natural resources, and conservation of cultural heritage.

Community-based ecotourism, as a logical component of community development, requires a multidisciplinary approach, careful planning (both physical and managerial), and strict guidelines and regulations that will guarantee sustainable operation. Only through involvement by multiple sections of the community will ecotourism truly achieve its goals. Governments, private enterprise, local communities, and NGOs all have vital roles to play. I firmly believe that every country, particularly the less developed ones, should set up regional tourism plans that should include clear ecotourism strategies and guidelines. Regional ecotourism councils, with representatives from all sectors involved in the ecotourism process, have recently been created in several countries with promising results.

Before ecotourism can be expected to fully achieve its potential and avoid pitfalls, well-founded principles and clear guidelines must be established for the appropriate active involvement of local communities: park managers, NGOs and private entrepreneurs, in-depth regional and site-specific research on the socio-economic and environmental impacts of ecotourism; the development of national and regional strategies, and the establishment, monitoring, and assessment of selected pilot projects.

Apart from the natural resources mentioned above, it is equally important to perform an analysis of local cultural resources, both of the past and the present, including archaeology, as well as available infrastructure and local services in the site and its vicinity. This analysis will also provide important input for the subsequent design and construction stages.

Analyze Cultural Elements, Both Past and Present:

- Specific ethnic groups.
- Traditional settlements.
- Local traditions and folklore: language, architecture, clothing, handcrafts, dance, music, ceremonies, magic, and religion.
- Archaeological features.
- Potential for integrating design with cultural environment.
- Ways of avoiding negative impacts on local culture.

Available Infrastructure and Public Services

It is critical to analyze the local availability of the following infrastructure elements and public services:

- Transportation means: highways, roads, harbors, trails, tracks, airports, landing fields, railways, docks, etc.
- Conventional systems for providing electricity, drinking water, sewage, telephone lines, public lighting, etc.
- Postal service, garbage collection and disposal, medical services, schools, commercial facilities, etc.
- Local means of transport: motor vehicles (bus, taxi, rent-a-car), regular commercial air charter or private flights, motor boats, cruise ships, yachts, ferries, railways, etc.

It is important to maintain that, frequently, due to obvious reasons, there are sites which are more appropriate for environmental development because of lack of infrastructure, isolation and remoteness.

ECOTOURISM DEVELOPMENT STRATEGY FOR GHARB SEHEL VILLAGE

The Nubian village and home, as well as Nubian women, are the most idealized symbols of Nubian identity in Egypt today.

From Aswan, Gharb Sehel village is reached most quickly by boat. The village is located on the west bank of the Nile, to the south near the Aswan Dam on the road to the airport. A village visit is often combined with a number of activities via either sailboat (called falluca) or motorboat (lanch). These activities may include a visit to West Bank antiquities such as Pharaonic tombs, a Coptic monastery, the Agha Khan's mausoleum, or the Botanical Island and Elephantine Island. Tourists may arrive in

Gharb Sehel by camel after a short ride from the monastery. A trip to one of the villages, accessible by bus and car, can also be combined with any of the numerous sites of Aswan, including the dams, other temples and Pharaonic sites, and the tourist markets within the city itself.

A walk around a Nubian village plus a visit to a local home is a very common item on the Aswan tourism itinerary, perhaps more so than a visit to the Nubia Museum, a relatively new site. Tourists arrive in Aswan on Nile cruisers, by bus from Luxor, and by airplane and train from Cairo.

Nubian women's work in tourism reinforces the discourse of authenticity, yet may subvert the gender norms in Aswan in terms of what is appropriate women's work and tourism-related work (as tourism involves bringing not only strangers but foreigners into the home). Many families have built up a clientele of Egyptian tour guides who may bring up to ten groups per day to their family home in the winter high season.

How is this Nubian community represented in and by its women, in the authentic original space of the Nubian village home? How do women within the community represent Nubianness to outsiders, both Egyptian and foreign? How do they claim the authority of authenticity for themselves? Do they care about the preservation of traditional practices, objects, and customs? In the space that we present as an authentic village home, how do these women challenge stereotypes of what is authentically Nubian? How do they transform this authenticity into income? How do women negotiate the dichotomy between primitive, ancient, unchanging culture, and a modern domestic sphere?

Nubian villages surrounding Aswan's urban area, such as Gharb Sehel, are a regular stop for foreign tour groups who choose half- or full-day boat and bus tours of the Pharaonic, Christian, Islamic, and modern landmarks of Aswan. From their perspective, foreign tourists aren't necessarily visiting a Nubian village in particular, but rather any home in any village in Egypt.

Among Nubians, Gharb Sehel village represents the look and feel of a village in Old Nubia, when compared to the government-built concrete homes in New Nubia. West Aswan villages comprise about a half dozen villages that remain in their original locations below the Aswan and High Dams on the Nile opposite Aswan City. Because they were downstream from the dams, they have never been flooded and relocated. The mud-brick architecture and way of life are understood today to represent the survival of the appearance of Old Nubia. In this sense, they are genuine Nubian villages in comparison to New Nubia with its concrete block, government built homes in Gharb Sehel, or the even more isolated Sehel Island, which represents what Old Nubia really used to look like.

Aswan's Nubian villages were accessible and therefore often photographed, filmed, and observed by national and international audiences. It's not only foreign tourists who come to the Nubian villages of Aswan looking for an authentic experience. Egypt's most famous architect, Hassan Fathy (1900 – 1989), had heard about the use of mud-brick, barrel-vault architecture in homes in West Aswan. During a visit in 1941, Fathy sought out mud-brick roofing techniques, which he later used in his quest to use local materials for architecture for the poor in Aswan. He wrote: "I realize that I was looking at the living survivor of traditional Egyptian architecture, at a way of building that was a natural growth in the landscape, as much a part of it as the dom-palm tree of the district. It was like a vision of architecture before the fall: before money, industry, greed, and snobbery had severed architecture from its true roots in nature." (Fathy 1973: 7)

WOMEN'S WORK IN TOURISM

Nubian women working in tourism in their homes in the villages around Aswan are considered within their communities to be working in the domestic sphere of the home. This is in contrast to working in tourism in public hotels, agencies, restaurants, or sites as men do. Women's work outside the home could include agricultural labor or selling goods like dates and fruits in the markets of Aswan. Women may also engage in various kinds of home-based labor: raising poultry, baking, sewing, and making beauty preparations, including henna for brides.

In presenting a Nubian tradition as interpreted through tour guides' perceptions of them, women make concessions to authenticity designed to recreate Old Nubia, like that expressed in producing local crafts. The majority of their home is not maintained like a museum exhibit. The rooms where tourists are hosted retain the feel of today's regular, slightly shabby living room. Tourists have been known to ask to buy "souvenirs," which were not souvenirs at all, but actually a homeowner's baskets, necklaces and bracelets of beads, Nubian hats of needlework, and henna tattoos. These "souvenirs" are unlike the rare "Genuine Nubian Products" as advertised in Nubian souvenir shops in Aswan and the artifacts on display in the Nubia Museum from the pre-Dam era.

Nubian houses that regularly host tourist groups have begun to exhibit more of a museum-like trend. The interior of the home, which used to be much like any other in the village, has acquired a more exhibit-like décor that draws on new visual themes, including ethnographic exhibits from the Nubia Museum and images of sites in Nubia. Recent additions included murals painted on the walls by local artists, hired to reproduce some typically Nubian scenes, including a basket-making woman and portraits of Nubian women and men, as well as the name of the homeowner, written in English capital letters both inside and outside the front door.

Since Gharb Sehel is a unique village, it is of utmost importance that the main cultural and natural ecosystems found there be conserved for posterity. These conservation efforts will have to be carried out in harmony with a sustainable development framework, which should provide improvement in the living standards of the local populations.

Due to the high vulnerability of Nubian villages, both naturally and culturally, any tourism development to take place should be of an ecotouristic nature. No massive tourism activities should be allowed in Gharb Sehel, since they would irreversibly damage the fragile natural and human environment. If managed correctly, community-based ecotourism activities should bring many benefits on behalf of conservation of the village's culture, but also to the local inhabitants.

Community-based ecotourism should also provide important political benefits to Egypt, improving the national image abroad and generating a constant flux of foreign exchange to the country. It should also provide many opportunities for the tourism industry and generate many new jobs. It must not be forgotten that any tourism activity, including ecotourism, is a business, and successful operation leading to profit should be sought. A tourism venture associated with a protected area that loses money and fails to produce enduring socio-economic benefits for the locality and the tourism industry will simply cause more problems for the protected area than those that already exist.

Since community-based ecotourism is a new phenomenon of a complex and interdisciplinary nature, it is very important to develop a strategy for its sound development in the Nubian villages of Aswan.

The goals of this strategy are:

- Conserving the natural and cultural environment.
- Enhancing the quality of life of the resident community.
- Providing a high-quality conservation product and world-class reputation.
- Producing cultural benefits to the country of Egypt, in the areas of foreign exchange, good business for tourism-related activities, and new jobs.

The following are the main elements that constitute the community-based ecotourism strategy for the Gharb Sehel village. Each one of these elements identifies an issue, a specific recommended action, and a how-to approach.

PROMOTION OF ECOTOURISM CULTURE

Issue

In general, Egypt now recognizes that the growth of community-based ecotourism can become an important factor in the sustainable development of the country by providing additional foreign exchange and new jobs, as well as serving as a vital instrument for conservation and rural development. However, since ecotourism is a relatively recent phenomenon, it is still not widely known or understood throughout Nubia and all of Egypt.

Action Recommended

A true ecotourism culture has to spread among the different sectors of Egyptian society, including Nubian villages, so that all key players are properly involved and benefit from the process. An intensive and extensive training and capacity-building programme is required. Community-based ecotourism must be positioned to play a key role in future development of Gharb Sehel and, if carried out appropriately, will contribute to attracting considerable foreign exchange to Egypt, sustainable development options for the local population, profitable business for the tourism industry, as well as a very attractive and positive international image to the country.

How

Tourism must be strengthened by carrying out an intensive ecotourism promotional and training programme, including workshops, courses and seminars at different levels among the different sectors (locally and nationally), as well as by developing advertisements, publications and TV programmes. The Ministry of Tourism, Aswan government, and the private tourism sector all have an important role to play in this field. Also, the local tourism bureau in Aswan must be strengthened to actively participate in future ecotourism training activities, raising ecotourism and environmental awareness among the local populations, and a practical knowledge of ecotourism operation. Local guides must be trained and licensed. Already, a number of community-based ecotourism training courses have been carried out, both in the Aswan mainland and in Gharb Sehel village by the Nubia Museum (within the framework of this Aswan Government Pilot Project and also within the work carried out for the World Tourism Organization (WTO) Committee on Sustainable Development of Tourism and Egypt Tourism Development Authority (TDA)). This training programme should continue uninterrupted over the next three or four years, involving different stakeholders.

AVERTING THREATS OF MASS TOURISM

Issue

Due to the vulnerability and uniqueness of the landscape, views of the Nile, and cultural traditions of Gharb Sehel, it is quite clear that the tourism model must be a sustainable model (mainly ecotourism). Otherwise, it will be difficult to avoid the temptation of using harmful mass tourism practices, that would undoubtedly destroy the rich, but very fragile, singular natural and cultural heritage of the area.

It would be regrettable if thoughtless and greed oriented mass tourism should destroy the unique character of Gharb Sehel, forever. Also, it has been seen around the world that mass tourism normally does not benefit the local populations. On the contrary, they have frequently had to migrate elsewhere, seeking new job opportunities because the cost of living usually rises dramatically. Mass tourism usually sees local populations as a hindrance and finds ways of displacing them. Also, mass tourism may provoke a clash with traditional religious values.

Action Recommended

To counter any initiatives towards mass tourism, the model of community-based ecotourism has to be urgently implemented in the other Nubian villages in Aswan as a viable tool for conservation of cultural heritage and sustainable development. The economic viabilities of this implementation are key considerations and should be diligently analyzed. Ecotourism should not be seen as a means for stopping development. People have a right to develop their resources, and ecotourism gives them the opportunity to advance in that development in a sustainable and participatory manner. The involvement of key private firms will also be vital. Raising the awareness and knowledge of community-based ecotourism among the key stakeholders of government representatives, the private sector, and local populations will be vital in providing concrete guidelines and mechanisms.

How

Leverage must be applied to obtain full support from the highest political and economic forces of Egypt toward low impact, sustainable tourism in Gharb Sehel, versus the implementation of mass tourism. The role of the WTO is vital in respect to the adoption of Egypt's Aswan National Declaration for Livelihood and Income from Sustainable Tourism and Community-based Ecotourism.

In the case of this project, an important contribution is the implementation of the Ecotourism Master Plan for Gharb Sehel. This plan includes the identification and classification of ecotourism attractions, zoning aspects, development of ecotourism itineraries, physical planning aspects, and promotional and marketing strategy.

THE COMMUNITY-BASED ECOTOURISM MASTER PLAN

- Desiring to further increase Egypt's tourism contribution to economic growth and to diversify tourism products as the country's leading export sector, working to intensify the industry's importance to the conservation of natural and cultural heritage, supporting the principles of sustainable development, and providing for the growing role of local communities in tourism development and services.
- Appreciating the importance of sustainable tourism and ecotourism

as a catalyst for influencing policies in favor of increased community participation and integration in economic development.

- Recognizing the necessity of meeting the needs and aspirations of local populations in high growth tourism regions and nature conservation areas, and the need for greater public awareness of environmental and cultural preservation.
- Creating awareness that ecology, culture, and people constitute the greatest asset of Egypt's different regions as international tourism destinations.
- Taking account of the multiple roles of local communities in development and conservation, and the need to give full support and provide facilities and opportunities to enable them to undertake their roles effectively.
- Building on past policies and commitments issued to support sustainable tourism principles and practices in the different regions of Egypt, including the South Red Sea and the Marsa Allam Ecotourism Declaration of 2004.

In the context of redefining tourism development policies and conservation management regimes adopted in tourism development regions and nature-based destinations, in the spirit of strengthening national and regional cooperation, collaboration and coordination for the purpose of advancing the role and contribution of local populations in the progress of the various regions, economically and sustainably, Tourism Development Authority shall, either individually or collectively, endeavor to:

First: Promote and implement the equitable and effective participation of local communities whenever possible in tourism development and nature conservation at various levels: political, economic, social, cultural, national, regional and international, especially their role as a productive force to attain the full development of the country's potential.

Second: Enable local communities to undertake their important role as active agents and beneficiaries of national and regional tourism growth, particularly in promoting sustainable tourism development, either through increased economic and social benefits or contribution to the conservation of natural and cultural resources.

Third: Ensure that sustainable tourism and ecotourism is integrated into land use policies, conservation plans, community support programs, and socio-economic development to improve the key environments that may be affected by development, and reduce the socio-economic disproportion and the unbalanced provision of tourist facilities in remote regions, nature-based destinations and protected areas.

Fourth: Implement livelihood improvement programs that involve the participation of local communities and nongovernmental organizations in the planning, development and operation of tourist establishments and natural areas towards strengthening regional coherence and sectoral harmonization of objectives and of implementation.

Finally: Emphasize that direct government funding and subsidization for the management of biodiversity are not sustainable and that ecotourism, eco-lodges, and nature reserves managed for both conservation and tourism should be the leading source of revenue for managing culturally rich and environmentally sensitive areas, while meeting social objectives, involving the local people in the regional economy, and empowering them to act as key partners in the development process and in the management of resources and the environment.

Ossama A. W. Meguid

Ossama A.W. Abdel Meguid lives and works in Aswan, Egypt, where he is the director of the Nubia Museum. He travels widely lecturing on the Nubian People and Egyptology. His education includes a bachelor's degree in Archaeology from Cairo University and a PhD in Museology and Egyptology from the Reinwardt Academy, Lieden University, The Netherlands. He is actively involved in the UNESCO Creative Cities Network as a representative of Aswan.

Promoting Literature in Your City
by
Alison Bowden (Director)
and Lorraine Fannin (Founding Trustee)
Edinburgh, UNESCO City of Literature Trust

In October 2004, Edinburgh became the very first UNESCO City of Literature, pioneer in the new UNESCO Creative Cities Network. It is a permanent title, a highly prestigious award, and was the culmination of two years' work by a dedicated group of people working within the literature sector in Scotland, who had conceived and developed the idea and presented it to UNESCO for validation.

Edinburgh has a unique reputation as a city built on books, and is the capital of a nation renowned throughout the world for its writers, past and present. The city is home to the world's biggest international book festival, numerous libraries and prestigious collections, and booksellers, both new and antiquarian. Leading publishers and publications originated in the city, and a thriving publishing industry continues today. It is a noted centre of education, and has shared its expertise in learning all over the world. Edinburgh has been the inspiration for many classic works of literature, and world-famous writers live and work in the city.

To make the most of the UNESCO City of Literature designation, a charitable trust of the same name was set up in 2005 with the following purposes:

- To promote awareness and prestige of Scotland's literature, nationally and internationally.
- To celebrate Scotland's contemporary literature and literary heritage.
- To provide a focus and co-ordination for literary activity, to encourage greater participation at all levels of Scottish society, and to attract new initiatives to Scotland.
- To develop partnerships with other cities with strong literary profiles and aspirations.

In its first four years as a UNESCO City of Literature, the trust has worked hard to promote literature in Edinburgh. Our work has focused on four areas—events, providing information, providing opportunities for writers and readers, and co-coordinating literary activity.

Bookcrossing in Edinburgh.

We have attracted high-profile literary events and awards to the city (including the prestigious Man Booker International Prize), coordinated a series of free literary events in the city, supporting new talent as well as established and international authors, developed special performances for literary festivals in Scotland and abroad, and held conferences to assist other cities in their applications to be cities of literature. We work closely with the Edinburgh International Book Festival each year to offer an information desk for literary Edinburgh and Story Shops, a series of free readings of micro-stories showcasing Edinburgh's new emerging writers.

Kidnapped performance.

PROVIDING INFORMATION

This is key to what we do—sharing the story of Edinburgh as a literary city. In 2006, we launched a literature hub website at www.cityofliterature.com, that provides an overview of literary Edinburgh, an interactive literary map of the city, and a What's On section that gives a full literary events listing for the city. The content grows each day. We produced a book called, *We Cultivate Literature on a Little Oatmeal*, which provides an introduction to Edinburgh as the first UNESCO

City of Literature and is available as a free download on our website.

The recent additions to the website include Stories in Stone, a free audio-visual download which provides a tour of the built and literary heritage of the city and is used by our national tourism agency. We have commissioned a series of free literary trails of the city, including trails focused on specific books (most recently *44 Scotland Street* by Alexander McCall Smith), in the Literature Quarter area of the city, as well as trails focusing on authors (most recently Robert Burns in Edinburgh).

PROVIDING OPPORTUNITIES FOR WRITERS AND READERS

Over the last four years, we have promoted the cultural exchange of writers, including exchanges with the famous writers' centre in Varuna, Australia, Cove Park in Scotland, and the Institute for the Translation of Hebrew Literature in Tel Aviv, Israel. In 2006–2007, we ran a series of literary residencies across the city, with writers in residence in venues including arts centres, a hospital, the Festival of the Middle East, a museum, and a prison.

We support the Edinburgh Makar who is the poet laureate for the city and who acts as the city's literary ambassador. We have renewed a literary salon tradition with monthly City of Literature gatherings at a city centre bar for the Edinburgh literary community to meet and network. From this simple monthly gathering, authors have found publishers and been booked for events, and it's given us all a better sense of who works in the area of literature in our city.

COORDINATING ACTIVITY

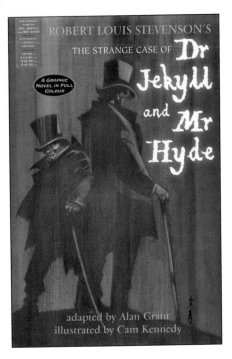

Perhaps our most successful large scale projects are our citywide reading campaigns. We have coordinated and delivered Edinburgh's three citywide reading campaigns. Launched in February 2007, One Book—One Edinburgh, saw 25,000 free copies of three new editions of Robert Louis Stevenson's *Kidnapped* distributed around the city through libraries, and all primary and high schools, as well as through restaurants, cafes, partner organizations, etc. A month of public, school, and community events supported the campaign. A specially commissioned graphic novel version of the book was published as part of this initiative.

Strange Case of Dr. Jekyll & Mr. Hyde book cover.

In February 2008, 10,000 free copies of Stevenson's *Strange Case of Dr Jekyll & Mr. Hyde* were distributed around the city and supported by a week-long series of public, school, and community events. The most recent reading campaign, February 2009, has seen the city come together to read *The Lost World* by Edinburgh-born author Sir Arthur Conan Doyle. This campaign was part of the UK's largest collaborative reading initiative, and saw Glasgow and cities across England join us in reading the same book at the same time. As with previous campaigns, we brought together a wide range of organizations. In 2009 the campaign brought 52 partners together. In Edinburgh, a programme of events supported the specially created books that were distributed for free, and a performance was commissioned that toured the city. A fantastic web animation series, *The Lost Book*, was also launched as part of the campaign, as a way of reaching out to new audiences (www.thelostbook.net).

Isobel enjoying her Scots language graphic novel of *Dr. Jekyll & Mr. Hyde.*

This gives you a sense of the work of our small organization—we are two full-time staff members. As an independent company, a lot of our time is spent securing funding and sponsorship, dealing with day-to-day inquiries from partner organizations seeking advice or information, and answering inquiries from the media and the general public about literary Edinburgh. There is a wide range of information on our website, as well as more detailed information and evaluation reports about our citywide reading campaigns. To find out more about our city of literature, visit www.cityofliterature.com.

Literature: writers and books are powerful cultural ambassadors for Scotland in the international arena. Scotland excels in the written word.

For many people around the world, Scotland's cultural image is defined by its literature, from Burns and Stevenson to Rankin and McCall Smith today. The country's writers have been translated into numerous languages; Scotland has provided dictionaries, atlases, and academic texts to a global education market. In calling on illustrators, designers, and photographers as well as writers, this sector of the creative and cultural industries has a major impact on Scotland's international reputation.

One of the great affirmations of this was the designation of Edinburgh as a UNESCO City of Literature, the first in the world, the first Creative City, a leading role for Scotland. At this point in time, we have a perfect opportunity to pull together cultural and international aspirations, together with a commitment to help in other parts of the world. There is also an opportunity to expand the outreach of our writers and the output of our publishers through strategic projects that will deliver the work abroad, and there is a willingness by institutions and organizations to work together on programmes to deliver a lasting effect.

So this is our story, which is what literature is about. Literature is often how other countries recognize and judge us, and support for the creation of good literature usually falls within the scope of cultural policy. But how literature reaches the public, the reader, the audience to provide a cultural experience, is via the publishing of the work in book form—or using new technology. That is seen as an economic activity, a business, not just for the publisher; it is also the way the writer, the creator, makes a living.

Cultural activity includes literature, fiction, poetry, and playwriting, but there's also a need for educational material, reference, and academic material that reflect the world of the reader. Often, these flourish in the same company. Similarly, creative skills cross boundaries; writers, illustrators, and designers need people with business skills to bring income from their intellectual property.

I want to look at how these multiple roles came together in our quest to designate Edinburgh as a UNESCO City of Literature, but first I think it's useful to have some facts and figures on book publishing in the UK.

In the UK as a whole, there was an estimated total consumer book purchase of £2.31 billion in 2006. Exports from UK publishers are estimated at a net invoice value of £1 billion. The creative output of UK book publishing is one of the highest in the world in terms of new title publishing, producing almost 200,000 new books and editions each year, ranking only marginally behind the US and China whose populations are much larger. The UK also has a positive balance in trade in intellectual property rights in the book industry. It is estimated that income from rights and co-editions may be around £300 million. A major part of this income goes directly to the author, the creator.

Scotland, lying on the edge of Europe, has a population of five million, of which 20 percent live in its two major cities—Edinburgh, the capital, and Glasgow, which is in fact the larger city. Parts of the Highlands of Scotland are sparsely populated, but the country is home to a very high number of writers, attracted to the lifestyle. In Scotland, we can establish that its publishing sector has more than 10 percent of the invoiced value of the total UK industry, though we don't have definitive figures on the total book market. These statistics do, of course, mask significant patterns and problems. More than 50 percent of the total UK consumer market is dominated by four major multinational groups and the academic market by two. Removing these groups from the picture changes it radically.

In Scotland there are 100 book publishers. Many of these are small, lifestyle companies formed specifically to publish certain work, rather than to grow a business. The fastest growing companies are small to medium enterprises, typically with fewer than 25 staff and a turnover between £500,000 and £5 million. They also outsource work to a workforce of freelancers with a wide range of creative skills, many of whom also work for companies based south of the border.

Support for book publishing in Scotland has largely come through culture funding mechanisms, and has provided crucial funding for the sector since the 1970s, when it had become little more than a cottage industry with the exception of the large companies. The radical effects of globalization, especially in the 1990s, left the sector without head office control of the larger companies, and led to a reduced workforce and output in Scotland. The importance of the independent publishing sector has therefore been greater than in the UK as a whole, given Scotland's—and especially Edinburgh's—former pre-eminence as a world centre of publishing.

Support for the sector also rested on the fact that every country regards its publishing industry as a vital tool in recording its life, history, ideas, and creativity. Literature in Scotland is a pre-eminent art form, and Scottish writing plays a significant role in cultural tourism.

In recent decades there has been a changing landscape in the delivery of the written word, and Internet information and sales channels made it more possible to promote to and engage with readers around the world. The dominance of English is also an advantage, though the work of Scottish writers is translated into many languages. There are also major global changes, technological changes, in how literature is delivered, which require business development, in supporting education or culture.

Despite forecasts, the death of the printed book is not seen as imminent. It remains the most easily accessible format for many functions. However, the range of new formats and technologies allow a multiplicity of choice, depending on material and use, and in addition, it is now recognized that the written word, however it is delivered, remains the basis for much creative enterprise, from scientific research papers to story treatments that form a basis for film.

All of this indicated that books, publishing, and literature should be flourishing; there has been a need for a strong focus, investment, and market development.

So it happened that a group of individuals, discussing the literary world over a glass of wine, developed an idea. It was simple, really. Here is a city, Edinburgh, with a marvelous literary pedigree, over the centuries home to some of the most eminent writers of their day; it is a city where celebrated writers of today live and work: including J.K. Rowling, the most successful children's author of all time with her Harry Potter series, Alexander McCall Smith, creator of the No. 1 Ladies' Detective Agency, and Ian Rankin, crime writer. The city has the largest monument to a writer in the world, the biggest book festival in the world, and 50 publishing companies.

Ian Rankin supporting the reading campaign for *The Lost World*.

How could we focus attention, both at home and abroad, on those achievements? How could we gain more support for the ongoing work of the many organizations connected to the written word? How could we help the small publishing companies, to keep them from falling under the wheels of giant corporate juggernauts?

Edinburgh was already a World Heritage Site, a designation given by UNESCO. We approached UNESCO, then formulating a Global Alliance of Creative Cities. Literature was not on the list of designations for the programme, but after discussions, they agreed it should be added, and the Edinburgh team worked with UNESCO to look at criteria for inclusion. The outcome was that Edinburgh became the first city of literature in the network, and in fact the first in the global alliance. Since then, the team in Edinburgh has worked to pull together partnerships and projects to benefit those working in the world of books and writing, readers in the city, and as a by-product, to support literary and cultural tourism.

This has brought attention to the publishing and books sector. The 2007 One Book–One City campaign brought a great publishing partnership venture. Four publishers joined together to produce five different editions of *Kidnapped*, each for a different readership. The scriptwriter and illustrator of Star Wars and Judge Dredd comics—both Scots—were contracted to produce a stunning graphic novel.

Kidnapped reading campaign editions.

The success of our projects to date inspires us to continue finding new ways to bring the story of literary Edinburgh—literary Scotland—alive in new and exciting ways, for audiences of all ages.

Alison Bowden

Alison Bowden is director of Edinburgh UNESCO City of Literature Trust. She has 10 years experience in book publishing in Scotland, in various roles, working as a commissioning editor at Polygon, and later as rights manager at Edinburgh University Press. In addition to publishing, she has many years experience in the Scottish arts and culture environment, on committees, and working as advisor and guest speaker, as well as work within the music sector as a promoter.

Lorraine Fannin is a founding trustee of the Edinburgh UNESCO City of Literature Trust and was formerly chief executive officer of Publishing Scotland. The organisation has responsibility for the support and development of the publishing sector in Scotland, working with companies, organisations and individuals in the industry, and co-ordinating joint initiatives and partnerships.

CREATIVE CITIES NETWORKING IN CANADA
by
Elizabeth Keurvorst
Executive Director
Creative City Network of Canada / Réseau des villes Créatives
du Canada Suite

The presentation by the Creative City Network of Canada (CCNC) focused on the case study of this organization that has been successfully networking communities across Canada on the issue of cultural development. The session was presented by Elizabeth Keurvorst, Executive Director and Dr. Nancy Duxbury, Adjunct Professor at Simon Fraser University and lead researcher at CCNC.

Who is CCNC? Municipalities are playing a growing role in the development of arts, culture, and heritage in Canada. The CCNC is an organization of municipal staff working in communities across Canada on arts, cultural and heritage policy, planning, development, and support. It was incorporated as a not-for-profit organization in 2002 and has 109 Canadian Cities as active members. The largest city is Toronto at five million people, and the smallest is Houston, BC at 3,100. The CCNC exists to connect and educate the people who do this work and share this working environment, so we can be more effective in cultural development in our communities. By sharing experience, expertise, information, and best practices, members support each other through dialogue, both in person and online.

Our goals are: to provide a way for communities, large and small, to access each other's experiences and expertise; and to develop tools and resources for the community of practice in community development across Canada.

SERVICES OFFERED BY CCNC

Networking: Our listservs allow practitioners in the arts and cultural fields to interact and communicate directly with one another. Participants can solicit advice and information from colleagues across the country.

Online Resources: The Creative City website is host to a plethora of resources. The documents, research, and links that we have compiled are essential for anyone working in arts and culture.

In Person Meetings: Since 2002, the Creative City Network of Canada has been holding highly successful national annual conferences and summits. Our 2009 conference will be held September 9–11 in Fredericton, New Brunswick. CCNC also regularly organizes regional workshops.

Publications: The Creative City Network of Canada is pleased to publish the free e-newsletter, Creative City News, and our popular Special Edition Newsletters. The CCNC has also published Cultural Planning and Cultural Mapping Toolkits. A Public Art Toolkit is currently in the works and will be available in 2009.

What sets the CCNC apart is the focus on the municipal bureaucracy, the rather boring but vitally important part of a creative city. Referring to themselves as a community of practice and creative bureaucrats, these workers don't fit well in either the world of art makers or municipal workers. Or rather they do work well in either camp, but can be misunderstood in both. They have to negotiate the different cultures; one is the not-for-profit world—which is how most arts groups are organized—and the other is the bureaucratic culture found at the city organization, where their salaries come from.

These workers view the city as an ever changing cultural landscape, not a static place. They infiltrate city halls with difficulty. Many of our members lead from behind. One of the biggest challenges is to see civic resources going to crime fighting and risk management with a loss of creative imagination to solve problems. The key understanding that these workers bring to their cities is that the way to truly engage a community is through culture. Some examples of cultural infiltration at the city hall level included art being featured before council meetings, and using city trucks as public art opportunities.

The CCNC defines the creative bureaucrat as, "Someone who, in spite of, and often because of, the challenges of the established bureaucratic system, strives to move the organization into new ways of providing services."

The creation of the CCNC provided a sort of support mechanism for these workers, as well as an opportunity for professional development not found anywhere else. It began in 1995, in Metro-Vancouver at the local/regional level with in-person roundtable meetings between cultural managers from a dozen cities. What was realized from that opportunity was terrific growth and innovation in the participating communities. Policy development, facility improvements, and even reciprocal speaking engagements (experts from "away" speaking to one another's councils) took place, and very quickly participants were realizing the benefits of being part of a community of practice.

The movement then grew to incorporating listserv technology in 1997 (this is before social networking tools we are used to today such as FaceBook). Culture-L included the original Vancouver regional group, Montreal region, Toronto region and Ottawa, and quickly grew to include many other cities. Federal incorporation and formal membership followed in 2002, along with the first face-to-face national meeting. Provincial and federal levels of government joined the initiative to provide funding.

Currently there is an international outreach with other city cultural networks in the USA, Sweden, Ukraine, Sri Lanka and Australia, to name only a few.

The success of the network can be attributed to, first of all, recognition that there was a shared need to create one. That it is a community of practice; so right off the bat there is a shared understanding and peer support. And key to the network is that the members are trusting with one another, generous in their willingness to help each other succeed, and non-competitive. The CCNC provides resources, tools, and strategies that meet a need and ultimately build the knowledge base of the profession. We are now serving second and third generation practitioners, where in some cases no one was doing the job for a city a few years ago.

Specifically, the tools provided include a balance between in-person and digital communication, credible research conducted by CCNC, and knowledge sharing between the practitioners, stemming from a shared responsibility to the development of the profession.

Elizabeth Keurvorst

Elizabeth Keurvorst has extensive municipal experience including leading an international cultural development project for a city in Sri Lanka. She has also performed a variety of communication consultation work in the private sector. She has recently left her position as executive director of the Creative City Network of Canada to pursue other interests. Before joining the Creative City Network, Elizabeth worked for the City of Port Moody as manager, Cultural Services and then director of Communications and Culture. She also worked for the Municipality of Cumberland as manager, Cultural Services. Elizabeth has her Master of Arts degree in Professional Communications from Royal Roads University, her Professional Project Manager Certification from the Project Management Institute, and a Business Administration Diploma from Fraser Valley University College.

MUSIC, FESTIVALS AND GASTRONOMY
by
Benedetto Zacchiroli
Foreign Affairs, city of Bologna

Music, festivals and gastronomy. These were the three themes that most involved me at the International Conference on Creative Tourism held in Santa Fe, New Mexico. All three can be simultaneously the main or secondary interest when you talk about tourism.

Today, a host of people, the numbers of which are not easy to ascertain, are moving about the planet looking for their festival, their music, or the satisfaction of their palate. The world is becoming smaller and smaller and Creative Tourism is growing by leaps and bounds. Creative Tourism means looking for an authentic experience, one about which we can say we have not simply been in a place, but that we have lived that place.

It's the search for the uniqueness of a situation, of an experience that cannot be duplicated except in one's memory. It's the experience of ordinary daily life made up of the extraordinary.

Taking the time to reflect on this theme means reflecting first and foremost on mankind at this beginning of a new millennium—about men and women who, from time immemorial, have been searching for happiness, longing to be carefree, but who are no longer content to be mere spectators of something great or exceptional.

Modern man expects to be able to participate, to be a protagonist of his own touristic experience. He no longer can imagine himself with a guide book in one hand and a camera slung around his neck. The man of today wants to enter into the heart of the experience to which he has been exposed. Accustomed to technology that brings him ever closer to virtual reality, the tourist asks to be able to experience reality in the same way.

We tried to look at the issues from the perspective of those who organize tourism for individuals. Organizing an international festival is not an easy task per se, whether the subject is music, literature, or film. But the challenge is how to create a welcoming approach that honors those who visit. There are no longer any events in which the distance between the protagonists and the onlookers is clearly defined. The lines of demarcation no longer exist and involvement is total.

An important issue is the involvement of municipal governments, and the efforts cities can make as representatives of public authority and the public-sector economy.

Creativity cannot be improvised. Creativity needs its own ecosystem to emerge, develop, and progress. Creative ideas and creative environments attract people, and with them comes an added economic value.

When we confront these issues in a meeting such as the one organized in Santa Fe, it is important to look at them from the most general perspective. Individual festivals, individual experiences should be seen as starting points in an attempt to formulate general rules.

Global and local are constantly being mixed. "Glocal" is the challenge of creativity. We speak to a global public with a global language, but the destination remains local.

This is what the creative tourist is looking for and this has to be what the Creative Cities Network strives to achieve—succeeding in making one's own work a "glocal" effort. It is not easy to bring cities together from all continents, with their different histories and traditions. Only an international organization such as UNESCO can succeed in taking this kind of strong and consistent approach.

For the past several years, we have grown accustomed to confronting each other, learning the other's language, and collecting the most varied stories and traditions.

But this is the challenge we face today—even in tourism. We cannot do without it. The richness of the Creative Cities Network and the contribution it can make to the debate could become a terrific asset.

I personally witnessed all of this in Santa Fe during the Conference on Creative Tourism. I saw an enormous potential beginning to express itself. I saw individuals willing to mix different experiences to find a common recipe. This is the first step. Santa Fe, Bologna, Seville, Popayan, Buenos Aires, Montreal, Berlin, Edinburgh, Aswan and all the other Creative Cities can accomplish much; because they have UNESCO as an international sounding board. And UNESCO, in turn, must highlight the richness of a network such as this one in which the experience of cities is fully communicated. We must not forget that more than half the world's population lives in cities. The experience of cities is the experience of those who, day-in and day-out, get together to discuss real urban issues, including that of receiving tourists. What services cities provide and how they are organized must be examined. Tourism is not just the business of large multinational corporations; it is an issue that involves all cities as receiving communities which must lay the groundwork for its future development.

This theme goes to the issue of interculturalism. Just as the creative tourist goes in search of varied cultures, so those who receive must be attentive to cultural differences and not treat the subject as something exotic. Interculturalism is the winning formula in welcoming the tourist. Being open to what is different needs to be learned in the community from a very young age.

Interculturalism is one of the basic ingredients for the development of creativity. Becoming accustomed to diversity and feeling troubled by standardization is necessary in today's world.

Once again, the challenge is a "glocal" one. Succeeding in injecting a breath of internationalism into a local situation is a role that local organizations should be the first to take on. Knowing how to receive and welcome tourists cannot be improvised, and only the teaching of culture and art will lead to satisfactory results.

Culture and art, which are universal languages, help us to describe every type of message. They motivate us to be attentive and they stimulate our curiosity. Culture and art help us to grow accustomed to creativity which in its diversity, finds its indisputable richness.

Learning a subject like music when one is very young accustoms a person to understanding that to play a symphony or to compose one, one has to pay attention to all the instruments, even those different from one's own, and that one cannot play out of tune, or play more loudly in order to be heard; to do so would ruin the final result. An individual has to pass through this phase in order to grow. Living in a symphonic community is necessary. Local governments are in charge of this, and they must encourage it. What counts is not the individual event. The basic ingredients are creativity in diversity and the continuity of the action. Man is still a creature of habit, and learning how to warmly receive those who are different requires constant effort.

Along with the role of the public sector, the role of the private sector must also be examined, and here the first rule is quality. If you want to talk about global, quality has to be at the top of the agenda. Improvising events is of no use to anyone and is an enormous waste of resources. And even in this sense, the role of the government in individualizing a community can be helpful.

Many experiences were presented in Santa Fe from every part of the world, and what they all had in common was a high level of quality.

The conference in Santa Fe made a "glocal" meeting possible. It stimulated ideas, and these will lead from reflection about individual, specific experiences to the more general. It was a first step—an experience that should definitely be repeated, an experience that should involve, more and more often, the UNESCO Creative Cities

Network. Comparing and sharing ideas is necessary, if we are to achieve satisfactory results.

Public and private together—global and local. Everyone working to bring together and merge differences into a creative response to an ever more urgent demand for quality. We see this demand cropping up from all corners of the world. We have begun to respond. We must not stop here.

Benedetto Zacchiroli. Photograph by Linda Carfagno.

Benedetto Zacchiroli. Born in Bologna, Italy in 1972, he obtained his diploma in Bologna at "Istituto Magistrale Laura Bassi" a high school for future teachers. He graduated from the Vatican University San Tommaso D'Aquino with a degree in theology in 2001. Since 2002 he has been a member of the staff of Sergio Cofferati who became mayor of the city of Bologna in 2004. Mayor Cofferati gave him the responsibility of Foreign Affairs in his Cabinet.

SEARCHING FOR OUR OWN 'PUEBLO'
REFLECTIONS ON A VISIT TO THE MAGIC
CITY OF SANTA FE

by
Jin Minhua
Reporter and Deputy Director,
Creative Industry of Culture Section
Shenzhen Economic Daily

The tour of Santa Fe at the turn between summer and autumn was quite interesting. In the hinterland of the North American continent, the city may not be the farthest from Shenzhen, a coastal city on the west coast of the Pacific. However, the cultural and historical contrasts are huge and stimulating.

One is a 28-year-old, high-tech city in an ancient country; the other is a 400-year-old city of Creative Tourism and artists in a young country.

The rise of Shenzhen began in 1978 when China launched its reform and opening-up drive. An ordinary town of 300,000 inhabitants neighboring Hong Kong, Shenzhen was chosen as China's first special economic zone on August 26, 1980, a date later regarded as Shenzhen's anniversary. The population subsequently ballooned to more than thirteen million by the end of 2007.

The city became the earliest gateway to China for capital, talent, management, and technology from the outside world. Shenzhen soon became known as the World's Factory. This land of less than 2,000 square meters is regarded as the epitome of China's rapid growth in the past three decades. As the saying goes, "Xi'an showcases China's past 3,000 years, Shanghai the past 100 years, while Shenzhen the past thirty years."

Shenzhen has topped the country in import and export volume for fifteen consecutive years. It is the power of trade that seems to have shortened the distance between Shenzhen and Santa Fe. The Yantian International Container Terminal (YICT) in eastern Shenzhen is part of Shenzhen Port, the fourth-largest container port in the world. Maersk's container liners depart from there every Tuesday, Friday, and Saturday, en route for Los Angeles, after voyages lasting fifteen to seventeen days across the Pacific. The containers are then sent to Santa Fe by rail. Maersk is only one of many shipping companies that operate on the route.

The boom and bust of the global economy may enlarge or shrink this Ocean Silk Road from time to time. However, Shenzhen has begun ridding itself of the label, factory, in the past ten years, and has started to transform itself into a high-tech, creative, and knowledge-based city.

During the process, Shenzhen has attracted increasing world attention. Rem Koolhass, then a professor at Harvard University, shifted his studies to the Pearl River Delta, the fastest growing region in the world, between January 1996 and January 1997. He interviewed urban planners, architects, officials, professors, scholars, and students in six cities, including Shenzhen, during his research and wrote a book on new conditions for urbanization, the *Pearl River Delta*, which was shown at the Kassel Art Book Exhibition in Germany. Koolhass' 2002 book *Great Leap Forward* was based on his research on Shenzhen and other cities.

In 1999, as a model for urban planning and construction of a fast growing city, Shenzhen was nominated for UIA's Sir Patrick Abercrombie Prize, the highest honor for an Asian city since the award was inaugurated forty years ago. Shenzhen was also China's first city to win the Nations in Bloom award (in 2000 for Category E, cities with a population of at least one million).

In the research program, Emerging Metropolises in the Next Decade, by Scott Lash, who is teaching cultural industry courses for a master's degree at Goldsmiths, the University of London, Shenzhen was listed along with Bombay and Dubai. In the new book, *Who's Your City* by American urbanization scholar Richard Florida, the Hong-Zhen corridor is among the forty cities he lists as mega-regions, defined as conurbations with huge populations, powerful economies, creative industries, and a pool of talent. Shenzhen is concentrating efforts to become a city that spearheads China's development, a city that looks to the future.

The visit to Santa Fe was undoubtedly an important step for Shenzhen to become a city of design. Shenzhen was the first Chinese city to apply to be included in the UNESCO Creative Cities Network. At the Santa Fe conference, Shenzhen was the first Chinese city to take part in an official event of the network. Shortly after the Santa Fe conference, Shenzhen became the first Chinese city to be included in the network.

Starting out with a manufacturing base thirty years ago, and now redefining its role as a creative hub, Shenzhen is demonstrating a growth curve. In Santa Fe, we clearly felt the welcome, acceptance, and curiosity from conference organizers and attendees towards the eight-member Shenzhen delegation. Most participating cities were represented by a single person while the Shenzhen delegation included the mayor's envoy, cultural officials, city marketing officials, foreign affairs officials, journalists and a cameraman. This showed the special interest Shenzhen took in the Santa Fe conference.

Then, what did the 400-year-old Santa Fe give the 28-year-old Shenzhen? In other words, what did I see during my four-day stay in Santa Fe?

Starting from the rustic Albuquerque airport, what I saw were sights filled with all the elements of Native American culture. Posters about local opera and music festivals could be seen everywhere in the hotel. It was said the opera festival there was a pioneer in the United States. The Palace of the Governors near the historic Plaza and the Native American handicraft market in front of the historical museum seemed to remain unchanged from what I had seen nine years earlier. The farolitos on the rooftops and in the central courtyard of the Santa Fe Community Convention Center were still there. The spectacularly huge farmers' market was as friendly and warm as a family get-together. Of course, pueblo-style buildings and the best restaurants, were must-sees. The grilled cakes at the Mexican restaurant were really delicious and diners still paid at the cashier's desk. The Land Eagle works displayed in the shop windows demonstrated the agony, silence, and hardship of Native Americans in a powerful way.

Similar to Shenzhen, a city of migrants, Santa Fe's culture is pluralist, mixed, and inclusive. The Mestizo culture itself is a mixture of the Native American, Mexican, Spanish, and Anglo-Saxon cultures.

In my view, pueblo-style architecture may be the best identity for Santa Fe. This suggests that cities, like humans, need to search for their identity and roots. In other words, the fast-growing Shenzhen must forge consensus, seek an identity by residents, and gradually transform from a materialistic city into a humanist city, and from a city of migrants into a city of citizens.

Although modern Shenzhen has a history of only twenty-eight years, Shenzhen as a border town has a history of 7,000 years of civilization. As the original inhabitants, the Hakkas deserve protection and promotion of their culture and heritage. Design and creativity will play an integral role in this regard.

In fact, starting from the Tulou project by local architects three years ago, Shenzhen has begun to search for its cultural roots and forge its own lifestyle against the backdrop of its own culture.

This pursuit needs an international perspective, as well as modern presentation skills. At the Santa Fe conference, besides Santa Fe (UNESCO City of Craft and Folk Art); Edinburgh, City of Literature; Montreal, City of Design; Seville of Spain and Bologna of Italy, Cities of Music; Aswan, Egypt, City of Craft and Folk Art; as well as Kobe and Nagoya of Japan; Iowa City of the United States; and the three other candidates for the UNESCO Creative Cities Network were all inspirations for Shenzhen in its pursuits. This enabled Shenzhen to savor the values of the Creative Cities Network as an exchange platform for creative industries. It also enabled Shenzhen to realize the responsibilities and urgency in creating its own lifestyle and industry development model on the roots of its culture.

Perhaps we can say: Shenzhen's dream of becoming a city of design sprouted in Paris and took root in Santa Fe. It will grow and prosper in the land of Shenzhen.

SHENZHEN: A DYNAMIC AND CREATIVE CITY

What we are introducing is Shenzhen, a city full of legends, vitality and creativity.

In 1980, a small frontier town on the South Sea coast in China named Shenzhen was fortunate enough to become China's first special economic zone. This had been advocated by Deng Xiaoping, and it was the first mainland city to open up to the outside world.

Since then, the city has made great strides to join the list of modern, metropolitan cities within only 28 years and enjoyed fame as an overnight city at home and abroad.

Just 28 years ago, Shenzhen was a tiny fishing village with only one street and a population of 30,000. Today, it is a modern metropolis with more than 10 million residents and a beautiful environment. It was awarded by the UNEP's affiliate as a city of Nations in Bloom.

The GDP of Shenzhen 28 years ago was less than 200 million yuan. But the figure soared to 676.54 billion in 2007, an increase of more than 3,000 times. An average annual growth rate of 26.9 percent in 27 years is a miracle in the history of the world's modernization and industrialization. "Shenzhen speed" has become a catchphrase and is known in every household in China.

Just as Chinese Premier Wen Jiabao pointed out not long ago, "The Shenzhen Special Economic Zone is a flagship in China." Growing at an amazing speed, the city has become a vivid example of China's success in its opening-up process, and a window to showcase China's dream and future.

This is a dynamic city, with innovation and creativity as its character. Being the youngest city in China, populated mostly by immigrants, the city has a population with an average age of 30.8 with 98 percent coming from different parts of China as well as foreign countries, resulting in a typical migrant culture that features pursuit of innovation and excellence, and tolerance of failures.

The capacity for innovation is strong in Shenzhen. The city is now recognized by the Chinese government as one of the national comprehensive bases for high-tech industries and one of the national demonstration cities of intellectual property rights (IPR). In 2007, 35,808 patents had been granted to Shenzhen enterprises, among which 19,198 were innovative designs, the highest in China for the second consecutive year.

Shenzhen enjoys a good reputation around the world as a manufacturing center. The city is home to 80 Chinese brand-name products, and tops other mainland cities by creating 30 percent of China's world labels.

Shenzhen enterprises, especially high-tech enterprises, are vibrant and high achievers, owning more than 70,000 home-grown labels. The city is home to international, heavyweight high-tech enterprises like Huawei, ZTE, Skyworth, and Tencent. China's insurance giant, Ping An Insurance Company of China which is also based in Shenzhen, is now one of the Fortune 500 companies.

A modern design industry took shape in Shenzhen as industrial manufacturers expanded and the market economy developed. The earliest generation of Chinese designers was trained here. A magnet to arts graduates from universities all over the country, Shenzhen is still the first choice for young designers, making it a hub for Chinese design talent. Young or old, designers are allowed full exposure to media and modern design concepts from the West.

Home to most influential designers and leaders in the nation's design industry, Shenzhen has more than 6,000 design companies employing more than 60,000 designers. In 2005, the output value of the city's design industry reached US $1.9 billion, and that of the creative industry as a whole accounted for four percent of the GDP. The number is expected to grow to ten percent within five to ten years.

The business scope of Shenzhen's professional designers ranges from graphic design to industrial design, fashion design, toy design, handicraft design, timepiece design, jewelry design, package design, architecture design, interior design, animation design, game design, communication design, and software design.

Shenzhen delegation members with Georges Poussin of UNESCO

Jin Minhua is a reporter and deputy director of the creative industry of culture section for the *Shenzhen Economic Daily* in Shenzhen, China. In 1999-2000, he was a visiting scholar in the Journalism Department of the Univeristy of Illinois at Champaign-Urbana. He serves as a member of the Shenzhen, China UNESCO Creative Cities Network team.

SECTION 3

CREATIVE ENTREPRENEURS:
THE ECONOMIC CONNECTION

INTRODUCTION AND COMMON THEMES
by
Tom Aageson
Executive Director, Museum of New Mexico Foundation

"Artists know better
than anyone that places
hold meaning."
—Eric Maisel

Visitors enjoy "small" experiences at least as much as they enjoy the "large" cultural experiences of museums and monuments. Human things appeal to human beings. These human things are called "authentic experiences" in the cultural tourism and Creative Tourism literature. —Eric Maisel

CREATIVE TOURISM ENTREPRENEURS

Creative Tourism is a relatively new concept for many, yet Creative Tourism entrepreneurs began building their Creative Tourism enterprises years ago. These entrepreneurs paved the way for this new bouquet to appear in the field of cultural tourism and led to the first International Conference on Creative Tourism in Santa Fe. These entrepreneurs saw that people wanted more than a passive experience in their travels but one where they can involve themselves in an authentic, educational cultural experience. They sensed that people wanted to express themselves through their own creativity and grow in their own development. Creative entrepreneurs had a vision of an enterprise that created income for them and others while giving visitors an experience that contributed to their personal growth.

Barcelona Creative Tourism was designed to counterbalance the trend of mass tourism putting Barcelona at risk of losing its friendliness. The program's goal is to "humanize" the relationships between visitors and inhabitants by using creativity, a universal attribute, as the motive of collaborations between travelers and locals.

"Cultural tourism is becoming mass tourism."
—Greg Richards

Mass media is moving to individual media, YouTube, FaceBook, blogs, and podcasts. Similarly, Creative Tourism is the leading edge of tourism moving from mass, passive experiences to individual, involved authentic experiences. The desire to enter into a community, know its artists and cultural heroes, is at the heart of Creative Tourism. The Experience Economy and the Creative Economy merge around Creative Tourism.

Creative Tourism entrepreneurs are visionaries who take risks to start their own enterprises. They work in a sector of the economy that often does not recognize their added value to the economy yet and often are operating on market instinct. They combine vision, mission and market in a balance that requires long hours and personal capital. These entrepreneurs are often ahead of a market and by nature are innovators, creative in their own right and they create the new markets.

CREATIVE TOURISM ENTERPRISES

Creative Tourism enterprises are commercial ventures, both for profit and non-profit that connect creative experiences with people seeking a deep, creative moment in their lives. These enterprises market goods and services that are bundled in creative experiences. Every business practice and skill is required, including product development, pricing, production and promotion. Creating the products calls for creativity and often comes out of a passion.

In Santa Fe we have photography workshops, porcelain workshops, Native American cooking, creative writing, painting, healing arts, etc., all of which came out of the individual entrepreneur's passion for a unique creative process. They have creative capital, or some might call it intellectual property, accumulated in their life experience. This creative capital is the core of the business venture and the new enterprise is built on it.

Human capital and financial capital are blended together with this creative capital to build the foundation of a Creative Tourism enterprise. Blending together vision, passion, innovation and risk taking with creative capital are the essential ingredients of the new Creative Tourism enterprise.

CREATIVE ENTERPRISE BUSINESS MODEL

The business model for creative enterprises has all of the essential ingredients found in businesses. The product, pricing, promotion, placement and production must all be planned. The business plan is critical to building a solid footing.

Product: The product is the experience. The visitor might make something that is a result of the experience, but this is not the product one is selling. The time together and the lingering memory are in the experience. The perceived value is in the experience and what is learned and the relationship that is developed.

Pricing: Pricing is structured around several levels, tied to different experiences. The visitor is buying the experience, and elements that affect price are time and level of involvement (beginner to expert, with and without grand children, for example). Activities might run from the short experience to the deluxe experience, and it is important to address each market. Remember that there are compact cars and sedans and speedsters that all achieve the same objective; they get you to the store and back. Wrapped around each is one's personality and budget.

Promotion: Promotion includes advertising, public relations (PR) and sales. Each is a tactic; each has its own objective and accordingly a budget.

Place: Where the experience is held is key to success. It might be in an exciting destination like Santa Fe, or on a Native American reservation, or in a canyon, or out on the trails, painting. The environment is very important to the total experience.

Production: Who teaches the creative process is essential to an excellent experience. This is "free-choice learning," as each customer/visitor has made a conscious choice to venture into the creative process. This is not a required course, but an educational experience to improve one's development and expand one's interests.

Financing: The Creative Tourism entrepreneur is important in creating a critical number of offerings in a community. There are several strategies for financing a Creative Tourism enterprise that range from private to public sources.

- Private support from personal funds, family and friend investors.
- Government support through any number of strategies:
  - Business Improvement Districts.
  - Arts and Culture Districts.
  - Main Street Program.
  - Micro/SME Loan Fund.
  - Tax Incentives.

- ⧠ Cultural Industries Office.
- Debt financing from financial institutions or private sources.

DEVELOPING AND PROMOTING CREATIVE TOURISM

"Visitors want safe, sanctioned experiences."
—Eric Maisel

The development of a strong Creative Tourism sector takes private and public support. Setting high priorities and cooperative marketing will lead to the development of a collaborative destination for a new market of visitors.

This tourism segment will grow when cities, states and countries begin to promote their Creative Tourism experiences. Before doing that, it is necessary for tourism groups to train and prepare owners of Creative Tourism enterprises to have a minimum standard of services such as consistent hours, predictable pricing, an effective reservation system, a welcoming working space, a trustworthy payment method, a web site, etc. "Creative Tourism New Zealand's (CTNZ) role was redefined to focus on helping tutors develop and promote their workshops effectively to visitors. In other words, tutors became CTNZ's primary customers rather than workshop participants. A handbook was written for tutors outlining what had been learned about best practice in workshop provision and CTNZ began to promote itself to potential tutors throughout New Zealand as a cost-effective way to promote their workshops in a cluster." —Crispin Raymond.

". . . destination managers need to become more creative . . . and start thinking about their role as enablers of tourist creativity." —Greg Richards

The market today is ill defined, yet presents an emerging opportunity for artists to engage with visitors while building another source of income. It is doubtful that the term "Creative Tourism experiences" will mean much to potential visitors so the marketing will have to be positioned in a different fashion. *"Promote tutors' workshops as a cluster.* This will involve developing a good website and using traditional and web-based promotion: e.g. blogs, Internet forums etc. It could also involve encouraging local festivals to include some of the tutors' workshops." —Crispin Raymond. Aggregating the Creative Tourism experiences into an area of promotion is important. Advertising and PR based around words and concepts such as learning, experiencing, authentic, expertise and unique creates and positions Creative Tourism in the market for people interested in these experiences. PR initiatives will be key to building the market. Eric Maisel points out that, "Every local government should have a Meet Our Artists! brochure that helps visitors understand that their city supports visitor-artist interactions."

SUMMARY

This section includes the presentation of three creative entrepreneurs/enterprises.

Eric Maisel's, Bridging the Artist-Tourist Gap, discusses creating new public opportunities for artists and introduces a pragmatic Creative Tourism model for likely stakeholders.

Hayes Lewis, in Creative Tourism in Indian Country: More than Beads, Feathers and Casinos, explores the unique history of what indigenous Native Americans bring to economic development and tourism; emphasizing the importance of making connections to places and gatherings. Hayes also demonstrates the opportunities for strengthening people through authentic tourism development.

The section concludes with Becky Anderson's inspirational story titled Yester-morrow: Using a Region's Heritage and Culture for its Economic Future. Commencing with her poignant description of North Carolina headlines in the mid-1980s of massive unemployment, failing furniture factories, water and sewer infrastructure collapse and struggling schools; this article proceeds to delineate specific ways HandMade in America turned these negative trends around by building a new economic model around the region's culture and heritage. Key to this turnaround was the development of community-based tourism, which perfectly exemplifies the sustainable type of tourism being promoted by this conference—place-based tourism.

Thomas Aageson is the executive director of the Museum of New Mexico Foundation (MNMF) in Santa Fe, New Mexico, a non-profit organization that provides private support to the Museum of New Mexico's four museums and six state monuments. Mr. Aageson was recognized as one of *New Mexico Business Weekly's* "Ten Power People in the Arts" in New Mexico for 2005 and "Top 100 Power People in New Mexico" in 2006. He co-founded the International Folk Art Market and was a recipient of the Mayor's Arts Award for this new event in Santa Fe. He led the development of *New Mexico Creates*, an award-winning economic development initiative that markets the work of New Mexico artists and artisans in the MNMF's museum shops and on their Internet shops. Santa Fe Mayor David Coss

Thomas Aageson.
Photograph by Linda Carfagno.

proclaimed October 24, 2006 as "Tom Aageson Day" to recognize his outstanding contributions to the community. In 2007, the United Way, Santa Fe selected him as "Humanitarian of the Year."

Aageson advises the UNESCO Division of Cultural Expressions and Creative Industries, created the Santa Fe Cultural Leaders group and led the economic development planning for Santa Fe's arts and cultural industries in 2003-2004. He chaired the formation of Creative Santa Fe 2004 – 2006, a non-profit organization that brings together diverse constituencies to strengthen Santa Fe's creative economy. He also chaired the University of New Mexico Bureau of Business and Economic Research study, "The Economic Importance of the Arts and Cultural Industries in Santa Fe County." Aageson is a frequent speaker on the subject of the Cultural Economy and Co-Founder and Chairman of the Global Center for Cultural Entrepreneurship.

BRIDGING THE ARTIST-TOURIST GAP
by
Eric Maisel
Author of *Creativity for Life*

Artists know better than anyone that places hold meaning. That's why they hunger for Paris, Berlin, San Francisco, Greenwich Village, and the other stops, small and large on the International Bohemian Highway. They contrive to spend a year in London or Tokyo because those places hold special meaning. Yet most artists do not consider that the visitors who come to where they live are also hungry, also hoping to be stirred, and also looking for an experience that has nothing to do with room service breakfasts and garish souvenirs.

Because so many artists are in survival mode, struggling to make ends meet; because they are squirreled away in their studios painting, writing, or practicing their instruments; because like everyone, they are over busy and over anxious and because they tend not to think about the visitors to their community as potential audience members, they rarely connect with these fellow human beings, who are themselves looking for some meaning. This is a shame, as visitors are primed and ready. In the Creative Tourism movement, artists who live in locations that attract visitors, that attract tourists, conventioneers, and people passing through, would pay new and special attention to these readily available and always changing audience members.

Let's say that you are a writer, actor, musician, craftsperson, visual artist, or some other creative individual. You live in your neighborhood, possibly far from the tourist haunts; across town, a million annual visitors pass through your city taking in the customary sites. They know that they must visit three churches, two museums, and that famous shopping street—but what else? Is there a way for you to be that what else? Is there a way for you to make some useful contact with these visitors, contact that serves both of your ends?

First of all, who would have a say in making such contact happen? Naturally, you, the artist, would have the first say. Unless narrowing the gap that currently exists between you and the people who visit your locale interests you, nothing will happen. That opportunity falls squarely on your shoulders. Visitors, too, will have their say; if they do not show up at the event you plan, if they show up but leave immediately or if they show up and stay, but feel no connection to what you are offering, not much will have changed. This is the age-old dynamic: the artist not only must make a Herculean effort to create, but must also seduce or convince her audience to pay attention to what she is offering.

There are five other constituencies that have a vested interest in seeing this gap bridged. Government officials, whose help artists will want to enlist, will also have their say, because they have the power to announce upcoming events, the power to support artists' initiatives, and also the power to prevent the use of public spaces. Also involved are tourist industry professionals, who can trumpet the fact that artists are transforming their city into a creative hotbed, or who can ignore those efforts. Also in the mix are local businessmen and women, the hotel managers, restaurant owners and the like, who count on tourist dollars and who want to see tourism increase. Another constituency is made up of art industry professionals—gallery owners, theater directors, museum officials, publishers, and so on. Last but not least are a locale's residents, the other people who live in your community who may benefit or who may be harmed by the activities of visitors and by your activities as well.

These, then, are the seven groups who have a stake in the matter: artists, visitors, government officials, tourist industry professionals, business owners, art marketplace players, and local residents. Each group will have to stretch a bit in order for the changes I have in mind to occur, but no group will be bent completely out of shape. I think, if presented well, this stretching will make sense to all seven groups, who will see how they can benefit from artists and visitors beginning to interact in new, small scale, personal ways.

Before I present my main argument, let me make a few observations.

First, artists are currently not content. I've heard personally from thousands of creative and performing artists over the past several years. More than 2,000 have come forward to receive the free creativity coaching I offer when I train new creativity coaches. I know exactly to what extent artists are having trouble meeting the emotional and practical challenges of a life in the arts. Artists do not earn enough, they experience a significant amount of angst related both to the difficulties associated with producing good work and the difficulties associated with selling their work, and they tend to feel isolated from their peers, from marketplace players, and from their audience.

That this discontent exists is not a good thing. But it does mean that artists are primed to make changes, because they know that they need things to be both different and better. If everything they created turned to gold, they could go on vacation and not worry about transforming tourists into fans. If they got so much out of their current social interactions that they felt no lack of human warmth, they'd feel that much less motivated to reach out to strangers. But as it is, artists need their landscape to change for the better. Therefore they are primed to make the changes that I intend to suggest, if and maybe only if, all of the stakeholders involved come on board to help.

Second, artists function as renewable resources. That geyser that brought visitors to your area may begin to dry up. That church that millions throng to may have to close for repairs. The roads that the tour buses chew up likewise may need repair and cost enormous sums to keep up. But artists renew themselves. They paint a mural and then they want to paint another one. They write a short story and then they want to write another one. They love what they do and need to do what they do, and this very devotion can be enlisted, if they are helped to make the connection, as motivational energy that will drive them to interact with visitors.

Not every resource can be renewed and not every site can be sustained. Writing tongue-in-cheek in a piece called *Cultural Tourism: Between Authenticity and Globalization*, Frans Schouten explained, "At a conference in Africa recently, someone involved in a cultural tourism development project in a tribal community announced that he had included in the village tour a visit to a ritual circumcision of a boy. Such an announcement raises many questions, the first of many being, "Might they run out of boys in the peak season, or how many times can you circumcise someone?"

Even in the peak season, you can't run out of an artist's creativity. If you run a small barbecue joint, you close your doors when the barbecue runs out. If you run a small city, you feel threatened when your revenues dwindle. The barbecue and the revenue are finite. But Pete Seeger can extend his concert set simply by singing another folk song. Van Gogh can turn every blank canvas in his vicinity into something memorable. As long as they live, and as long as they feel motivated, artists can turn the lead of everyday existence into the gold of art.

Third, visitors enjoy small experiences at least as much as they enjoy the large cultural experiences of museums and monuments. Human things appeal to human beings. These human things are called authentic experiences in the cultural tourism and Creative Tourism literature. A tourist may not even know that he is hungering for a small human experience from his visit to your place, and may suppose that he is coming for the shopping, the museums and the restaurants. But in fact, what he wants is to have his heart stirred for a moment. If he is landlocked at home, he wants to feel the breeze of the ocean hit his face. If his town is pitch dark by nine in the evening, he wants to see city lights and human beings still reveling at midnight. To repeat, he may not know that he wants these things, and all the constituencies I named at the outset need to help him understand that he does, but he surely does want and need these small, human-sized experiences. He will treasure them and he will return to your city again and again, simply because he holds a fondness for what happened there.

Visitors will crawl through the exhibits of even the greatest museum as much because it is an obligation as it is a pleasure. But if they encounter Mongolian chanters or Andean flute players in the open space in front of the museum, they will stop and listen with real pleasure. That will be the memory they take home and the reason they return. You can pour millions into your museums, or, for free, you can create an environment such that Mongolian chanters and Andean flute players arrive, make music, and create memories.

We should consider the tourist not only as he is but as he might become if he were presented with the right opportunities. As he is, he seems to want only shallow, simple, distracting experiences—nothing authentic, please. Those who cater to him often see as their goal, as described in an article called *The Fakelore of Hawaii*, to "mystify the mundane, amplify the exotic, minimize the misery, rationalize the disquietude, and romanticize the strange." They believe that they ought to provide as safe and cocooned an experience as possible. This may be one truth, but side-by-side with this truth is the contradictory truth that what tourists find most memorable are the human sights and sounds of the places they visit—the aroma of freshly baked bread, the lilt of a spontaneous song, the human things.

Fourth, residents and visitors alike love street life. There is a vast difference between bustling downtown streets filled with life and an overrun tourist attraction clogged with tour buses. In the raging debate about how much tourism is good for a place, it is important to make a distinction between adding life to the streets and adding visitors to the main tourist attractions. Residents may well balk if they experience their everyday life overwhelmed by tourists who are visiting local attractions. But they love and embrace street life and are happy to share that street life with visitors. Residents love and need their street fairs, their open air markets, their band concerts, and their people watching exactly as much as visitors do, and with respect to this bustling street life, residents do not mind that visitors share the wealth.

There is a great lesson to be learned from the failure of the urban redevelopment movement of several decades ago. It is the lesson that human beings need human life around them and want their environment to be built and lived on a human scale. We should remember that great pioneer Jane Jacobs, whose book *The Death and Life of Great American Cities* made a brilliant case against inhuman urban development, and who spent her life advocating for the humanization of cities. With fierce eloquence, she announced back in the 60s that the ideas promoted by urban planners to save cities were destroying those cities, and that urban planners, out of ignorance, an obsession with theory, partisan politics, or ties to corporate money were doing their constituents a disservice by not looking at and honoring what actually worked in cities.

She noted for instance a fact that should have been obvious to anyone; people like to look at one another. When you get right down to it, people who are attracted to visiting cities are attracted primarily because they get a par-excellent opportunity to people-watch. Denizens of cities are themselves made happy by well-used parks, rather than empty ones, by bustling common areas, rather than deserted ones, and by people coming and going on their own two feet, rather than driving by in cars belching exhaust fumes. Jane wrote, "The activity generated by people on errands or people aiming for food or drink, is itself an attraction to still other people. This last point, that the sight of people attracts still other people, is something city planners and city architectural designers seem to find incomprehensible. They operate on the premise that city people seek the sight of emptiness, obvious order, and quiet. Nothing could be less true. People's love of watching activity and other people is constantly evident in cities everywhere."

Street life is crucial to the vitality of a place. Artists can add to the street life of their cities and, in turn, to the culture of their cities, by taking their creative efforts public, by engaging visitors and residents in small-scale, street corner-sized activities and events, and by imagining the street as an extension of their studio. Street fairs and bandstand concerts are wonderful and valuable, but such events do not need to represent the sum total of public culture. Where people go—along the boulevards, into restaurants, waiting in hotel lobbies, gathering in train stations, standing in line at a great museum, strolling in parks—that's where artists should also be.

Fifth, visitors want safe sanctioned experiences. A very small percentage of travelers are genuinely adventurous. Virtually no traveler wants to court actual danger. Visitors want safe experiences, experiences that they know or feel are sanctioned by someone they can trust, whether that someone is a government official, a tourism professional, a hotel concierge, or an art gallery director. A tourist would probably not even consider attending a street performance happening in an edgy Manhattan or Berlin neighborhood, even if he found the description of the event intriguing, unless someone he trusted vouched for the performance and the neighborhood. Visitors will almost always opt for safety first.

If, however, he reads about the event in a publication he picks up at the tourist office, he will be more likely to attend it. If he sees a flyer for it at each of the galleries he visits along gallery row, flyers not dropped on the floor but presented in such a way that it is clear that the galleries are standing behind the event, he will be more likely to go. If he hears about it at the travel office back home, if it is one of those things he is told that he must do when he gets to Manhattan or Berlin, he will be more likely to go. If it is announced on the scroll in the lobby of the hotel where he is staying, he will be more likely to go. The more that these small, intimate, street corner-sized events are publicized and sanctioned by the various players in the tourism industry, the more likely it is that visitors will feel comfortable trying them out.

Sixth, government officials, tourist industry professionals, local business owners, and marketplace players, all of whom appreciate the value to their community's creative assets, nevertheless are not accustomed to promoting those efforts and are not particularly adept at working with artists.

There are many reasons why this is so. Government tourist bureaus are likely to find it hard enough just promoting the annual festival their place is known for, keeping up with the everyday demands of tourists for city maps and basic information, and supporting the big sights in town, the museums, concert halls, shopping districts, and so on. Local business owners are hard pressed just to keep their businesses going; a restaurant owner is much more worried about keeping his customers happy and his doors open than connecting with local artists. Players in the art marketplace, many of whom are operating on the tightest of profit margins, are much more likely to feel the need to focus their attention on gaining Internet customers or promoting their stable of artists than on supporting local artist-created events that they see as unlikely to drive customers to their establishments.

What this means is that the constituencies who need to be enlisted do not see themselves as being in much of a position to help. What would transform this picture and bring these constituencies on board, as overburdened as they already are, is the following. These constituencies—artists, visitors, local government, tourism professionals, local businesses, art marketplace players, and residents need a model to hang their hat on. When you have a model understood by all the players involved, conversations and cooperation are possible. The same is wanted here.

In the Creative Tourism model, individual artists and collections of artists dream up public, interactive experiences. I'll describe some such possibilities in a moment. Local officials, local businesses, tourism professionals, and art marketplace players support these small, human-sized activities by promoting them and legitimizing them. Tourists and other visitors are helped to understand the value of engaging in such interactions by virtue of the fact that the materials they pick up at tourist offices, the materials they find in hotel lobbies, the materials they encounter in the art galleries they frequent, and the information they receive from tourist industry professionals all reinforce the idea that there is value and joy in interacting with local artists.

In this model, artists begin to collaborate with local businesses and local government. For example, an artist makes an appointment with a hotel manager and describes an idea she has for how they might collaborate. She explains that if the hotel provides her with a hospitality suite one Friday evening a month, she will perform her magic act there for free. All she asks is that the hotel provides the space, sets it up, and begins to announce her presence, that is, begins to announce that she is an attraction. She, in turn, will be permitted to announce her other magic workshops, sell her magic videos, and invite the audience to her other magic gigs around town. For almost no cost, the hotel gets an attraction that no other hotel in town has, a resident magician, and the magician gets a regular venue and a platform from which to build her business.

In this model, artists who would never think of venturing out into their community with their wares, artists like writers or actors, would have a model to spark their imagination and help them create new public opportunities for themselves. A writer might approach the person in local government designated to handle such requests and be given a verbal go-ahead to set up in a local park, read from his current novel, facilitate a discussion and sell copies of his book. Rather than being restricted to formal bookstore readings, writers might come out and be encouraged by local government to come out and do park readings, mall readings, town square readings, and street corner readings.

This Creative Tourism model is a simple one. Artists, local government, local businesses, tourism professionals, and art marketplace players enter into new collaborations that make it easier for artists to interact in public with visitors and residents. Public here is construed in the broadest sense possible—small parks and large parks, inside a hotel or outside on a street corner, inside a restaurant or outside by the beach, inside a shop or outside in front of a church. Wherever people go, artists would go, supported and encouraged by the many constituents who gain when a city is full of life, activity, and creativity.

Naturally, there is a close affinity between this model and the community arts model, with the model of the artist working in her community and for the sake of that community. Thousands of artists are already engaged in the community arts model in disciplines like dance, literature, media arts, music, public art, theater, performance, and the visual arts. Some of the social contexts in which they work are activism, community development, corrections, cultural democracy, education, environment, and health. These groups and projects have names like the Community Arts Corps, the Prison Creative Arts Project, Culture for Development, and the Art for Healing Foundation.

The main difference between the Creative Tourism model and the community arts model is that in the community arts model, activism is the key. In the visitor arts model, interaction is the key. Individual artists design activities and events that promote interactions in public spaces with the people who pass through that space, or who show up because they have heard that something is happening. The community arts model is more frankly social and political; the cultural tourism model includes social and political work, but also includes anything an artist may dream up, from the political satire of the San Francisco Mime Troupe to open air watercolor workshops.

Here is one example of the cultural tourism model in action. Patrice, a visual artist in Honolulu, described her efforts at connecting with Hawaii's tourist trade. She explained, "I live and paint in Honolulu and create most of my watercolor paintings in public by demonstrating at two hotel gallery/shops in Waikiki. The work I do is of interest to the visitors passing me as I paint, and we often have interesting conversations about painting, life in the islands, and their visits here. People of all ages love to watch me work and there is a certain magic in watching a painting come to life, because only the artist has any idea of what might happen next.

"When visitors tell me that they like to draw or paint, I ask them to tell me what they like to create. When they bemoan the fact that they're not as good as I am, I tell the children that I'm older, and I tell everyone that I have been painting a lot longer than they have. When they tell me I make it look so easy, I explain it's my job. I encourage everyone to keep painting and drawing, and I tell them that the more they do, the better they will get. Who knew that old adage was really true?

"I also offer two-hour private watercolor classes to people of all ages. During that time, we discuss color as they fill in a color wheel and mix colors by combining complementaries. They paint their own painting, whatever subject matter they choose, and take their matted painting home with them, ready to be framed. I give them a folder of information including everything we've discussed; it's enough information for them to be able to continue to paint once they get home. Some of them keep in touch, sending photos or digital images of what they've created. One of my students lives in England and calls twice a year to keep me posted on his progress.

"My classes are titled, Be a Creative Traveler. I publicize them with rack cards and on the back of my business cards. Obviously, I'm fortunate to be living in such a wonderful tourist destination. But wherever we live, it behooves artists to reach out to the public. We can create relationships with those who feel they have no talent, but who appreciate art. We can educate others as to what it means to be an artist. When we make ourselves visible and known, we can begin to raise the awareness of what it means to actually live life as an artist in society today."

Here are some other Creative Tourism possibilities. Nonfiction authors who live in a given neighborhood can each give a weekly chat at some unlikely venue, like the neighborhood laundromat, to an audience of locals doing their laundry, and to visitors who have heard about the series and have come to listen. The chat can be followed by a conversation, a conversation that unfolds as audience members fold their clothes. As unlikely as this possibility sounds, exactly such a lecture series has been run successfully at a laundromat in the Bernal Heights neighborhood of San Francisco, where I recently lived. The series attracted many well-known authors and many interested audience members.

Filmmakers with films to show, faced with the massive problem of finding distribution for their films and venues for showing their films, might take their films out into the community and create a film series that uses the walls of schools as screens. As odd and outlandish as this might sound, exactly such a film series is a successful annual event in the same Bernal Heights neighborhood of San Francisco I just mentioned. Hundreds of residents and visitors pay to sit in schoolyards under the stars and watch films projected onto school walls. Naturally, these filmmakers are also submitting their films to festivals and looking for other venues and other marketing opportunities, but as they wait they are earning money and making some useful connections by showing their films in this public way.

Among the things I do, one is running a cyberspace artist bridge group made up of creative and performing artists who live in locales worldwide. I give them assignments to try out and ask them to report on their efforts. The following is one of the assignments that I gave. I asked them to consider the following. "Imagine that an event like a convention is coming to your locale. It doesn't matter how small your locale actually is—for this mind experiment imagine that there is some attraction in your area that is drawing people, and that a group is coming. Picture some number of people, whether twenty or 2000, arriving in your locale. In what new ways might you connect with them? Generate a list of several of these new ideas." Then I asked them to do this. "Take one of your ideas and translate it into a series of steps that you actually take to connect with people, visitors or locals, in your area. Take the first step this week and report on your efforts."

Here is one response to this exercise. Christina, a visual artist in Shanghai, explained, "The art installations that I make are not readily accessible to people who are not conversant with contemporary art, so at first I couldn't think of any convention that I would want to connect with. But then I realized that there were two art events in Shanghai that actually do bring in my audience, the Shanghai Biennale and the Shanghai Contemporary Art Fair. This audience of tourists from inside the culture industry would be interested in spending time in Shanghai in ways that are not necessarily easily available to them through traditional tours. Some of these tourists are artists themselves, others are interested in the creative process and how it is manifested here in Shanghai. So I quickly generated the following list of ideas.

"I can create tours for visiting artists to the markets from which they might buy inspiring materials—the fabric market, the notions market, the hardware market, etc., and also take them to places off the beaten track that would be inspiring, like the bird and flower market, the backstreets of the old city, the tinsmiths, my studio building, and the propaganda museum. I could include a play date in my studio, where visitors get to make a handmade souvenir, maybe a simple artist's book incorporating the local materials they just purchased. An extension of this might be having them rent a piece of my studio for the length of their stay, so that each day they could interpret what they'd seen. This could include coaching on my part about how one interprets one's experience of a place in order to imbue experience with meaning.

"Now I need to get started turning some of these ideas into reality! First, I'll approach several tour guides I know who do unusual custom tours and ask them to consider me as an option. Then I'll approach concierges at some of the high end, trendy hotels. Next I'll find out who does the marketing for these two events and get my new tour information to them. Fourth, I'll create a website whose name comes up when you search variations on artist studio, Shanghai, and creative tours. Fifth, I'll place a listing in all the ex-pat magazines, as newcomers to Shanghai might also love to know about this possibility. Okay, I see how this might work!"

In order for the cultural tourism model to work, all seven groups of stakeholders need to stretch—artists, visitors, government officials, tourism industry professionals, local business owners, art marketplace players, and residents.

Artists need to be encouraged to stretch in the direction of going public. It is virtually another art form to lead a public discussion or to present an interactive workshop, and most artists do not see themselves as talented in these ways. They need to be helped to understand that there is a learning curve involved, that their first efforts may fall flat, and that trusting the process is everything, just as it is in the art-making they engage in daily. Here is a place where city government and tourism professionals could be of great help, by sponsoring workshops that teach artists how to go public with their efforts.

Visitors need to be encouraged to stretch in the direction of participation. Most visitors tend to prefer staged performances to reality, and the safety of observation to the perceived risks of participation. A concerted effort by government, local businesses, tourism professionals, and art marketplace representatives to present participation as a great way to make memories can help enormously in this regard. Every outlet, hotel lobby, restaurant, art gallery, bookstore, could have a "Meet Our Artists!" brochure on hand, a brochure created at the national or local level to explain to visitors the value of participation, to train them in the art of participation, and to reduce their anxiety about interacting with artists.

Government officials need to be encouraged to stretch in the direction of supporting artists who want to go public by providing them with easy access to venues like public parks and tourist sites, by providing them with workshops and trainings on how to effectively go public, by encouraging, rather discouraging, their efforts to bring their creativity into public view and, as a top priority, by announcing these artists' activities with as much energy and enthusiasm as they announce annual festivals, great museums, and other large cultural attractions. Every local government should have a "Meet Our Artists!" link on their tourist-oriented web pages that is kept up to date and that does a good job of directing visitors to cultural tourism events. Likewise, they should create a "Meet Our Artists!" brochure that helps visitors understand that their city supports visitor/artist interactions.

Tourist industry professionals need to be encouraged to stretch in the direction of adding visitor arts to the products they tout. Every tourist industry professional knows to tout free breakfast and three nights for the price of two. They know the allure of high-end shopping, fine dining, and world-class theater. Now they need to be encouraged to point out that certain destinations come with this added allure, that artists from all the disciplines provide public activities there. Aspen is not just its music festival; it is the scores of impromptu concerts music students provide on every corner and in every square. As a tourist industry professional, you can sell Aspen's skiing, dining, galleries, festival, mountain beauty, and cachet as a popular watering hole. But you can also sell it as a place where art and music happen everywhere.

Local business owners with a stake in the matter need to be encouraged to stretch in the direction of standing open to artists' ideas, to hearing artists out when they suggest, for instance, that they might be given space in the hotel lobby to interact with guests. This is a natural extension of what business owners already know to be true, that hanging an artist's show is good for their café, and allowing a mariachi band to play is good for their restaurant. This is the logical next step for local business owners, to see these new interactive arts activities as good for business, to support artists' initiatives, and to actively seek out artist collaborations and partnerships.

Art marketplace players need to be encouraged to stretch in the direction of thinking outside the box of gallery, crafts shop, theater, concert hall, and bookstore by inviting the artists they interact with and represent to go public. A painter will often ask the gallery owner who represents him, "What can I do to help?" Gallery owners typically have no idea how to respond beyond, "Send people to the gallery." Now, as active participants in this movement, a gallery owner can say, "Do a public workshop—I'll help you arrange it." A publisher can say, "Publicly interact with your readers. Here are some ideas for doing that." Art marketplace players can learn to support this movement and by doing so, increase their bottom line profits with no added cost.

Residents need to be encouraged to stretch in the direction of attending the activities made available to them, including new activities that creative and performing artists dream up. They need to be coaxed from in front of their television sets, charmed into attending what may seem like unusual and even edgy activities, and informed about the events happening down the street and across town. When residents experience these new activities as pluses, and come to anticipate them and enjoy them, the natural ambivalence they feel toward the visitors who flock to their place will be tempered.

Millions of artists are available to interact with the hundreds of millions of people who travel for business and pleasure. Artists have both personal and professional reasons for wanting to connect to these travelers. On a personal level, it helps counteract the isolation they often feel, and creates the warmth that only comes from human contact. On a professional level, it builds the artist's audience, and forces the artist to better articulate what it is that he or she is doing. An artist could work in her studio, create paintings, and look for gallery representation; that is the traditional model. Or she could work in her studio, create paintings, look for gallery representation, and take her paints, her spirit, and her expertise into the sunlight and interact with other human beings. That is the Creative Tourism model.

Eric Maisel.
Photograph by Linda Carfagno.

Eric Maisel has been coaching performing and creative artists for more than twenty years. He trains other creative coaches and has written more than thirty books, including *Coaching the Artist Within, Fearless Creating, A Writer's Paris, A Writer's San Francisco, The Van Gogh Blues, The Creativity Book, Performance Anxiety, Ten Zen Seconds*, and others. He has also written for many magazines, and is a well-known speaker on creativity issues and coaching. He holds master's degrees in counseling and creative writing and a doctorate in counseling psychology.

CREATIVE TOURISM IN INDIAN COUNTRY: MORE THAN BEADS, FEATHERS AND CASINOS

by
Hayes A. Lewis
Director, Center for Lifelong Education,
Institute of American Indian Arts

Indigenous trade and commerce have been integral aspects of Pueblo life experience since time immemorial.

Today, I want to provide those attending the Santa Fe International Conference on Creative Tourism with an Indigenous historical overview from a tribal perspective of the following: the experiences of Pueblo people regarding trade and commerce, as well as the conditions that existed at the time of first contact with the Spanish Europeans; an awareness of the trade patterns of Indigenous people in this region of the Southwest; a description of how early trade developed into what is now called economic development and tourism; and highlights of contributions and modern economic development initiatives among Pueblo tribes. I will also discuss some of the social-political-economic implications of recent developments.

The ancestral stories of our Pueblo origins are similar to those of other Indigenous people. The Indigenous tribes of this region, those residing in other parts of this country and on other continents such as Africa, migrated extensively as they searched for that final place they named as their homeland.

According to Zuni ancestral knowledge, after the emergence from the fourth world, the Zuni people were searching for the sacred middle place or "Idewanna." The name my Zuni ancestors have given our core community is "Halonawa Idewanna."

Our ancestors were led to this place after a great migration from the area of the Grand Canyon. Emerging from the canyon, they traveled southeast to found several important spiritual places of worship and for habitation. One of the important spiritual places that they visited is known as "Kothuwalawa," the village of the Katchina spirits, which the Zuni people acknowledge as Zuni Heaven. We believe this is where our spirits go when death causes us to transition from our earthly existence, just as others believe they go to a heavenly place beyond this existence.

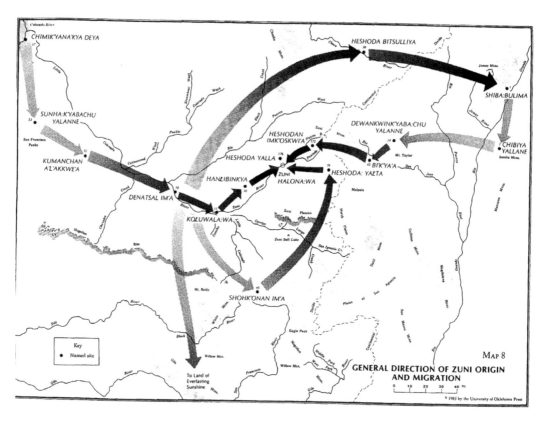

Zuni Origin and Migration Map
(Used by permission of author, T. J. Ferguson: Zuni Atlas)

In their search for the sacred Middle Place, the ancient Zunis traveled far to the north and south of the present reservation in New Mexico. Tribal oral history indicates that the Zuni visited a special place called "Hanthebinkya." At this place, the clans became fully designated; a governance/leadership structure was organized and religious/spiritual and cultural practices were initiated. However, this was also a place of division, because a strong factionalism occurred within the tribe.

The story of factionalism within the tribe occurred when our ancestors were searching for the middle place. When the conflict could not be resolved, elders and spiritual leaders decided to settle the factionalism using a special practice. Bird eggs were gathered. A leader from each side was told to choose one egg. One was very colorful and the other was a darker, speckled egg. Each group was told to nurture the eggs until they hatched. Whatever type of bird hatched would determine that group's destination. Each group would travel and reside in the homeland of their bird. The present-day Zunis are descended from the group that stayed in the north, because the leader chose the egg that hatched into a raven. This region of the Southwest is one of the natural homelands of that bird. The other leader and group went south, because their egg hatched into a macaw parrot, so they traveled to the "land of the everlasting sun." We have not seen our relatives since that fateful time. That is the experience of the Zuni in the place known as Hanthebinkya, and as our ancestors continued looking for the middle place, they traveled to this area, the modern-day Rio Grande corridor.

The ancient Zunis visited and lived in many sacred places. One such place was "Sipapulima," known today as the area near present-day Bandelier. The Zuni ancestors came to this region, traveled down to the Sandia Mountains, and then went back to modern Zuni Pueblo. Prior to the establishment of trade and commerce among Indian people in this region, we were all searching for that special place and we found it at "Halonawa," or Zuni Pueblo.

Modern trade and commerce is based upon ancient trade relationships developed among tribes in this region. The people living here at the middle and northern Rio Grande Pueblo region were known to our ancient Zuni ancestors. The early migrations established a familiarity among people; relationships and kinship ties were established, and minerals and other natural products located here became known and used for barter. Trade became established among Indigenous peoples of this region, as well as far to the west and to the south. In today's Pueblos you will see an abundance of feathers and natural materials from the south. The macaw feathers have been extensively traded since pre-colonial times. Indigenous traders from this region followed well-established trails to trade with the Puebloan peoples.

The Spanish Conquistadores followed well-worn trade routes north on paths created by Indigenous people who traded with those to the south. The Aztecs, Tarascans, and other Indians that live in Sonora, Chihuahua, and other places came north from Mexico to several of the Zuni villages and into the Chaco area.

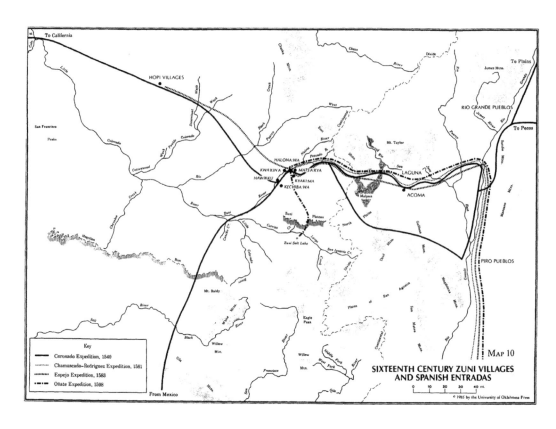

Ancient trade routes lead Spaniards north. Spanish Entrada Map.
(Used by permission of author, T. J. Ferguson: Zuni Atlas)

The trade was extensive between tribes throughout the region. Shells from the Gulf of Mexico, salt, dried medicinal and food plants, seeds, skins, and other natural products—clays, pottery, baskets, pigments, and minerals used for painting and ceremonial purposes, and feathers were but a few items passed from tribe to tribe through trade. "Hawikuh," a western village of Zuni, is the site of the first official military contact between Pueblo peoples and the Spaniards.

The trade of feathers has been extensive since prehistoric time. The use of macaw feathers is attributed to the trade among Indigenous people from central Mexico.

Last year while watching a Katchina dance at Zuni, I was reminded of pictures I had seen from Mexico of Aztec and Mayan dancers and their extensive use of parrot feathers. During the Katchina dance at Zuni, two Katchinas had macaw parrot headdresses of the entire bird. The colors were brilliant and very reminiscent of the Mexican Indians' use of feathers in ceremonial headpieces.

During the initial violent encounter with the Spaniards, our Zuni ancestors were subdued after a battle near Hawikuh village. After resting and refitting, the Spanish conquistadores proceeded on to the Rio Grande area. Along the way, they entered the Acoma or Haku villages. Then they travelled north along the Rio Grande, over to Pecos Pueblo, then on to Taos Pueblo and into the Great Plains region.

The early European explorers, following trails and trade routes established by Indigenous traders were able to find their way rapidly over rough terrain and unknown lands and to conquer the Pueblo tribes in their search for the mythical Seven Cities of Cibola (the golden cities).

In any discussion related to Indigenous commerce, trade, and development, there must be recognition of the relationships that developed and the kinds of events that occurred in ancient days. From the middle place, Zuni traders traveled extensively from their home village to trade with other tribes in distant locations. The map shows the kinds of materials traded.

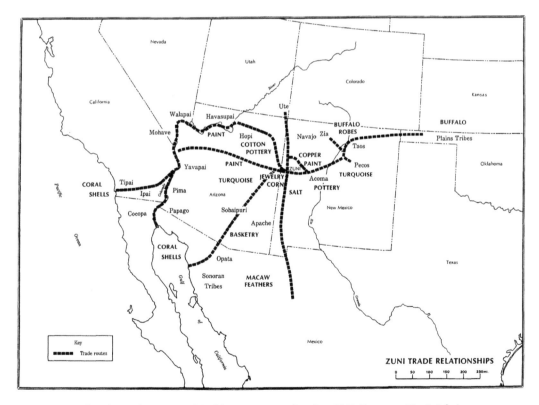

Zuni Trade Relationships Map. (Used by permission of author, T. J. Ferguson: Zuni Atlas)

A Different Sense of Time and Space

There was an expanded sense of time and space in ancestral days. Those involved in trade took whatever time was required to travel from one place to another. Travel might have taken a week, sometimes two weeks, or more than one month. An important aspect of relationships that are built upon trade is making friendships, establishing valuable personal connections, and visiting. Early Indigenous traders would meet those Indians from the south, trade for macaw feathers, shells, minerals, and the trades people from the south would spend time in the region, visit relatives (many Indigenous warriors who accompanied the Coronado expedition chose to remain and intermarried with villagers from Zuni and elsewhere), and then went back to their homelands with salt, minerals, paint, weavings, arrow making materials, corn, and other dried products.

The Zuni people traded with other tribal groups, all of which are, with a few exceptions, still in existence. Zuni traders came to the region and brought their shells and other highly valued products, which included extensive amounts of turquoise. They traveled to the east to the area known as the panhandle of Oklahoma. Near Pecos, which is a Pueblo southeast of Santa Fe, there is an ancient village called San Marcos. It is now a national monument. Here, one may find examples of pottery—glazed wares—that were brought from Zuni to Pecos.

Ancient Trade Relations: The Precursors to Modern Commerce

The trade, commerce, and relationships that were initiated in ancient times by our ancestors really are the precursors to the trade that is enjoyed today. The place names that are referenced in our prayers, Bandelier, the Rio Grande, and the Sandias, are reminders that our ancestors passed these locations, and those memories are kept alive.

All of the trade products were carried on peoples' backs. There were no horses, burros, or wagons. The people traveled in groups and, most of the time, they were accompanied or led by a Bow Priest, which is comparable to a war captain in other Pueblos. There were Bow Priests, warriors as well as other people, who were a merchant class of people and who carried on commerce. Times were dangerous and challenging. The development of trade and relationships led to intimate knowledge of other people, the land, and environment and familiarity with needs and wants. Because the products traded were very useful and important, there was more of an acceptance of these new relationships. As relationships developed and acceptance continued, diverse people became allies.

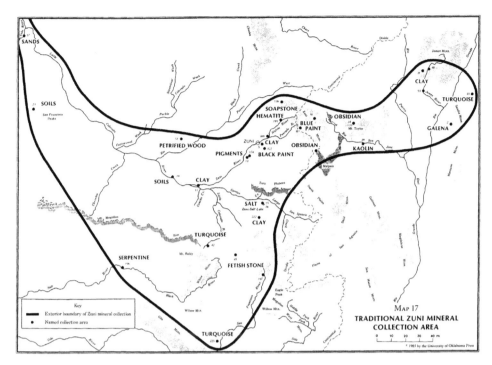

Mineral Collection Map. (Used by permission of author, T. J. Ferguson: Zuni Atlas)

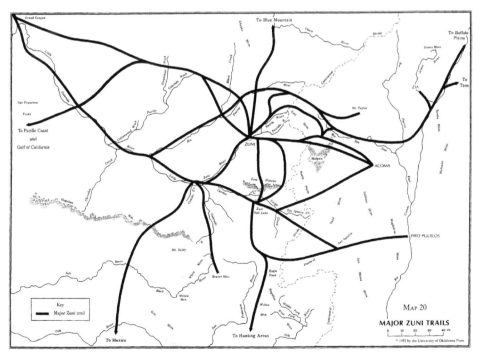

Major Trails Map. (Used by permission of author, T. J. Ferguson: Zuni Atlas)

There is a myth about Pueblo Indians being a kind, docile, gentle, peaceful people. This picture is not entirely accurate. Our ancestors were very hard people, known for their tenacity, courage, and persistence. They were also very warlike in many ways and able to defend themselves. The stories of courage and competence in warfare regarding our Bow Priests and our warriors are amazing. While they protected themselves, they maintained the trails and patrolled—an early form of law enforcement—to make sure that important trade and commerce proceeded along the trails.

Pueblo people have the shared experience of ancestral trade and relations. Through this perspective, I wish to acquaint you with where we're coming from as Indigenous people. Trade, commerce, and tourism didn't start with the coming of the white man; it was already well established and has been built upon by successive generations. So, we have some important lessons to learn about the trade and relationships. Early tribal relations with the Europeans, were a brutal experience. The Spaniards and other missionaries came with a bible in one hand and a sword in the other. Our ancestors suffered many extreme encounters, and many died due to diseases and warfare. But, they left other things behind. As we learned to coexist and work together, we saw that we do have a commonality; the creativity and the strength of people have been interfused in many different ways—through inter-marriages, trade relationships, and friendships.

IMPACTS OF COLONIZATION AND TRADE RELATIONS

We have remnants of ancient Spanish families living in various part of New Mexico. The Spanish did recognize, particularly for the Pueblo tribes, the need to grant land by official decree. A number of the Pueblos, if not all of them, were granted tracts of land that are still recognized. Indigenous lands and territories were recognized by the Spanish representatives of the King of Spain. In 1848, when the Mexican-American War ended with the Treaty of Guadalupe-Hidalgo, the Spanish land grants made to Pueblo tribes were recognized by the United States Congress. Those grants of land became the basis of modern Pueblo Indian reservations.

Even though the colonization process was hard on people and presented a number of extreme challenges, our Pueblo tribes have legal recognition and acknowledgement by successive colonizing governments. Developments and changes to modern tribal councils, as in any colonial relationship, were imposed and influenced primarily by the Spaniards. Our ancestors had different cultural models of leadership and governance prior to the first European encounters, and even though many say we have traditional models of leadership and governance, we cannot discount the Spanish influence. The Spanish influenced and modeled Indigenous tribal ways of decision-making and leadership in a likeness of theirs—as they wanted one person to be the tribal chief, or spokesperson.

TRADE AMONG INDIGENOUS PEOPLE IN THE SOUTHWEST

In pre-contact times, this region of the Southwest was highly populated. One of the major precepts the Europeans used to justify the conquest of lands and the subjugation of people was the concept of "terra nullis," the notion that the lands "discovered" were empty of humans. However, there were large numbers of people who were moving around, trading with each other and forming many kinds of relationships. As evidenced at Hopi and Zuni, one may see how cultural influences played out in the cultural practices among Indigenous peoples of this region. Those influences and cultural exchanges go back in history and perpetuate relationships established generations ago.

As we examine how these relationships were established, we must consider how this plays out today, in terms of commerce, trade, and tourism. Early traders carried their goods on their backs and valued the relationships developed from trade, interaction, and friendships. Throughout all this people movement, there was little negative environmental impact on the ground and surrounding landscape.

CONTEMPORARY MODELS OF TRADE, COMMERCE, AND DEVELOPMENT

The contemporary models of tourism either chosen or imposed on tribal communities are corporate—industrial models with a one-size-fits-all mentality. Some of these developments are evident in areas of Oklahoma, the Navajo Reservation, or even in the Pueblos to the immediate north. There are corporate models exemplified by franchises, casinos, fast food establishments, grocery outlets, and other kinds of business development, such as gas stations—basically strip malls. This predominate model was initiated during the 1970s and has extended to the present.

INDIAN GAMING: A NEW FORM OF ECONOMIC COLONIZATION

Many people do not realize that many gaming tribes entered into management contracts with casino management corporations from Nevada, and elsewhere. Indian casino gaming is a multi-billion dollar revenue source for everyone, including the management corporations, the state (via gaming compact concessions), and financial backers. The tribes, while deriving revenues, must pay an exorbitant percentage under state imposed compacts. Tribes involved in casino gaming spend a great deal of money to obtain the expertise of management corporations.

HUMAN AND ENVIRONMENTAL COST

Many tribes throughout the United States became involved with casino gaming because it seemed a quick route to economic development, and they hoped for economic self-sufficiency. Unfortunately, this option has not benefited all who have chosen this path. Many tribes are now strapped with unanticipated human, social, and cultural costs on top of the price of doing business. Casino gaming represents very little in actual economic benefit to grassroots tribal community development, while the scale of the carbon footprint and environmental damage has become larger.

North of Santa Fe, the largest, monolithic gaming casino in northern New Mexico has been developed on tribal lands. The sheer size, scale, impact, and stress this enterprise places on the network of fragile earth and environmental resources will be evident well into the future. Did tribal officials and their non-Indian planning firms seriously consider the issues of waste disposal, environmental damage, electricity use, water usage, aquifer depletion, etc? Where is the trickle-down effect? Yes, some people have been employed, but at the same time, this type of development does not sustain viable economic development into the communities in appropriate, dependence-free ways. Artisans, craftsmen, farmers, and tribal members gain strength from cultural enterprises of a smaller scale that are linked to spirituality, ecology, culture, and the sacredness of place and space. In the Pojoaque Valley, the hope and rhetoric that casino gaming might contribute in some lasting way to a large scale cultural revival and renaissance for the Pojoaque tribe is an empty dream.

The gaming establishments are not places one goes to find a cultural experience, because the casino does not represent Indian culture. Go to an Indian casino to gamble. However, do not look for a cultural experience in a casino, because it just will not happen.

During my experience with the Zuni tribal government, there were a number of presentations by casino experts and other off-reservation entrepreneurs looking for investment on tribal lands. They offered casino gaming and other related economic development opportunities. Zuni is not on the beaten tourist path, and besides, the primary population that might use any casino-type development would be the Zuni people themselves. They asked—as an alternative to casino gaming, does the tribe want a mall, with a restaurant, a gas station, or fast food outlets? These colonizing and dependent economic models are evident and being peddled to tribes all over the Southwest. Where are the connections to community, traditional values, sacred space, and spirituality in such enterprise?

TOURISM—FOR WHAT PURPOSE?

As tourism has developed in Indian Country, we see many tour buses coming into tribal villages, to see what? To see the Indians. This type of tourism places the tourist in a passive/observer situation with little else to hold their attention. They walk around on unguided visits, never having an encounter that is meaningful, or even learning a bit of the lives and culture of the people. Often, tourists come to the tribal building and ask, "Where is the Pueblo?" and they are told, you're standing in it. They comment, "It doesn't look like the pictures we've seen." Of course the modern Pueblo does not resemble old photos because of the development and evolution as a tribal community. Sacred spaces within tribal communities are off limits and need protection from curious outsiders. I recall a time in Zuni when there were so many tourists off-loaded during ceremonial dances that our people couldn't view their own religious ceremonies. The Zunis had to literally fight their way to the front for a viewing space. These situations have sometimes led to a closing of ceremonial dances and activities, much to the anger or embarrassment of local tourists. Many times there were so many anthropologists hanging out and discussing what they thought would be the next sequence or meaning of a ceremony—as if they knew. At first, the inclination is to argue with them, but what's the point, because they already think they know everything.

Tribes have come to a period of re-examining—what are we doing and how are we doing it, in terms of economic development, commerce, and tourism in our communities? While the casino, gaming, or industrial mall initiatives are models that have worked to some degree within some tribal communities, these models are not the only answer to our economic and community development needs. There has to be a transition of how we empower people to make a variation in strategic models, and we must adjust these to strengthen people in a way that makes a difference and is appropriate. We must also reduce the environmentally and socially damaging impacts of the mega-casino development model. The answer isn't building larger casinos and strip malls.

Shared Knowledge—Shared Learning

So, it is important to make these connections in places and gatherings such as this one, to critically examine the prevalent economics so we can learn from each other. There are more appropriate ways to create economic development in Indigenous communities with resources that will strengthen people and provide a sense of contribution, efficacy, and investment in community.

In ancestral times, the practice of leaving less of a footprint was very intentional because our ancestors had to live off the land and use the natural resources in an economical way to sustain and support themselves. The creation of relationships was not just a human endeavor—there were the animals, environment, ecology, and land to consider. Some of those practices and lessons deserve reconsideration.

Re-examining Tribal Community-based Economics

Even though strip malls and casinos exist, we must look at how we might plan for the creation of smaller and viable economic environments, so life may become more meaningful for people living within our tribal communities. During one of the

Creative Tourism planning sessions, I was impressed with the representatives from Aswan, Egypt. They spoke about cultural tourism in terms of involving families and communities, using the cultural strengths of people to be the catalyst for tourism. The art, culture, and place were used as a means of giving the tourist an experience that is more holistic and more meaningful. As a tourist, if you enter an Indigenous community and you are on a self-guided tour, you cannot make a meaningful connection with people. Just as in the past times, we must reconsider the basis of commerce and tourist development as based on meaningful relationships and friendships, and as giving a measure of consideration by leaving less of an environmentally damaging footprint.

Indian tribes must re-examine the models that have been imposed on them, along with the ones they have chosen. Tribes have accepted the corporate and industrial models. Tribal and community leaders need to learn from others, and conduct forums to examine what is happening within their communities, and to protect the cultural and spiritual base while they create economic enterprise. At the same time, they must find ways to empower and create efficacy among tribal members to create enterprises for themselves and in connection with families, so that a smaller impact will be evidenced on the environment and resources. For instance, water is very scarce in New Mexico. Tribal leaders and planners must be mindful about the limited amount of water that is pumped from the limited aquifer sources. Other areas include effective ways to recycle waste and examination of the impacts of extractive methods to produce electrical power.

Throughout the centuries, our ancestors have visited this place and migrated over the land. Today, Santa Fe and the surrounding areas are populated by very creative, energetic, and visionary people. We have many human resources that can be used in different ways and in different collaborations and partnerships with tribal communities. We need to proactively and productively coexist, make enterprise for ourselves, and connect with the spiritual base of the people and land.

NURTURING THE CREATIVE SPIRIT AT THE INSTITUTE OF AMERICAN INDIAN ARTS

The region is a very spiritual space and place. In our area of Santa Fe, we are grateful for the Rancho Viejo development, because they donated 145 acres to the Institute of American Indian Arts (IAIA) to create our college for our students and our artisans. This type of generosity is rare, but you can find it here in this place called Santa Fe. In developing our campus, we critically think about how we may serve people and how we can use our resources, expertise, and experience so tribes can benefit.

As IAIA develops its outreach and connections with tribes, particularly in relation to economic development and enterprise, we must consider our core values as Indigenous people, as well as the core values of people in the communities. We must all remind ourselves to be mindful of the footprints we leave. We must consider alternative sources and uses of energy, build environmentally compatible buildings that meet either LEED certification or match environmental standards. The building we have planned as our Tribal Conference Center will be a LEED gold-certified facility because of the use of material, recycling, heating, and cooling of the facility and other environmentally supportive features. The more that cities and industries start looking at how to conserve energy and our resources, the better off we all will be. Everyone must to be able to walk the talk. If you say you're going to be working in creative enterprise, supporting each other, creating new relationships and networks, and you're all here for that purpose, that makes us feel good, because we also have to do the same thing in all the relationships with the people and communities we work with.

There are many small beginnings that will blossom into larger activities and impact more people. We have the programs at the IAIA in terms of art and culture, and we also have new courses in the business of art, teaching artists how to create enterprises for themselves and how to promote their own businesses in collective as well as individual ways. This will make a difference. We have a lot of alumni and artists in this community, both Indian and non-Indian, friends who are using their home spaces as galleries. Find out where those are and visit them. That, in my opinion, is really what cultural and family enterprise is about. Many times, while the artists have to struggle along, you need to look around and realize there are families involved in this enterprise, and they're as much a part of the endeavor as the person who has the name or is selling the product. So, the more we get away from this very individualistic type of development, especially in tribal communities, the more that we can connect with and use the natural power and strength of families.

Although IAIA is designated as a tribal college, we are accredited by two accrediting agencies in the United States—the North Central Association of Colleges and Universities and the National Association of Schools of Arts and Design.

After a visit to Africa this summer, we will be hosting at least six people from that continent, who want to come to IAIA to experience some of the cultural activity for artisans in this region, as well as to learn about the business of art—how to go about developing and connecting with people who can market their product so they can eliminate, to the largest extent possible, the middle men, which happen to be NGOs in the region of Botswana. As we discovered on our trip, the NGOs are making all the money.

CONCLUDING COMMENTS

The same thing is happening worldwide. These Indigenous people in Africa are looking for opportunities to connect with other Indigenous or like-minded people, to market and sell their products, even using the Internet and web-based marketing. They also want to strengthen their connections with us and other Indigenous people, so we can learn from each other. It's not a one-way street and no one person has all the answers. We all have some piece of the puzzle, and we need to interact in positive and creative ways to gain from each other.

So many creative, energized, and knowledgeable people live in Santa Fe. This is a very special place, from ancient times to the present. It is very special because of the people here. And, as we always say in our gatherings, any time you have a gathering for the purpose and intent of doing something positive and good, then this is a sacred place as well. All of you represent that in your own individual themes and collectively. Just as our ancestors' ancient trails have led others to come to our country and homeland, we still honor the values and trails of the past, as we bring everyone together here and make those connections that are so important for sustaining ourselves and our community.

I would encourage you, during your time here, to visit the surrounding Pueblos, because the enterprises you see next to the thoroughfares—the malls and casinos—are only one part of who we are as Pueblo tribes. The other part is in the villages, our communities, and with our people. We have a beautiful environment and I encourage you to take the time to look at those places. When you decide to go to one of the Pueblos, you need to check in with the Pueblo Governor's office because that is the protocol.

I thank and greatly appreciate all of the sponsors of the international conference for the opportunity to share a little of my ancestral past, in terms of the historical perspective of commerce and trade, and how it has impacted contemporary economic development. While the impacts of colonization haven't been enjoyable for Indigenous people, we have been left with many things we can still value, such as new technology,

friendships, and ties to the land and environment. As we go into the future and as our pasts converge, we find a convergence of interest and enterprise in this place called Santa Fe. We consider all of you as resources and thank you for your contributions to your communities and nations. I wish you all success and good health for the future.

We appreciate all of you being here today and being part of this International Conference on Creative Tourism.

Hayes Lewis. Photograph by Linda Carfagno.

Hayes Lewis is a member of the Zuni Tribe of New Mexico. He is the director of the Center for Lifelong Education, Research and Cultural Exchange (CLE) at the Institute of American Indian Arts (IAIA). The CLE is funded by the W. K. Kellogg Foundation and expands IAIA's outreach services to tribal governments and Native communities in nine priority areas. Target constituencies include Indigenous people in regional, national, and international locations.

YESTER-MORROW: USING A REGION'S HERITAGE AND CULTURE FOR ITS ECONOMIC FUTURE

by
Becky Anderson
Becky Anderson Consulting

Yester-morrow strategies, which use a region's heritage and culture for its economic future, have proven to be effective in hard economic times. These strategies are sensitive to the natural environment and take into account culture, traditions, and talents, allowing new economies to be built around them.

YESTER-MORROW STRATEGIES IN TOUGH TIMES: AN EXAMPLE FROM NORTH CAROLINA, USA

In a twenty-three county region of western North Carolina, more than 25 percent of traditional manufacturing vanishes and in some counties more than 50 percent disappears. Unemployment is at eight to ten percent regionally, exceeding 18 percent in some counties. Financial institutions are failing, even closing. Road systems, water, and sewer infrastructure are in need of repair and expansion. School systems are struggling with high dropout rates.

Sound familiar? Sound like your community's morning newspaper? Yes and no. Actually, this data made the headlines twenty years ago in the mid-1980s and early 1990s in the mountains of western North Carolina, where the traditional manufacturing economy of furniture and textiles began to die out, and the region's agricultural crop of tobacco had lost its market. It was in this place and at this time when new economic development strategies, yester-morrow, strategies, were initiated.

How Did We Do It?

We looked at the land; all 1,200 square miles of our region, where the mountains, home to the highest peaks in Appalachia, stretch across 150 miles. More than 50 percent of the land cannot be used for development because of watershed regulations, steep slopes, corporate holdings, and vast areas of government land.

We looked at our people; more than 1 million residents, who were becoming an older population, intensified by the numbers of retirees moving here. We faced pressure on land use with demands for golf courses and gated communities, on health care, and on taxation issues such as tax revenue support for schools and social services.

We looked at our economy; although employment in traditional manufacturing had steadily declined, the entrepreneurial spirit abounded with small business jobs increasing by 23 percent annually.

We responded. We employed a variety of strategies that value community uniqueness and sense of place. Western North Carolina returned to its roots of the handmade object or craft as one response to this transition and its economic and community development challenges.

The Blue Ridge and Great Smoky Mountains of our region have long been identified with beautiful and functional handmade objects. The area is home to the nation's finest craft schools and its oldest continuing craft organizations, and to the fourth-largest concentration of craftspeople in the United States. Most native North Carolina industries, such as pottery, paper, textiles, and furniture, grew out of handmade traditions.

In 1993 we established an organization called HandMade in America to create an economy around the region's craft heritage. In 1994 we completed an economic impact study that revealed the business of the handmade objects contributed $122 million annually to the region's economy. A 2008 economic impact study revealed that it had grown to $213 million annually.

The first economic impact study revealed that 67 percent of all craft purchases were made by visitors, who number 22 million a year in our region. In addition, the impact of tourism on a community raised the following questions: How do you meet the request from craftspeople to find a way for them to stay in their studios making their work and not always at a fair, trade show or a market? How do you meet their request to show them as they truly are: how they live, and how they work? How do you integrate the visitor into the community?

COMMUNITY-BASED TOURISM

One approach is community-based tourism, where the community determines the tourism venue. We met three times in each county, aware of the community divide in each meeting. We asked only three questions per community: What and where are your sacred places? Where do you not want visitors to go? What places that reflect your craft and cultural heritage would you share with a visitor?

These meetings resulted in the establishment of a series of self-guided auto trails throughout a twenty-five-county region, taking people into rural areas and small towns. The trails contained studios, historic craft sites, shops, galleries, local restaurants, and lodgings. The first *Craft Heritage Trails of Western North Carolina* guidebook was published in 1996 and the companion guide, *Farms, Gardens and Countryside Trails*, was published in 2001. They became so popular that the guidebooks have been updated and republished three times with 250 new sites listed each time and more than 70,000 copies sold. Many crafts people, local businesses and tourism organizations partnered for packaged weekends and promotions.

The results were a 23 percent increase in incomes for crafts people and a 28 percent increase in incomes for shops/galleries.

How do you prepare small towns and rural communities for tourism? This is where authenticity is key. A community must identify its assets and heritage to improve and restore its Main Street. Through a program of mentoring, technical assistance, self-help projects, and learning from each other and neighboring communities, twelve small towns, ranging in population from 103 people to 1,000 people, often without a town manager, have been able to build more attractive downtowns, public spaces, greenways, creek walks, inviting gateways, signage, and wayfinding, landscaping, and entertainment venues for residents and visitors alike. The towns discovered authenticity is the key and assets were given priority over needs.

Together over a twelve-year period they have worked to: restore 152 facades; renovate 187 buildings; create 1,184 jobs; establish 294 new businesses; provide an investment of $40 million; commit a total of 175,000 volunteer hours; increase tourism lodging by 38 bed and breakfasts, inns, and cabins; and create 28 new craft shops/galleries.

PLACE-BASED ECONOMY

How do you merge a region's cultural heritage with technology? How do you increase new craft businesses, and at the same time utilize a community's worst real estate? Try a strategy called the place-based economy, where the economy is so tied to place for its natural amenities that it must remain there and cannot be outsourced or clicked away. Try landfill craft business incubator programs called EnergyXchange and the Green Energy Park. Establish craft business incubators for glass, ceramics, and metal smithing at abandoned landfills where the incubator space, glass furnaces, ceramic kilns, and metal smithing forges are fueled by methane gas captured from the closed landfill; add greenhouses for endangered native plants to be wild harvested from mountain woodlands; add galleries and a bio-diesel fuel production program, and it becomes a high-tech facility located at a closed landfill. And oh yes, don't forget that each facility is reducing enough greenhouse emissions from the atmosphere to be comparable to removing 22,000 automobiles off North Carolina highways.

EnergyXchange craft business incubator.

SUSTAINABLE DEVELOPMENT STRATEGIES

How do we look to future economic and environmental challenges that will utilize the region's craft heritage? Try sustainable development strategies. Currently, the city of Asheville and Buncombe County have a commission to look at new business and adaptation of current businesses to meet the new environmental challenge of global warming. HandMade is at the table along with medical, technical, research, and climatic clusters to determine new approaches. Participants are exploring ways for the fiber/weaving industry to produce medical fibers and heat resistant fibers—placing looms back on the floor of textile firms. They are investing in the use of diseased woods and the revival of bark housing with wood turners and furniture makers, and the utilization of the landfill greenhouses for medicinal plant production. New housing construction techniques that utilize craft in architectural elements and home furnishings—unifying craft and architecture as it was in the Renaissance—have resulted in a showcase HandMade House built in a new housing development.

Rendering of showcase HandMade House.

CIVIC LEADERSHIP

But none of these strategies would work or would even be initiated without the most important ingredient of all—civic leadership! For it is in the hard work of our citizens and their unwavering belief in community that their impact is felt:

> By twenty citizens placing sod in a public park at 11:00 pm in a cold rain by the headlights of their cars and the town fire engine.
>
> By a 78-year-old woman, who writes the town landscape ordinance, chairs the town appearance commission, and walks 1.5 miles to show where to plant each tree, and then is elected to the town board for two terms.
>
> By twenty-five citizens who meet for ten cold December nights in a tobacco warehouse to tie evergreen roping to decorate bridges, lampposts, and the town hall in a traditional manner, reflective of the town's history and heritage.
>
> By a postmistress who locks everyone's mail box until a personal commitment is made to assist with the town's revitalization efforts, and then rewards them with a smile, cup of coffee, and a cinnamon bun.
>
> By a town where each merchant buys a lamppost to install and maintains and pays for the electricity, because the town's budget is needed for a new water system.
>
> By twelve small towns that refused to compete with each other for state funds until the state changed its rules to permit them to share lesser amounts of funding as a collaborative, so that all towns came equal to the table.

We have discovered that civic renewal and creative economies don't come from outside visiting experts but from within, by acts of neighborliness, by a love of precious things, by a passion for work, and by the wish to be at home. It is yester-morrow, the best of our past for a better future.

Becky Anderson

Becky Anderson. As executive director of HandMade in America, Becky Anderson built this pioneering organization located in Asheville, North Carolina. HandMade promotes economic development, sustainability, and heritage tourism through its support for handmade objects. As executive director, Anderson oversaw operations that involved 3,000 citizens and 20 regional partnerships. She now serves as a consultant for cultural and economic development programs related to crafts. Previously, she was director of economic development for the Asheville Chamber of Commerce. She has held several positions in community and economic development and helped establish the first federal day care program in the region. She was named one of America's Top Twenty Visionaries by *U.S. News and World Report* in 1999.

SECTION 4

SANTA FE
CREATIVE EXPERIENCES
AND NEXT STEPS

Introduction and Common Themes
by
Sabrina V. Pratt
Executive Director, City of Santa Fe Arts Commission

This section describes two aspects of the conference that fulfilled goals set from the start of the planning: the Creative Tourism Experiences Track and the Creative Tourism: Your Stories, Your Ideas sessions. Goals agreed upon by the UNESCO Creative Cities Network representatives involved in the conference planning included having the conference focus on exploration of Creative Tourism and providing meaningful interactions between participants. The articles in this section outline two ways in which the conference met these goals. In addition, the second article gives the reader conference participants' thoughts on next steps they would like to pursue.

In the first article I discuss the Creative Tourism experiences offered in the Creative Tourism Experiences track of the conference program. The workshops offered at the conference were designed to be representative of everything offered in Santa Fe. In assembling the creative experience conference track, we researched available Creative Tourism product. Through this research and the conference we were able to activate the people and institutions that are working in this field. This continues today as we further develop communication and promotion of Creative Tourism.

In her article, "Open Space Technology Sessions," Jackie M covers another hands-on experience during the conference. On the last two days of the conference registrants were invited to attend

Creative Tourism: Your Stories, Your Ideas and with the help of professional facilitator Toby Herzlich, discuss any aspect of the conference or other ideas they wished. This was done using Open Space Technology, which allows the participants to determine topics and direct the discussion. This use of conference time was chosen to allow conference participants to work in groups of their own choosing and make connections with other people working in the same field or having the same interests.

Both articles discuss aspects of the conference that allowed participants to pursue their interests, explore new ideas and exchange information. The creative experiences were an opportunity to connect with the arts and cultures of Santa Fe and see a variety of formats of Creative Tourism. The Open Space Technology sessions allowed for active learning and reflection on round table conversations, panels and speeches that occurred earlier in the week. These very interactive conference sessions helped meet the goal of fully exploring Creative Tourism and providing opportunities for interaction among all participants.

Exploring the Cultures of Santa Fe
The Santa Fe Creative Tourism
Experiences Track
by
Sabrina V. Pratt
Executive Director, City of Santa Fe Arts Commission

What does Santa Fe have to offer in the field of Creative Tourism? How did Santa Fe present itself through culture-based workshops and other events at the Santa Fe International Conference on Creative Tourism? What could a conference registrant learn about Santa Fe's cultures? This article is an overview of the Creative Tourism Experiences Track and other related aspects of the conference. Participants had a choice of up to eight different workshops each day. In general, these were held in the afternoon after a morning of speakers and panels. Evening events also had creative experiences woven into them, giving visitors more opportunities to delve into Santa Fe's cultures.

Planning for the Conference Track

At a meeting of the Creative Cities Network held in October 2006 for the purpose of planning the Santa Fe International Conference on Creative Tourism (2008), discussions included defining Creative Tourism and creating the format of the proposed conference. It was vitally important to the group that the conference be presented in an experiential and participative manner. Planning started from this Creative Tourism definition developed by the group: "Creative Tourism is travel directed toward an engaged and authentic experience, with participative learning in the arts, heritage or special character of a place, and it provides a connection with those who reside in this place and create this living culture."

The 2006 meeting was planned with one Creative Tourism experience included. The Creative Cities representatives all gathered at the Santa Fe School of Cooking for hands-on lessons in roasting chile and the preparation of New Mexican specialties. The chef educated everyone about the local ingredients, including red and green chile, posolé and beans. He presented his recipes with stories of his grandmother's cooking, including the lessons she taught him about cooking chile and how to roll out flour tortillas.

Green chile roasting. Photograph by Linda Carfagno.

The goal was set at the 2006 planning meeting that the 2008 conference would not have the routine presentation formats of most conferences. Benedetto Zacchiroli, the mayor of Bologna, Italy's staff member for foreign relations, stated at one point that this conference "should be like speed dating so that everyone would be able to talk with each other." Conversation was to be valued, versus presentation. The local Santa Fe planning committee for the 2008 conference kept these points in mind, working to keep a good balance and promote quality interaction.

As preparations began for the 2008 conference, Santa Fe started looking more closely at the available Creative Tourism offerings. One of the primary sources of Creative Tourism experiences is entrepreneurial artists. Another is institutions such as museums, arts centers, performing arts companies, and the like that present the work of artists. Dena Aquilina, at that time executive director of Creative Santa Fe, began collecting information. Through a large email list she put the word out. She also called artists and businesses that she knew were offering Creative Tourism opportunities. Word started to spread, which resulted in many people contacting her. Some of the less obvious ones came to her attention this way. At the end of her project, we had a database of 50 Creative Tourism experiences. Aquilina believes that this is only the surface of what is offered and could be offered in Santa Fe.

In keeping with the goals of the conference planning group, experiences organized for the conference were scheduled at the convention center, in studios, and in other settings to allow participants the maximum impact of the appropriate environment. This was important for two reasons: the commitment to make this conference an experiential one and to offer Creative Tourism at its best in culturally meaningful settings. The result was that the Creative Tourism experiences took place in natural settings, museums, artists' studios and homes, a cooking school, performance spaces, a foundry, and the convention center.

The experiences offered were: Porcelain Workshop, Chile Amor Cooking Class, Nature Journal Making, A Circus Arts Sampler, Hand-built Clay Vessels, Poetry Workshop, Science and Art Demonstrations, Theater Workshop, Tea Ceremony and Chinese Brush Painting, Rio Grande Weaving and Colcha Embroidery, Amulet Making, Watercolor Workshop, Encaustic Painting Workshop, Digital Photography, Photo/Porcelain Tile Workshop, Cooking Demonstrations, Pastel Workshop, African Dance Class, Glassblowing Demonstration, Sculpting Class and Foundry Tour, Writers Workshop: WORDHARVEST, Straw Appliqué, Traditional Adobe Oven Building, Native American Cooking and Pueblo Pottery, African Drumming, Creating Travel Journals, and Tribal and Oriental Dance. The local conference planning committee chose these workshops to give conference registrants choices from Santa Fe's historic and present day cultures.

To give the reader a feel for the experiences, descriptions of some of the workshops follow. They are organized in the categories of ceramics, Spanish colonial art forms, New Mexico's foods, performing arts, and other visual arts.

CERAMICS

Santa Fe's deep history of pottery making dates from the area's long history of Native American inhabitants. Today clay is a material still widely used by Native Americans and also by people of many other backgrounds. Widespread interest on the part of artisans and collectors with the support of educational institutions results in a thriving ceramics community. Three workshops were offered in which participants had the hands-on experience of throwing pots on a wheel, hand building with locally dug clay or applying photographic images to pre-made tiles. Participants reported great excitement about engaging in the process of making things, discussing their work, and having an artwork and/or a memory to take home.

Heidi Loewen teaching wheel-throwing workshop. Photograph by Seth Roffman

Spanish Colonial Art Forms

Northern New Mexico has a vibrant community of artists involved in Spanish art forms that have been practiced here since colonial times. Workshops were offered by two institutions that help keep important traditions alive: the Espanola Valley Fiber Arts Center and the Museum of Spanish Colonial Art. The participants in these workshops learned about Rio Grande weaving, an unusual embroidery form called colcha, and straw appliqué. At the evening event at El Rancho de las Golondrinas, attendees made small punched tin work with the help of Christine Carey, a local award-winning artist.

New Mexico's Foods

Since food is an important cultural element and gastronomy is one of the disciplines of the Creative Cities Network, emphasis was placed on the foods of New Mexico and our sister creative cities. The cooking classes and demonstrations were provided by two Santa Fe cooking schools, Las Cosas School of Cooking and Santa Fe School of Cooking. As is evident from the titles, these experiences were rich and delicious. Our Corny Heritage—Masa through the Ages focused on corn and how it is used regionally. The Chile Amor Cooking Class was all about cultural traditions surrounding chile. Through these experiences, conference participants learned about the history of cooking in the Rio Grande Valley. Cooking the local foods and understanding history through food gave the participants a multi-faceted experience.

Cooking Class.
Photograph by Seth Roffman.

Southwest Barbecue at Las Golondrinas.
Photograph by Seth Roffman.

A particularly popular event at the conference was the Taste of Creative Cities. At this evening event, conference attendees from other countries were amazed to see the generosity of local Santa Fe restaurants that served samples of the best of their menus. The wide selection of appetizers, entrees, and desserts originated in many different countries, reflecting the worldwide nature of the UNESCO Creative Cities Network and the talents of Santa Fe chefs. This wonderful array of food was complemented by wine provided by a New Mexico winery and a local wine distributor.

PERFORMING ARTS

The performing arts were included both in the Creative Tourism experiences track of the conference and as an element of the evening events. Theater Grottesco, a Santa Fe-based ensemble theater company, taught physical theater arts, based on their work of 26 years performing in Europe and the United States. Other local companies presented dance workshops and African drumming. Instrumental music was featured at each social event, played by Santa Fe musicians specializing in marimba, jazz, country-western, and flamenco.

During the Southwest Barbecue and Dance held at El Rancho de Las Golondrinas living history museum, country-western dance lessons were offered. A

Canadian conference participant commented afterward that she really understood the concept of Creative Tourism after that evening of eating local food and dancing. Putting those together and experiencing them physically made it real for her.

Theater Grottesco, seen here performing 12ᵗʰ Night, offered a physical theater workshop at the conference. Photograph by Marc Romanelli.

OTHER VISUAL ART WORKSHOPS

Other art forms common to Santa Fe are sculpting and glass work. A visit to Shidoni Foundry and Tesuque Glassworks gave a group the opportunity to observe and participate in an arts center in Tesuque Valley, just north of Santa Fe. Large lawns filled with sculpture are bordered by the bronze foundry and indoor art galleries, a river, and a glass-blowing studio and gallery. Local artists led this tour and a sculpting class, giving the participants an experience based in the modern-day Santa Fe visual arts scene.

The contribution of the local landscape to our culture was demonstrated in a digital photography workshop held at the Pecos National Monument. This historic site features 12,000 years of history and wide open vistas. Conference participants who attended this workshop were treated to a beautiful two-hour journey out of the downtown built environment into history and the landscape, with far-away views of unpopulated land and mountains. The experience of the landscape surrounding Santa Fe was an opportunity to further understand the magnificent place in which people have made their homes for centuries.

As a result of collaboration between New Mexico Arts, the state government arts agency, and many artists, New Mexico has a Fiber Arts Trail modeled after the HandMade in America trails through North Carolina. (Refer to Becky Anderson's article). In addition, artists have recently put together their own ceramics trail in northern New Mexico. One conference session was devoted to an offsite tour of a selection of trail stops. While not a hands-on creative experience, this session gave attendees an inside look at artists' home studios and sales spaces. Santa Fe's large number of artists per capita results in many regional, weekend studio tours through the year as a means of bringing artists and their work to the attention of the public.

REACTIONS OF CONFERENCE PARTICIPANTS

Creative Tourism Experience Track participants interviewed post-conference were enthusiastic about what they learned. Engagement in the creative process was inspiring and exciting. Anticipation was high for participants who had to wait for their work to be returned to them, after a kiln firing, for example. Enthusiasm was great for taking the work home and having it as a reminder of the visit to Santa Fe.

Artists and other workshop providers were pleased to engage with people from around the world and make connections that will help them build their businesses. For a city of 69,000 people Santa Fe has an unusually high number of artists. According to one study, the number of people who identify themselves as artists is 10 percent of the population. However, artists do not necessarily make their living entirely through the arts. In fact, many people pursue the arts purely as an avocation, deriving no income. It is common in Santa Fe for artists to have other jobs that give them a steady income. Sometimes these jobs are related to the arts, such as working as a teaching artist; in other cases these jobs are unrelated to the arts. Creative Tourism offers an alternative to less interesting part-time jobs for artists and artisans who are interested in sharing their expertise and culture with other people.

CONCLUSION

A surprise result of the experiences offered at the conference was the reaction of a conference participant who was born and raised in Santa Fe. She participated in a workshop presented by La Morena Artworks. This was about hand-built clay vessels, and the artist's work is based in her own and Santa Fe's Spanish heritage. When asked to present her clay work at the podium, this conference participant said that she had particularly enjoyed the experience because it provided a reminder of and connection to her own culture. The value of these types of experiences not only to visitors but also the local population was underscored by this comment.

Conference participants working with artist Mary Lou Cook. Photograph by Seth Roffman.

The Creative Tourism experiences offered at the conference were not all ones that are offered everyday in Santa Fe. As a result of holding the conference, the city of Santa Fe is building this group of product offerings as part of Santa Fe's economic development efforts. The conference web site is being revised to allow people to find listings of Creative Tourism experiences. The listings will allow the site visitor to connect directly with the Creative Tourism experience providers and to book an experience grounded in the people and culture of Santa Fe. We see this as an excellent income generator for Santa Fe area artists and a means of adding to the quality and uniqueness of visitors' experiences in Santa Fe. Through the Creative Tourism experiences, conference attendees were able to participate in and appreciate many aspects of our culture: the landscape, the food, dance, and the work of artists and artisans. We expect these brief experiences and insights into the culture of Santa Fe and the southwestern United States will stay with the participants and bring them back for more.

Sabrina V. Pratt

Sabrina V. Pratt has been the director of the City of Santa Fe Arts Commission (www.SantaFeArtsCommission.org) since 1990, furthering and developing programs that increase access to the arts. Major programs that she oversees are grant programs totaling $1 million in 2009, Santa Fe's Art in Public Places program, which was doubled to 2 percent of City bond issues in 2006, and the Commission's Community Gallery, established in 2008. Youth-oriented programs include ArtWorks, founded in 2001 to deliver aesthetic education in public elementary schools and the Community Youth Mural Program which ran from 1996 to 2009. Since the city of Santa Fe's appointment to the UNESCO Creative Cities Network, Pratt has served as the staff liaison. She has a Master of Public Administration degree from the University of New Mexico and earned her bachelor's degree at Vassar College.

OPEN SPACE CREATIVE CONVERSATIONS
by
Jackie M
Director of Education and Public Programs
Georgia O'Keeffe Museum

OPEN SPACE MARKETPLACE

The International Conference on Creative Tourism planners wanted to provide participants with a forum for addressing the issues they personally felt most important. Using a self-organizing process called Open Space Technology, the attendees proposed discussion topics related to Creative Tourism. Each session that followed was based on a proposed topic convened and documented by the person who suggested the topic. Instructed to work from a place of passion for the issue, participants could choose to attend as many of the sessions as truly interested them.

WHAT IS OPEN SPACE TECHNOLOGY?

There are four principles in Open Space Technology and one law:

- Whoever comes are the right people—whether it is one person or many, whoever is there is someone who cares about the topic.

- Whatever happens is the only thing that could have—letting go of expectations: whatever is, is; work with it.
- Whenever it starts is the right time: a reminder that creativity does not happen according to a schedule.
- When it's over, it's over: it doesn't matter if it is through in 10 minutes or if it needs to keep going.

The Law of Two Feet: if at any time, you find that you are neither learning nor contributing, use your two feet to walk to another discussion session. Some folks will attend several sessions and cross-pollinate ideas, while others may never attend a session, but provide insight or ideas in a discussion held outside of the meeting room. The Law of Two Feet takes care of those who hog the floor and bore the group.

Open Space Facilitator Toby Herzlich with Santa Fe Mayor David Coss.
Photograph by Seth Roffman.

WORKSHOP SESSION: "PROSUMER" CREATIVE TOURISM

Convener: John McDermott, President, Angel Fire Area Economic Development Group, Angel Fire, New Mexico, jjm@jkintl.com.

This session explored the role of community members as the producers of the events and programs that they also consume. Given that a number of Creative Tourism experiences are developed for community members as well as visitors, what considerations should be taken into account when a tourist attraction is meant to serve a local audience as well? The group discussed examples of work being done in Barcelona, Spain, and Boston, Massachusetts through its First Night Celebration. When communities produce their Creative Tourism experiences, they tend to be non-commercial, rely on the arts, or are artist driven, and include festivals that have both structured and non-structured events. The public can simply show up to participate, and that means visitors to the community at the time of the event as well as locals. The Internet provides a method for marketing these events which may take place with or without an overarching manager, and may happen at multiple locations simultaneously. Community-produced events tend to reflect the soul of the place, and it is this quality that a visitor may or may not find to be the big draw.

WORKSHOP SESSION: COMMUNITY GARDENS

A community garden can act as a gathering place for locals and visitors with benefits that go beyond the harvesting of food that is grown. There are educational opportunities for community members of all ages, including students. Local businesses engage in supporting these not-for-profit gardens and oftentimes the arts community becomes involved in programming. Foods indigenous to the area are of interest to tourists as well as culinary experiences using local produce. Agri-tourism is a positive draw that can be capitalized upon through Creative Tourism marketing.

WORKSHOP SESSION: MASS TOURISM TO QUALITY TOURISM AND HOW TO CREATE A COMMUNITY ART SPACE

Convener: Jackson L. Burnside, Architect, Artist and Chairman of the Creative Nassau Committee, Nassau, Bahamas, jburnside@jbl-design.com.

How does a community offer an authentic experience of place when it is widely known as a tourist destination? How can communities attract a discerning visitor who is interested in learning about the real place instead of packaged experiences that could be offered anywhere, as happens in the cruise ship industry? Do it yourself, artist-controlled experiences present an option for visitors who seek quality and diversity. Promoting small scale, educational opportunities that are connected to the spirit of the community draw families as well as repeat visitors.

Communities would benefit from linking with institutions that help them reach a global, targeted market. Tourism networks could be valuable resources to small communities. Art trails provide tourists with a tool for personal exploration and connecting with cultural creatives living in the vicinity of ports of call. By promoting studio visits, direct encounters with artists, and a spirit of travel adventure, communities could engage visitors, who have typically passed through their cities on the way to another generic travel experience. The Internet blogs provide a cost-effective method for marketing the first-hand experiences available to visitors.

WORKSHOP SESSION: CREATING A NETWORK OF CREATIVE CITIES, USA

Many of the participants at the conference were interested in maintaining a network of Creative Tourism providers. The advantages include cross-marketing opportunities, shared learning, connections among artists and cultural groups working with the tourist industry, and the ability to raise the standard of tourist experience available in small towns across the United States.

The creation of destination marketing strategies that are in alignment with core community values, including authenticity, culture, arts, human-scale, and place-based, might present a challenge for the network. Could it effectively cross-market tours or cities themselves, as well as major publications and national groups such as National Geographic, Preserve America, AIA, etc? The network would need to be an advocate of local efforts to raise the value and appreciation of their culture and their arts as in-reach. Establishing cross-community relationships is essential for success. Utilizing social networking such as Facebook might spawn community enthusiasm, realizing that keeping it simple and accessible is key.

An American network of creative cities might encourage a cultural exchange between cities and artists at conferences and conventions. A strategy for getting such a network going might be to first identify 10 people to join the board to brainstorm and establish a process for developing the network, coordinate both big and small ideas, and find capital to jumpstart the efforts. The organization will need a clear statement of purpose. Each community representative would be seen as an ambassador and need to work to spawn community enthusiasm.

Photograph by Seth Roffman.

WORKSHOP SESSION: MARKETING CREATIVE TOURISM

Convener: Katherine McDermott, Artist and owner of Angel Fire ArtSpace Gallery, President of the Moreno Valley Arts Council and the Northeast New Mexico Arts Alliance, Angel Fire, New Mexico, artzkat@jkintl.com.

As a new concept, Creative Tourism could benefit from intra-city marketing plans that foster intelligent collaborative campaigns and intra-community connections and cooperation. A better vocabulary needs to be developed to convey the Creative Tourist experience. Marketing can communicate the value of a Creative Tourist experience with slogans such as: "open yourself to innovation" or "it's worth the investment." The Internet will be the tool for marketing intra-city. By partnering, institutions, businesses, and artists can all benefit from intelligent collaborative campaigns. By knowing who the target consumer is and who the partners want to attract, Creative Tourism can be an arts-based engine for economic development in the community.

WORKSHOP SESSION: PRACTITIONER MODELS AND STEPS FOR ENHANCING THE GUEST/ VISITOR EXPERIENCE

This discussion focused on developing new perspectives, exclusive experiences, and alternative options in established tourist areas. Several case studies were examined:

The Eastern Shoshone Tribe (Wind River, WY) deals with a public that includes visitors to Yellowstone National Park and Jackson Hole. This public wants access to the community and its values. The community wishes to maintain its authenticity and integrity. A museum and heritage project developed as a research project could offer the resources the visitors are asking for without changing the community itself, if long range planning is involved.

Aswan Nubian Villages in Egypt offer tourists who arrive by boat opportunities to experience Nubian hospitality and their way of life. There are five participating villages where visitors can be in a park environment in the desert, enjoy a camel ride, witness a Nubian woman's way of life, and learn about the culture. A donation box allows visitors to contribute to the well being of the communities without compromising the spirit of hospitality.

In North Carolina, managed Creative Tourism that uses a trail system provides visitors access to artists year-round. As a result of this program, artists saw a 23 percent increase in their income. There is cross-marketing of the artists and the trails paid for by money from not-for-profit organizations, foundation grants, and the state.

The Hopi tribe of Arizona is selective in terms of the visitors they want to receive. The villages are along state scenic byways or trails and there are state parks in the area as well. Visitors can take a walking tour provided by the tribe, hear aspects of the oral history, taste local foods, and purchase locally made arts and crafts. The philosophy is come, visit, and appreciate the Hopi culture.

In order for communities to maintain their way of life, yet benefit from visitors, they need to look at the experiences they offer as a form of product development. What are the experiences or products they want to share with the public; what are the costs involved; who will teach and how will the community need to support the experience providers; and finally, what is the overall community vision, ownership expression, and value of the experiences being developed? If creative experiences are practices that promote sustainability, they need to involve the community members by offering things that are value–added for themselves as well as the visitors. This form of economic development can be transformative when it is structured to include the critical components of community, leadership, values, spirit, and place.

WORKSHOP SESSION: NEXT STEPS FROM THIS CONFERENCE

Convener: Jackie M, Director of Education and Public Programs, Georgia O'Keeffe Museum, Santa Fe, New Mexico, jackiem@okeeffemuseum.org.

There are big ideas to take away from the conference and work that can be carried on to move the Creative Tourist concept forward. Using email and the Internet, attendees can connect with their national creative cities movements. It is important for Santa Fe to update the website periodically and distribute DVDs of the recorded talks for sharing with local communities, government, artists, and the local tourist industry. Before planning another international conference, consider using web conferencing, and sharing models and practices through continued contact via email distribution lists. To spread awareness of the Creative Tourism movement, present papers, offer workshops, and schedule discussions at other conventions, including destination marketing association meetings, American Association of Museums and ICOM conferences, and other non-governmental organizations' meetings, as well as cities' economic development summits, and UNESCO Creative Cities Network efforts. Publishing a book or perhaps an e-book that organizes the many ideas and presentations could summarize the tracks, including the important ideas submitted by panel chairs. Jointly construct Power-Point presentations on Creative Tourism by soliciting one slide created by each attendee and add relevant local information.

By using an evaluation process such as Survey Monkey, participants can share the key learning points of the conference, and how they are using this now.

The evaluation should include comments on the basic structure and function of the conference, as well as specific international needs and concerns. This information will be helpful for use in future planning and creating global strategies for local application of conference content. In addition, the survey will help with developing themes for future conferences on how to energize a community, dialogue with other cultures/society, connect cultural diasporas for joint participation, and create methods for deeper involvement of youth. By simply sharing the evaluation comments, the conference will offer further exchange of ideas to the participants.

Jackie M

Jackie M is the founding director of education and public programs at the Georgia O'Keeffe Museum. Past positions include curator of education and public programs for SITE Santa Fe and Santa Fe coordinator for Very Special Arts. Jackie helped start the Santa Fe Gallery of Photography and the Performance Space. Jackie was awarded the 2006 Mayors Award for Excellence in the Arts. In 2008, the O'Keeffe Art and Leadership Programs for Girls and for Boys received national recognition from the President's Council on Arts and Humanities, the NEA and the NEH for excellence in programming. Jackie is a past chair of the board of Creative Santa Fe, an organization that supports the creative industries and past co-chair of the ArtTable Southwest Regional Alliance. Jackie M has also worked in New Mexico as an artist-in-residence and toured internationally as a performance artist. She has a BA in art history from the University Michigan, Ann Arbor and was in the Masters program in the history of photography at the University of New Mexico.

LaVergne, TN USA
18 December 2009
167538LV00002B